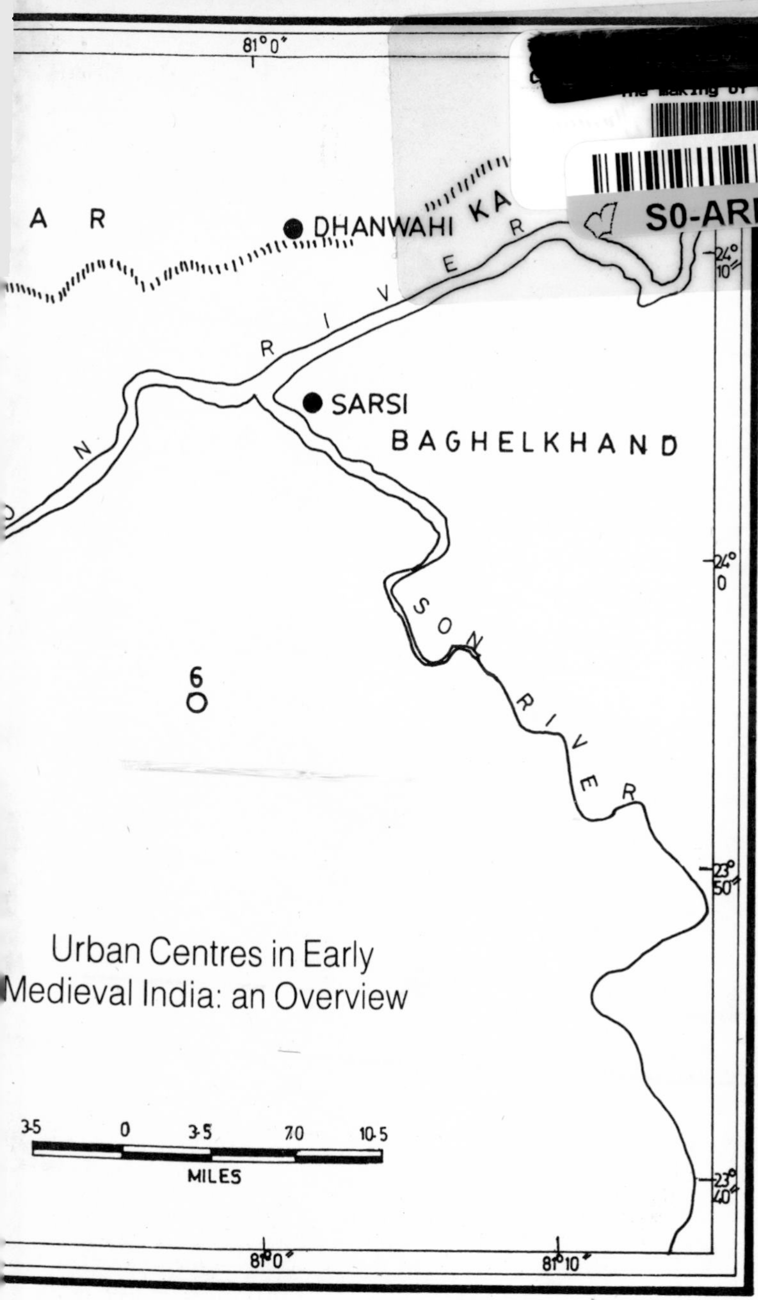

Dhavala: *āhāra* or administrative unit in which the village of Challipataka was located; identified with Dhawaia, 4 miles south of Dighi.
Challipāṭaka: village given by the prince; identified with Chilhari, about 11 miles east of Dhavala.
Antarapāta: appears to have been another donated village; identified with Amaturra, 7 miles east of Karitalai.
Vatagartikā: donated village; identified with Barhati, 10 miles west by south of Karitalai.

The Making of Early Medieval India

THE MAKING OF EARLY MEDIEVAL INDIA

BRAJADULAL CHATTOPADHYAYA

DELHI
OXFORD UNIVERSITY PRESS
[redacted]

Oxford University Press, Walton Street, Oxford OX2 6DP

Oxford New York Toronto
Delhi Bombay Calcutta Madras Karachi
Kuala Lumpur Singapore Hong Kong Tokyo
Nairobi Dar es Salaam Cape Town
Melbourne Auckland Madrid
and associates in
Berlin Ibadan

ISBN 0 19 563415 2

Typeset by Rastrixi, New Delhi 110070
Printed in India at Pauls Press New Delhi 110020
and published by Neil O'Brien, Oxford University Press
YMCA Library Building, Jai Singh Road, New Delhi 110001

For my mother
Surama Devi

Contents

Preface

Early medieval India has long remained a much maligned period of Indian history both among those who possess a passing acquaintance with India's past and with specialists. The Indian history to be found within most textbooks is still redolent with 'dark ages' and 'periods of crisis', in much the same measure as 'golden ages'. Characteristics generally associated with early middle age have burdened this period and dressed it up as one of the key 'dark ages' of Indian history. The value judgements of historians on personalities, as on periods of history, are carried over as axioms in historiography; early medieval India has not yet been able to shake off axiomatic pronouncements upon it; this despite the fact that recent researches look at the period from many more angles and have succeeded, to a very substantial measure, in rescuing this epoch out of its dismal maze of dynastic genealogies, chronological charts and chronicles of military success and failure.

The papers in this collection were written over a rather long span of time, alongside papers on other periods and themes, and so they are not really products of a systematically designed research project on early medieval India. They represent my explorations and ideas on the nature of the change which distinguishes the period following the decline of the Guptas in the middle of the sixth century from the one preceding it. Initially, the idea was to focus on the nature of change in a select region, namely Rajasthan. But an inevitable drift, generated by my curiosity over other areas and other themes, prevented any stringent thematic unity. What holds these papers together is the attempt to analyse different manifestations of the historical processes at work in the post-Gupta period. The introductory chapter was especially written for this collection of papers—which were published earlier in scattered academic journals—so as to provide a framework.

The suggestion that I put together my meagre output on early medieval India came from young friends and colleagues; I hope my decision to do this will not reflect adversely on their judgement. My interest in early medieval India and the urge to re-examine the dominant formulations regarding the period began when I was, for about a year, a Fellow at the Indian Institute of Advanced Study, Simla. I acknowledge with thanks the many facilities made available to me by the Institute. I am grateful to my colleagues Professor Muzaffar Alam and Dr Neeladri Bhattacharya for the interest they have taken in the publication of this collection; to my students Ms Nandini Sinha and Sri Shyam Narayan Lal for the help received from them in the preparation of the manuscript; and to Oxford University Press for having patiently awaited the final script.

May 1993 B. D. CHATTOPADHYAYA

Acknowledgements

Acknowledgements are due to the following for permission to reprint these papers: Chapter 2: *Journal of the Economic and Social History of the Orient*; Chapters 3 and 7: *The Indian Historical Review*; Chapter 4: *Social Science Probings*; Chapter 5: Professor S. Settar, Department of History and Archaeology, Karnatak University, Dharwad; Chapter 9: Professor P. Jash, Visvabharati University.

Abbreviations

ARIE	*Annual Report on Indian Epigraphy*
ARRM	*Annual Report on the working of the Rajputana Museum, Ajmer*
BSOAS	*Bulletin of the School of Oriental and African Studies*
EI	*Epigraphia Indica*
IA	*The Indian Antiquary*
IAR	*Indian Archaeology—A Review*
IESHR	*The Indian Economic and Social History Review*
JBBRAS	*Journal of the Bombay Branch of the Royal Asiatic Society*
JESHO	*Journal of the Economic and Social History of the Orient*
JPASB	*Journal and Proceedings of the Asiatic Society, Bengal*
JRAS (JRASGBI)	*Journal of the Royal Asiatic Society of Great Britain and Ireland*
PIHC	*Proceedings of the Indian History Congress*
PRASWC	*Progress Report of the Archaeological Survey, Western Circle*
ZDMG	*Zeitschrift der Deutschen Morgenlaendischen Gesellschaft*

1

Introduction: The Making of Early Medieval India

> 'Omission and simplification help us to understand—but help us, in many cases, to understand the wrong thing; for our comprehension may be only of the abbreviator's neatly formulated notions, not of the vast ramifying reality from which these notions have been so arbitrarily abstracted'.
>
> — Aldous Huxley, Foreword to *Brave New World Revisited*

'Early medieval', when used as an historical phase and marked off from other historical phases such as 'Ancient', 'Medieval', and 'Modern', may not be of very recent usage in Indian historiography;[1] what is comparatively recent is the fact that these terms, when used simply as convenient substitutes for 'Hindu', 'Muslim' and 'British', are questioned.[2] N.R. Ray, for example, urged almost three decades ago that the practice of using chronological terms in descriptive senses needed to be replaced. He argued for analytical attempts to see if chronological labels could be understood in terms of specific attributes associated with them. Since then there have been

[1] For example, the practice, now given up, of calling one of its sections 'Early Medieval' was followed in the Indian History Congress; see *Proceedings of the Indian History Congress*, 13th session (Nagpur, 1950); 14th session (Jaipur, 1951). However, the scheme of periodization followed in the Indian History Congress involved dividing 'ancient India' into two segments (upto 711 and 712–1206) and assigning 1206–1526 as 'early medieval'.

[2] For some relevant discussions, see Romila Thapar, 'Interpretations of Ancient Indian History', in *Ancient Indian Social History: Some Interpretations* (Delhi, 1978), pp. 1–25, and R.S. Sharma, 'Problem of Transition from Ancient to Medieval in Indian History', *The Indian Historical Review*, vol. I, no. 1 (1974), pp. 1–9. For an interesting analysis of how indigenous notions of historical time were gradually overcome by notions of Hindu and Muslim regimes, see Partha Chattopadhyaya, 'Itihāser Uttarādhikār' (in Bengali), *Bāromās*, April 1991, pp. 2–24(3).

some meaningful attempts in this direction. Discussions around the appropriateness or otherwise of chronological labels are now expected to relate to the theme of periodization, i.e. around the problem of historical change, and to whatever the scales and processes of historical change may have been. The problem therefore now involves—given the obvious elements of continuity in Indian history—the selection of variables which would purport to separate one historical phase from another. This task obviously implies abstraction and not simply the putting together of empirical evidence; in other words, the constructs of both what is early medieval and what leads to early medieval are problems related to the kind of vantage point a historian wishes to take, keeping long-term Indian history in mind. This introduction represents one more attempt to understand, along with the other essays as empirical support, the abstraction which the term 'early medieval' may represent, both as a chronological phase and as a signifier of processes of change which correspond to the phase. Of necessity, this involves a review of the current historiographic position on 'early medieval', as also how the passage to 'early medieval' has so far been viewed.

By accepting the idea of the medieval—or more specifically early medieval—as a phase in the transition to medieval, we subscribe to one way of looking at the course of Indian history. This is the perspective from which, despite an awareness of the elements of continuity, the course of history is seen in terms of stages of change.[3] In other words this use of chronological labels like early medieval and medieval, despite the overtones of European historiography which these labels evoke, implicitly rejects the notion of the changelessness of Indian society.

It is necessary to underscore this point because the notion of India's social changelessness, which derives essentially from particular perceptions of India's cultural characteristics and is inextricably associated with the major premises of *Orientalism*,[4] has not been given up. The notion persists under different camouflages; sometimes it stretches to

[3] N.R. Ray, 'The Medieval Factor in Indian History', General President's Address, Indian History Congress, 29th session (Patiala, 1967), pp. 1–29.

[4] For a recent discussion of this in the context of Indian history and a critique, see Ronald Inden, *Imagining India* (Oxford and Cambridge, Mass., 1990), *passim*.

declarations that attempts at reconstructing Indian history are essentially hopeless and futile.[5] The rejection of some of the premises of Orientalism, especially by Indian historians, and the insistence on analyses of social change as well as on redefining the periodization of Indian history, need to be clarified. The perception of change has not been altogether absent in earlier researches on historical India, nor has there been a general homogeneity of thought as to what the stages of change were—or in fact how change has to be viewed in the Indian context.

For the present discussion, three points need to be noted. First, the nature of the change which is the subject of critical debate when one discusses the move from ancient to early medieval, involves constructing in clear contours an image of what tends to be called ancient. Second, it involves providing a construct of early medieval. Third, it involves the methodological problem of causation, for if we use a term like 'early medieval' to suggest a time span as well as an historical phase, it is fair that we also try defining it in terms of what brought it into being. The term 'early medieval' has been in use in various senses, as has the term 'ancient'.

This leads us to an exercise in historiography, an exercise somewhat tenuous because the nature of the available historiography no longer allows us to construct 'ancient' to everybody's satisfaction. So long as

[5] For example, Madeleine Biardeau: 'in spite of a sizeable collection of inscriptions on stones or on copper plates, which have by no means all been studied or even published, this evidence scarcely enables us to reconstruct what *one would call a history* . . . Kingdoms, great and small, long lasting or ephemeral, even empires, succeeded one another, but brahmanic India continued to adhere to its own norms; *its thinkers and authors—all Brahmans*—have given her a *fundamentally timeless image* . . . This amounts to saying that change, when it does appear, is only *superficial and always refers back to a normative foundation* . . . There is simply a change of scale when dealing with India, because *one cannot 'periodize'* its history as one does for other areas, or divide it into territories as restricted as those of European countries . . . ' (emphasis added), *Hinduism: The Anthropology of a Civilization* (New Delhi, 1989), pp. 1–3. This long quotation was necessary because, as a reincarnation of Orientalist assumptions regarding India, it gives the lie to the assertion that biases represented by Orientalist assumptions are 'now less prominent than their converse—the biases of Indian nationalist history'. Brendan O'Leary, *The Asiatic Mode of Production: Oriental Despotism, Historical Materialism and Indian History* (Oxford and Cambridge, Mass., 1989), p. 268.

Indian history started with 'Aryan invasions' and suffered a major break with the coming of the Muslims, we had a simple view of the ancient. Despite the ups and downs of its ruling dynasties and the alternation of golden ages and dark ages, 'ancient' was seen to continue till the close of the twelfth century or thereabouts. Of course this was not the only view. The use of the term 'early medieval' in relation to a period which far preceded the Turkish invasions of northern India has been in vogue for some time, although the association of 'Muslim invasions' with the advent of the medieval period has remained, willy nilly, the dominant textbook point of view.[6] Altogether, clarifying what we seek to understand by the term 'ancient' is no longer so simple. For one thing, concerns with definitions have become much more acute than before, and second, in the Indian context a tremendous spate of archaeological excavations and explorations has added significant dimensions to how we view the ancient period of our history. Added to this is the growing awareness among many archaeologists and historians that we have to contend with the simultaneous existence of a wide range of cultures. 'Living prehistory' is very much a live concept,[7] and the view is quite strong that many meanings of the past can be successfully decoded only if live systems are simultaneously studied and analysed.[8]

[6] The equation between the establishment of Muslim rule and the beginning of a new era in Indian history which, as a sequel to 'ancient' has to be considered 'medieval', is quite strongly entrenched in Indian historiography. For example, even though R.C. Majumdar appears to deviate from the normal convention of historians of India by considering the time span 1000–1300 as part of a Hindu (and by implication ancient) period, in his reckoning the establishment of 'the first all-India Muslim empire on the ruins of the Hindu kingdoms' did 'usher in a new era in Indian history in which the Muslims played the dominant role for more than four hundred years'. R.C. Majumdar, ed., *The Struggle for Empire*, vol. 5 of *The History and Culture of the Indian People* (Bombay, 1957), Preface, xlvii.

[7] The expression 'living prehistory' was used by D.D. Kosambi in his article 'Living Prehistory in India'. For reference, see R.S. Sharma and V. Jha, ed., *Indian Society: Historical Probings (In Memory of D.D. Kosambi)*, second edition (New Delhi, 1977), p. 15, entry no. 125.

[8] Kosambi repeatedly stressed that what is visible in records from the past needs to be analysed in the light of contemporary realities. His insistence on the 'combined method' is well known. I cannot resist the temptation of giving an excerpt from a personal letter (dated 8 February 1964) in which, too, Kosambi underlines the need to be aware of the realities which surround us: 'I have an article in the *Times of India*

History, however, has to have chronological labels, and even at the risk of making a somewhat simplistic equation, I would say that what used to be perceived as 'ancient' now incorporates (sometimes inadvertently) a series of culture stages, not necessarily evolving unilineally. Instead of continuing to use the blanket term 'ancient' for all occasions, it has therefore become imperative to disentangle the various components of 'ancient' from each other; in other words, to redefine 'ancient'. One way of doing this is to identify the core cultural traits which constitute the required chronological construct. By viewing the transition to the 'early medieval' as representing a major social change, we would identify the phase preceding the transition as 'ancient'.

One may suppose that thus viewed, it is no longer necessary to label the entire pre-medieval or pre-early-medieval Indian society 'ancient'. The Stone Ages of the subcontinent, the Harappan civilization, the pre-Iron Age cultures of various regions, and even the early-Iron Age cultures (irrespective of whether some of them corresponded to a Vedic variant of culture or not),[9] need not all be aggregated together as 'ancient' alongside what developed later; rather, their cultural specificities may be highlighted. Perhaps if one insists on 'ancient' as a connotative term, the proto-historic cultures over a wide expanse of India through the Chalcolithic and early Iron Ages may be seen to represent a movement towards a historical stage which can be viewed as 'ancient'. Perhaps, even more appropriately, the current

---

Annual, due out in six months or so, on Krishna . . . You will see what Marxism can do, or can't do, when backed by field work. I should not have understood many elements of the Krishna legend without going to talk with the peasantry, and without my own boyhood in the village.' Basically, the same idea, expressed somewhat more strongly, exists in Obeyesekere's scepticism 'of the conventional "empiricist" historiography popular among the very best South Asian scholars . . . A historiography that relies exclusively on well documented and incontrovertible historical evidence, such as evidence from inscriptions, must surely be wrong since it assumes that the recorded data must be the significant data shaping history and controlling the formation and transformation of the institutions of a people. A more imaginative interpretation using a broad variety of sources—from myth, ritual, and popular literature—would correct this narrow perspective'. Gananath Obeyesekere, *The Cult of the Goddess Pattini*, first Indian edition (Delhi, 1987), p. 605.

[9] R.S. Sharma, *Material Culture and Social Formations in Ancient India* (Delhi, 1983), chs 4 and 5.

practice among historians in India is to term this phase 'early historical'. This term gives us a better idea of what chronological span and what kind of society we envisage when using it. 'Early historical' has, for example, come to denote a phase which started taking recognizable shape from the middle of the first millennium BC.[10] When historians talk about a transition from 'ancient' to 'early medieval' in Indian history, it is essentially the 'early historical' culture phase, which originated roughly in the middle of the first millennium BC which is the intended reference point. Even if we arrive at some kind of agreement on viewing the beginnings of ancient or early historical in this manner (and we are making a deliberate switch from ancient to early historical now), it does not necessarily mean that we are clear, to go by current historical writings, on either of these two counts: (i) what the major historical traits constituting the early historical are; and (ii) how far, chronologically, early historical would stretch.

The arbitrariness in the use of labels appears evident when it is noticed that both early medieval and medieval are used in relation to the Sultanate period of north Indian history, as well as in relation to the Cola period in south India, and equally to the Cālukya period in the Deccan.[11] It seems, then, that chronological labels need to be discussed afresh by taking up current views on periodization. It is these

[10] For the significance of this period in Indian history and for a discussion of such new trends as the emergence of territorial states, urbanization, the rise of heterodox ideas, etc., see R.S. Sharma, *Material Culture and Social Formations in Ancient India*, chs 6 and 7, R. Thapar, *From Lineage to State: Social Formations in the Mid-First Millennium BC in the Ganga Valley* (Bombay, 1984). The middle of the first millennium BC is taken as a chronological reference point, in comparison with other civilizations, as the 'axial age' of Indian history: H. Kulke, 'The Historical Background of India's Axial Age', in S.N. Eisenstadt, ed., *The Origins and Diversities of Axial Age Civilizations* (State University of New York Press, 1986), pp. 374–92.

[11] Cf. the chronological focus of, for instance, Burton Stein, *Peasant State and Society in Medieval South India* (Delhi, 1980); G.S. Dikshit, *Local Self-Government in Medieval Karnataka* (Dharwar, 1964); Om Prakash Prasad, *Decay and Revival of Urban Centres in Medieval South India, c. AD 600–1200* (Patna, 1989). David Ludden seems to speak of the 'last century of the medieval period' in the context of Cola–Pāṇḍya rule in south India, but it is not clear which century he refers to. See Ludden's, *Peasant History in South India*, first Indian reprint (Delhi, 1989), p. 205. By contrast, the time span 500–1200 is taken to represent 'early medieval' in R.S. Sharma, *Social Changes in Early Medieval India (circa AD 500–1200)*, The First Devraj Chanana Memorial Lecture (Delhi, 1969).

views which define, by implication, the attributes of the 'early historical', which is posited as a social formation radically different from 'early medieval'.

Despite variations, an image of the 'early historical' does emerge through this exercise, and, though schematic, the following may be taken to represent its major attributes:[12]

Political	*Economic*	*Social*
Territorial kingdoms ruled by *rājanyas* or *kṣatriyas*, finally crystallized into a highly bureaucratic, centralized state in which the hierarchy of power based on landholding was absent; its wide range of officials were all paid in cash.	Highly monetized economy, characterized by long-distance foreign trade, urbanization and urban crafts production. The rural units of production are seen to have existed in this phase in the form of village communities, with communal rights in land still quite strong.	Crystallization of the *varṇa* system in which the *rājanya/kṣatriyas* and the *brāhmaṇas* were appropriators of the social surplus, the *vaiśyas* as agriculturists and traders were the main taxpayers, while the *śūdras* provided servile labour. The existence of 'slavery' in various forms was also an attribute of the period. It is assumed that the proliferation of castes was largely absent, and that labour represented a pre-'serfdom' phase.

The society in which these attributes developed and operated is understood to have become pan-Indian and as having reached its high watermark by the third-fourth centuries AD. When we read about the transition to medievalism in the current historiography, the essential reference point seems to be what these attributes represent, for it is

[12] This statement is largely based on the substantial research output of Professor R.S. Sharma, among which the following may be cited as the sources of this abstraction: *Material Culture and Social Formations in Ancient India; Perspectives in Social and Economic History of Early India* (Delhi, 1983), chs 2, 9 and 10; *Urban Decay in India (c. 300–c. 1000)* (Delhi, 1987); R.S. Sharma, 'Problem of Transition . . .', 'Problems of Peasant Protest in Early Medieval India', *Social Scientist*, vol. 16, no. 9 (1988), pp. 3–16; *Aspects of Political Ideas and Institutions in Ancient India*, third revised edition (Delhi, 1991), chs 23 and 24.

through the transformation/inversion of these attributes that we arrive at a set of almost opposed attributes which mark the beginnings of 'medievalism'. To put it in terms persistently used, the route to medievalism, in what is currently the dominant school of ancient Indian historiography, was through 'Indian feudalism'. The belief in 'Indian feudalism' as an explanatory model for the transition has become so assertive as to inspire, in a recent important empirical contribution to the theme, this statement: 'the problem today is not whether India experienced a feudal development but rather what was the precise mechanism of such a development'.[13] What constituted medievalism and what constituted Indian feudalism are understandably perceived differently by different historians: the historiographical ground has been so well covered that it is pointless to repeat the discussion.[14] However, it is necessary to analyse sample views of the transition to the early phase of medievalism in order to understand shifts in the connotations of chronological labels, as well as shifts in the formulations of explanatory positions.

One type of statement on the transition, by Niharranjan Ray, attempts a multi-dimensional characterization of medievalism.[15] He locates the beginning of the process in the seventh century and says it became more pronounced from the eighth century; he envisages three subperiods within the medieval: (i) seventh to twelfth century; (ii) twelfth to the first quarter of the sixteenth century; and (iii) first quarter of the sixteenth to the close of the eighteenth century. Un-

[13] R.N. Nandi, 'Growth of Rural Economy in Early Feudal India', Presidential Address, Ancient India Section, Indian History Congress, 45 session (Annamalai, 1984).

[14] See in particular H. Mukhia, 'Was there Feudalism in Indian History?', *The Journal of Peasant Studies*, vol. 8, no. 3 (1981), pp. 273–310; Idem, 'Peasant Production and Medieval Indian Society', *The Journal of Peasant Studies*, vol. 12, nos. 2–3 (1985), pp. 228–50; D.N. Jha, 'Early Indian Feudalism: A Historiographical Critique', Presidential Address, Ancient India Section, Indian History Congress, 40th session (Waltair, 1979); Idem, 'Editor's Introduction' in D.N. Jha, ed., *Feudal Social Formation in Early India* (Delhi, 1987); B.D. Chattopadhyaya, 'Political Processes and Structure of Polity in Early Medieval India: Problems of Perspective', Presidential Address, Ancient India Section, Indian History Congress, 44th session (Burdwan, 1983); Idem, 'State and Economy in North India: 4th century to 12th century' (forthcoming); also, B. O'Leary, *The Asiatic Mode of Production* . . . .

[15] N.R. Ray, 'The Medieval Factor in Indian History'.

derstandably, Ray does not specify the major attributes of these sub-periods. Instead, he offers a broad package of characteristics which, for him, define Indian medievalism. Making pointed references to the nomadic incursions into Indian society represented by the Hūnas and their predecessors, and using these as comparisons with developments in Europe, Ray lists these major traits of medievalism:

1. All ruling dynasties became regional, and in this sense their genesis is considered comparable to the emergence of European nation-states.
2. The character of the economy changed from a money economy to a natural economy.
3. In various media of social communication (such as script, language and literature) there was the crystallization of a regional character—a process which offers, again, a 'striking parallel' with European developments.
4. The dominant feature characterizing religion was a proliferation of sects and sub-sects.
5. Art activities too came to be recognizable only in terms of 'regional' schools, such as Eastern, Orissan, Central Indian, West Indian and Central Deccanese; or in terms of such labels as Pallava and Cola, in which again the regional context is implicit.

When trying to identify the major traits of medievalism and situate these close to European parallels, Ray obviously saw the transition as deriving from a feudal process. His explanations for the genesis of the traits of *medievalism*, and his sweeping generalizations around the medieval 'factor', have given way in recent years to more specific concerns regarding the structure of early medieval India, as well as to a greater accent on substantial volumes of indigenous empirical material. All this has contributed to the effort to understand the gradual transformation of early historical society.

Recent writings have also largely bypassed D.D. Kosambi's idea of the dual processes operating towards the emergence of Indian feudalism. Kosambi's long-term view of what he considered feudalism, characterized by a two-stage development, namely feudalism from above and feudalism from below,[16] has not really had any followers,

[16] D.D. Kosambi, *An Introduction to the Study of Indian History* (Bombay, 1956), chs 9 and 10.

although, it needs to be stressed, the essential variables of the Indian feudalism construct are also present in his formulation.[17]

From what we have said above, two points emerge: (i) in the dominant view within Indian historiography, medievalism is present in the centuries preceding the establishment of the Delhi Sultanate, and the early phase of medievalism has to be understood in terms of the features of Indian feudalism; and (ii) Indian feudalism is a recent construct, and this construct (which has to be distinguished from earlier haphazard uses of the term feudalism) imbibes elements from different strands of historical writing.

However, despite the inevitable shifts which occur when explaining the formation of the structure which the construct represents, as well as when identifying the major political, social and economic variables of the structure, certain common variables figure as points of consensus. These variables exist in opposition to what are seen to constitute the ancient or early historical order. The essential points may be highlighted thus, particularly because they appear almost as the polar opposites of the attributes of early historical society:[18]

1. *Political decentralization*: The conventional duality of centrifugalism and centripetalism in Indian polity has been replaced by the image of a structure which provides a counterpoint to the centralized, bureaucratic state, the crystallization of which is located only in the post-Gupta period. The new state structure is characterized by decentralization and hierarchy, features suggested by the presence of a wide range of semi-autonomous rulers, *sāmantas, mahāsāmantas* and similar categories, and the hierarchized positioning of numerous *rāja-puruṣas* employed by royal courts.

2. *The emergence of landed intermediaries*: This is considered the hallmark of Indian feudal social formation and is seen to be linked both to the disintegration and decentralization of state authority and

[17] For example, Kosambi considered the decline of a money economy, the rise of village self-sufficiency, and the growth in the rank of 'fief-holding *Sāmantas* as hallmarks of Indian feudalism; these features seem to be common to most constructs of Indian feudalism thus far.

[18] Detailed bibliographical references from which these features are abstracted will be found in B.D. Chattopadhyaya, 'State and Economy in North India: 4th century to 12th century' (forthcoming).

to major changes in the structure of agrarian relations. The emergence of landed intermediaries—a dominant landholding social group presumed absent in the early historical period—is causally linked to the practice of land grants, the identifiable recipients of which in the early centuries of the Christian era (as also in later periods) were almost invariably *brāhmaṇas* or religious establishments. However, in the context of the post-Gupta period, 'fief-holders' and 'free-holders' are terms used in relation to secular recipients of such grants and to autonomous holders of land.

3. A change over from the market or money economy to self-sufficient villages as units of production, ruralization thus being an important dimension of the transition process. This change over is seen as deriving from the decline of early historical urban centres and commercial networks. This led to the practice of remuneration in land as a substitute for cash, to the migration of different social groups to rural areas, to an agrarian expansion, and to the crystallization in rural society of *jajmāni* relationships (relationships of interdependence between patrons and clients). According to one formulation, 'fief-holders' and 'free-holders' in rural society emerged as agents of social change in the later phase of early medieval society, generating once again such features of early historical economy as trade, urbanism and a money economy/market economy.[19]

4. *Subjection of the peasantry*: Likened sometimes to serfdom, characteristics of the subjection of the peasantry such as immobility, forced labour and the payment of revenue at exorbitantly high rates, all point to the nature of stratification in post-Gupta society. The condition of the peasantry in this pattern of rural stratification was in sharp contrast to what the agrarian structure in early historical India represented, since that structure was dominated by free Vaiśya peasants and labour services provided by the Śūdras.

5. *The proliferation of castes*: One dimension of social stratification is suggested by the proliferation of castes in post-Gupta society. Despite the presence of the idea of *varṇasaṁkara*, which explains the

[19] See R.N. Nandi, 'Growth of Rural Economy in Early Feudal India', Presidential Address, Ancient India Section, Indian History Congress, 45th session (Annamalai, 1984).

tendency of castes to proliferate in terms of uneven marital relations in the pre-Gupta period,[20] the intensity of the caste formation process is located only in the post-Gupta period.[21] As representing a comprehensive process of transition, the proliferation of castes was not marked by the appearance of major groups like the Kāyasthas alone, but by varieties of other groups as well. Further, many of the social groups associated with what was considered to be polluting manual labour came to constitute the degraded rank of untouchables.[22]

6. *The feudal dimension of the ideology and culture of the period*: The core of the ideology of the period is seen to be characterized by *bhakti*, which was feudal in content, since it accentuated the relationship of loyalty and devotion, which are believed to be hallmarks of feudal ties.[23] At the level of culture, the decline of what was urbane and cosmopolitan had its natural sequel in the degeneration of feudal courtly culture. The association of degenerate religious practices (such as Tāntric rituals) in princely courts, and the fact that the new agrarian structure created a leisurely class of landed magnates, provided congenial conditions for the rise of a feudal social ethos and feudal cultural traits.[24]

One cannot be sure of any consensus, even among those who study the transformation of *early historical* society in feudal terms, on reducing the 'vast ramifying reality' of post-early historical society to the features outlined above. However, what we are dealing with at the moment is current historiography. The rationale for projecting the image of the period, conceived as the early medieval period of Indian

[20] For the concept of *varnasamkara* as going back to when the Sūtras were compiled, see V. Jha, 'Varnasamkara in the Dharmasūtras: Theory and Practice', *Journal of the Economic and Social History of the Orient*, vol. 13, pt. 3 (1970), pp. 273–88.

[21] R.S. Sharma, *Social Changes in Early Medieval India (circa AD 500–1200)*.

[22] For the Kāyasthas, see Chitrarekha Gupta, 'The Writers Class of Ancient India—A Case Study in Social Mobility', *The Indian Economic and Social History Review*, vol. 20, no. 2 (1983), pp. 191–204.

[23] See the section titled 'Feudal Ideology' in D.N. Jha, ed., *Feudal Social Formation in Early India* (Delhi, 1987), pp. 311–401.

[24] See in particular, Devangana Desai, 'Art Under Feudalism in India (*c.* AD 500–1300)', reprinted in D.N. Jha, *Feudal Social Formation in Early India*, pp. 391–401; also Idem, 'Social Dimensions of Art in Early India', Presidential Address, Section I, Ancient India, Indian History Congress, 50th session (Gorakhpur, 1989).

history, in terms of these features is that they are posited as points of sharp contrast with features of early historical society. Indeed, in the available writings on the theme of transition from antiquity to the middle ages,[25] or more specifically from the early historical to the early medieval, the transition seems the crystallization of an opposition: early medieval is seen as a breakdown of the civilizational matrix of early historical India.

Breakdown implies social crisis, and it is precisely in terms of a social crisis that the breakdown of the early historical civilizational order has been envisaged. The historical events which signify crisis are identified differently by different historians, or at times by the same historian: sometimes it is the Hūṇa invasions,[26] sometimes it is the expansion of the scale of land grants,[27] at other times it is the decline of the early historical urban civilization which tears the fabric of early historical social order.[28] Recent writings attempt to show that the crisis can be analysed, in concrete historical terms, from the way the epics, the Purānas and other brāhmaṇical texts delineate Kaliyuga, namely as marking the fall from a normative social order which is assumed to have been the existing social order.[29] Kaliyuga, the contemporary

[25] The terminology is that of B.N.S. Yadava, 'The Accounts of the Kali Age and the Social Transition from Antiquity to the Middle Ages', *The Indian Historical Review*, vol. 5, nos. 1–2 (1979), pp. 31–64.

[26] N.R. Ray, 'The Medieval Factor . . . '. See also B.N.S. Yadava, *Society and Culture in Northern India in the Twelfth Century* (Allahabad, 1973), pp. 137ff.

[27] The genesis of Indian feudalism, through which the transition to early medieval Indian crystallized, was persistently traced by R.S. Sharma to the practice of land grants with administrative rights: R.S. Sharma, 'Origins of Feudalism in India (*c.* AD 400–650)', *Journal of the Economic and Social History of the Orient*, vol. I, no. 3 (1958), 298–328; Idem, *Indian Feudalism: c. 300–1200* (Calcutta, 1965).

[28] The point is particularly stressed in R.N. Nandi, 'Growth of Rural Economy . . . '. In providing an explanation for the genesis of feudalism in India, R.S. Sharma too has shifted the emphasis from the practice of land grants to 'urban decay', which according to him, was the social crisis equivalent to feudal decline, *Urban Decay in India (c. 300–c. 1000)* (Delhi, 1987), *passim.*

[29] For details of how Kaliyuga, which essentially signifies a period of deviation from ideal Brāhmanical society, is perceived as corresponding to actual historical trends after a particular period, see R.S. Sharma, 'The Kali Age: A Period of Social Crisis', in S.N. Mukherjee, ed., *India: History and Thought (Essays in Honour of A.L. Basham)* (Calcutta, 1982), pp. 186–203; B.N.S. Yadava, 'The Accounts of the Kali Age . . . '.

segment in the early Indian schema of cosmic periodization, is believed to be congruous with a segment of actual historical time span. This is because the brāhmaṇical texts use concrete social categories such as the state, human settlements, *varṇa*, and so on, to highlight an upheaval which heralded a rupture with the past. The transition to the early medieval period is located in this social upheaval. This is perhaps why what is perceived as the phase of transition to medieval society is seen to be composed of elements which were the opposites of elements constituting early historical society.

II

A detailed critique of the position summed up above would be redundant here; while one can insist on the empirical validity of what sustained research over the years has established, it is equally possible to detect explanatory incongruities in the way the transition has been constructed.[30] Detailed empirical and competent research presents us with the image of a society which was going through change, and no serious student of Indian history today would now view Indian society of the second and third centuries as having remained unchanged by the eighth and ninth centuries; we cannot now believe that the societies represented by these two time-segments were identical.

The question then really is: what made the eighth and ninth centuries (and of course subsequent centuries) so very different from the second and third centuries? The answer will emerge from the particular perspectives one chooses to adopt for viewing change in Indian history. It seems to me that an understanding of the making of early medieval India—as indeed the very rationale of the label 'early medieval' for a particular historical time span—has to begin by identifying the major historical processes in early India and examining the crystallization of these processes in their specific temporal and spatial contexts. Empirical evidence can be understood only if we are able to view it through these major historical/societal processes of change; else there is the danger of isolating a set of evidence from the total context, a sort of 'arbitrary abstraction'.

[30] See B.D. Chattopadhyaya, 'State and Economy in North India: 4th to 12th century' (forthcoming).

In the context of early Indian history, in particular, this methodological emphasis on societal processes in their specific temporal-spatial manifestations is important. This is because historians often depend on one set of evidence by virtually ignoring other categories with which comparisons ought to have been undertaken. A common example of this lapse is the historiography of the Mauryan empire. The image of this empire as a highly centralized and bureaucratic state apparatus operative over a largely homogeneous culture zone is constructed on the basis of certain categories of evidence. This image, with its roots in nationalist historiography (which justifiably hailed the discovery of the *Arthaśāstra*) tends to ignore the distinctions, in terms of their specific cultural patterns, between Madhyadeśa of fourth-third centuries BC and large parts of the empire such as the Deccan, where the dominant culture was still megalithic and in a pre-state stage.[31] Thus, when we talk of political fragmentation following the breakup of the Mauryan empire, we miss the major significance of the empire in its societal processes. The sequels to the formation of the Mauryan empire were: (i) the reaching out in different directions, of the cultural elements which the Mauryan state, with its *core* in the Madhyadeśa, represented; (ii) their interaction with local cultural matrices; and (iii) in subsequent stages, the formation of local states and empires in the Deccan. Looked at from this perspective, the breakup of the Mauryan empire did not bring a societal process to a close; rather, it needs to be underlined that, keeping

[31] The cultural variations within the Mauryan empire and their implications for the overall structure of the Mauryan state, the reconstruction of which still leans heavily on the *Arthaśāstra* evidence, have not been adequately underlined so far. For a continuing characterization of the Mauryan state as centralized—implying the existence of a uniform pattern of administration throughout the empire reaching down to all its units—see R.S. Sharma, *Aspects of Political Ideas and Institutions in Ancient India*, third revised edition (Delhi, 1991), ch. 23, Appendix to ch. 23 and ch. 24. For some recent relevant discussions, see G.M. Bongard-Levin, *Mauryan India* (New Delhi, 1985), ch. IV; Romila Thapar, 'The State as Empire' in H.J.M. Claessen and Peter Skalnik, eds, *The Study of the State* (The Hague, 1981), pp. 409–26; Idem, *The Mauryas Revisited* (S.G. Deuskar Lectures on Indian History, 1984) (Calcutta, 1987), pp. 1–31; G. Fussman, 'Central and Provincial Administration in Ancient India: The Problem of the Mauryan Empire', *The Indian Historical Review*, vol. 14, nos. 1–2 (1987–88), pp. 43–72.

specific regional/chronological dimensions in view, it accelerated societal processes of change.[32]

The major historical-societal processes in early Indian history will then have to be identified not by taking an epicentric view, but by keeping in mind the fact that historical-cultural stages have always been uneven over the subcontinent.[33] It seems to me that, viewed from this perspective, it should be possible to identify at least three major processes which were operative through all the phases of Indian history, and through early Indian history in particular. These processes were: (i) the expansion of state society through the process of local state formation; (ii) the peasantization of tribes and caste formation; and (iii) cult appropriation and integration. Obviously, these processes were not unrelated to one another, and together they constitute a cultural matrix which came to acquire over the centuries a recognizable shape at the subcontinental level, including in areas which had initially remained peripheral.[34]

Identifying these societal processes and underlining them as the

[32] For discussions relating to Kaliṅga and the Deccan, see S. Seneviratne, 'Kaliṅga and Andhra: The Process of Secondary State Formation in Early India', *The Indian Historical Review*, vol. 7, nos. 1–2 (1980–1), pp. 54–69; also B.D. Chattopadhyaya, 'Transition to the Early Historical Phase in the Deccan: A Note', in B.M. Pande and B.D. Chattopadhyaya, eds, *Archaeology and History (Essays in Memory of Sri A. Ghosh)*, vol. 2 (Delhi, 1987), pp. 727–32.

[33] For a statement of how geographers view the hierarchy of regions, and how such perceptions can relate fruitfully to the study of early Indian cultural patterns—not in isolation but in their interrelatedness—see B. Subbarao, *The Personality of India*, second edition (Baroda, 1958), chs I and II. Cf. also the relevant remarks by the Allchins: 'One of the distinctive features of South Asian culture in historic and recent times is the way in which it has encapsulated communities at many different cultural and technological levels, allowing them, to a large extent, to retain their identity and establish intercommunity relationships'. And further: 'We must recall that in the Indian subcontinent distinct, self-contained social groups, at different levels of cultural and technological development, survived right into this century. They include hunting and collecting tribes, pastoral nomads, shifting cultivators, traditional settled agriculturists, modern "developed" agriculturists, and several levels of urban industrial society, all co-existing and economically interdependent. This provides us with a basic model for past developments'. Bridget and Raymond Allchin, *The Rise of Civilization in India and Pakistan* (reprinted New Delhi, 1989), pp. 11, 62.

[34] This point was made earlier in B.D. Chattopadhyaya, 'Political Processes and Structure of Polity in Early Medieval India: Problems of Perspective', pp. 10–11.

mechanism of integration do not mean taking an epicentric position. On the contrary, they point to the need to understand how historical regions emerge with distinct personalities—not by being submerged by a single, predetermined cultural pattern but by responding to, and in turn reshaping with a broad range of variations, an ever dynamic pattern whose dominant political, social, economic and cultural dimensions could be recognized at a pan-Indian level. The making of early medieval India, if we adopt this perspective, may thus have to be seen in terms of the scale of certain fundamental movements within the regional and local levels, and not in terms of the crisis of a pre-existent, pan-Indian social order.

III

It is necessary to elucidate this position by referring to some of the important evidence which has a bearing upon the processes mentioned above. This evidence relates to specific contexts within the formation of regional societies. Chronologically, the period between the third and sixth centuries, but more particularly the period after the sixth century, was marked by an increasing scale of local state formation. This process is suggested by the emergence of different categories of ruling lineages distributed over regions which geographers like to put under different labels.[35]

To illustrate this process, I would like to cite examples from two time-brackets: the third-sixth centuries and the sixth-tenth centuries. In the Vidarbha region of north-east Maharashtra, archaeology reveals a sequence of cultures which, as in many other regions, stretches from the marginally Chalcolithic through the Megalithic to the early historical urban phase.[36] As a region, early historical Vidarbha was a part

[35] See note 33. The notion of regions, starting from what are considered 'perennially nuclear' to others down the scale, is present in O.H.K. Spate and A.T.A. Learmonth, *India and Pakistan (Land, People and Economy)* (Delhi, 1972), part 2. A familiarity with the notion of regions has proved of great use in understanding the differential chronology and scale of local-level state formation. This represents a distinct advance from the position which assumed the existence of states in all regions of India simultaneously, or which viewed the study of dynastic history as equivalent to the study of the state.

[36] For a brief statement on the sequence of archaeological cultures in Vidarbha,

of the major territorial kingdom of the Sātavāhanas, but the local state of Vidarbha, with an extensive agrarian base, came into existence only in the form of the Vākāṭaka lineage from the middle of the third century AD.[37] Going by the nature of the hypothesis being formulated regarding the breakdown of the early historical social order, one may encounter the suggestion that the agrarian kingdom of the Vākāṭakas was a consequence of the decline of the early historical urban centres of Vidarbha.[38] But the connection appears, even on the face of it, to be rather tenuous, and in any case impossible to validate empirically. Such a connection would also leave unexplained how the lineages of the Ikṣvākus, the early Pallavas and the early Kadambas (to name only a few) arose in other parts of the Deccan more or less in the same period.[39]

In the post-sixth century the scale of the formation of local states and the transformation of some of them into major, regional state structures became much more historically significant. These state structures, the rise of which can be located between the seventh and tenth centuries and which can be placed in all the major regions,[40] are

---

dating back, in limited finds, to 'aceramic microlithic' through the Chalcolithic to early historic cultures, see Amarendra Nath, 'Archaeology of the Wardha Wainganga Divide', *Puratattva* (Bulletin of the Indian Archaeological Society), no. 20 (1989–90), pp. 93–8. For a synthesis of data on the Megalithic cultures of the region, see K.K. Singh, 'Study of Some Aspects of the Megalithic culture of Vidarbha', unpublished M. Phil. dissertation, Centre for Historical Studies, Jawaharlal Nehru University (New Delhi, 1986).

[37] For a recent study of the agrarian base of the Vākāṭaka kingdom, based on a study of its land grants, see K.M. Shrimali, *Agrarian Structure in Central India and the Northern Deccan (A Study in Vākāṭaka Inscriptions)* (Delhi, 1987).

[38] For a brief resumé of the urban settlements of Vidarbha such as Pauni, Paunar, Kauṇḍinyapura, etc. and the extent of their chronological span, see R.S. Sharma, *Urban Decay in India*, pp. 74–8.

[39] For these post-Sātavāhana local ruling families which emerged in different parts of the Deccan and adjoining regions, see R.C. Majumdar, ed., *The Age of Imperial Unity* (vol. 2 of *The History and Culture of the Indian People)* (Bombay, 3rd impression, 1960), ch. 14.

[40] Since the primary concerns of early India's historians have been centred on reconstructing the genealogies and chronologies of ruling families, and on statements about dynastic achievements, the crucial dimensions which have generally been overlooked are: (i) how the emergence of ruling lineages in different areas bears upon the problem of local-level state formation and regional political structure; (ii) how

familiar to every student of Indian history. The point of significance is not their genealogical or military history but the fact that, examined closely, they all display trends which worked towards the formation of the regional political, economic and socio-religious order. These trends separate them from those of state formation in the early historical period. I shall return to this issue later.

I have picked on the process of local state formation, despite the presence of large territorial states in the early historical period, as exemplifying the process of transition. This is because when studied in the context of its local manifestation, state formation makes intelligible a wide range of relationships, whereas discussions regarding the state from 'the stratosphere of a rarified concept' rarely succeed in grasping such relationships. At one level, the process of state formation between the third-fourth and the sixth-tenth centuries resolved one outstanding issue: monarchy became the norm of polity. This vindicated Brāhmaṇical monarchical ideology, the view that anarchy pervaded the vacuums which signified an absence of monarchy.[41] The significance of this resolution was not limited to the political sphere, for even before the fourth century there was no opposition between heterodoxy and kingship; what it signified more importantly was the ultimate affirmation of the Brāhmaṇical view of the *varṇa* order in the political context. This was the most comprehensive framework of social stratification available, and its expansion in the form of *varṇa-saṁkara* was capable of both a horizontal and vertical spread. Since the framework was pliable, it left the working out of actual social details to their temporal-spatial contexts. Channels were available for the processes of social mobility, either in the form of movements

---

the phenomenon relates to local-level stratification and its agrarian order, and so on. For an idea of the scale and nature of the emergence of local ruling lineages in the two phases mentioned above, see R.S. Sharma, *Urban Decay in India*; J.G. De Casparis, 'Inscriptions and South Asian Dynastic Tradition', in R.J. Moore, ed., *Tradition and Politics in South Asia* (New Delhi, 1979), pp. 103–27; and B.D. Chattopadhyaya, 'Political Processes and Structure of Polity in Early Medieval India'.

[41] For a theoretical correlation between the absence of the monarch and anarchy, particularly within Brāhmaṇical ideology, see Romila Thapar, *From Lineage to State (Social Formations in the Mid-First Millennium* BC *in the Ganga Valley)*, p. 118; Idem, *Exile and the Kingdom: Some Thoughts on the Rāmāyaṇa* (Bangalore, 1978), pp. 10, 28.

within the hierarchy envisaged in the social order, or through the organization of protests against the ordering of the hierarchy.[42]

In addition to the dimension of ideology, to which was related the legitimation of royalty, the use of the term 'state' immediately implies (i) the existence of a resource base capable of generating a surplus; and (ii) the existence of a structure of relationships of domination and subordination. My contention is that if one were to examine the nature of the interrelatedness between the major societal processes identified above, we would reach an understanding of what precisely was activated by state formation. For example, if a recurrent motif of change in Indian society (and for the moment let us take this as an ahistorical abstraction) was the transformation of tribes into peasantry, then state formation, as a catalyst in the historical process, can be seen to accommodate several levels in the relationship of domination and subordination. Further, it points to the dominant strand in the total structure of such relations. In other words the extension of the state in pre-state societies, in those cases where state societies continued over centuries (either through conquest or through the emergence of local ruling lineages), inevitably brought about a range of changes in a region or in a community hitherto without the state sort of political formation. A state would integrate as well as disintegrate; it would

[42] This mobility took the form of segmentation and stratification within a community, with one segment emerging as an elite group, mostly by acquiring political power and an economic base. See B.D. Chattopadhyaya, 'Origin of the Rajputs: The Political, Economic and Social Processes in Early Medieval Rajasthan', *The Indian Historical Review*, vol. 3, no. I (1976), pp. 64–5; and S. Jaiswal, 'Studies in Early Indian Social History: Trends and Possibilities', *The Indian Historical Review*, vol. 6, nos. 1–2 (1979–80), pp. 1–63. There is also enough evidence to show that protests against the ordering of hierarchy as envisaged in the *varṇa* ideology (which gave predominance to Brāhmaṇas) were quite common. Dissenting groups such as the Siddhas rejected *varṇa* altogether (see notes. 67 and 68), and protests could also take the form of individual families, which wielded considerable political power, associating themselves with the Śūdra *varṇa* in order to claim a purity greater than the other *varṇas*. See S. Jaiswal, 'Varna Ideology and Social Change', *Social Scientist*, vol. 19, nos. 3–4 (1991), p. 47. The genesis of such early medieval ideas and movements as Vīraśaivism (which acquired a massive social following in the Deccan) lay in protests against *varna* hierarchy as well as against the ideological and economic dominance of Brāhmaṇas in society. See R.N. Nandi, 'Origin of the Vīraśaiva Movement', *The Indian Historical Review*, vol. 2, no. I (1975), pp. 32–46.

create a distinct stratum of ruling elites and, in doing so, cause ruptures within communities which had remained largely undifferentiated.[43] The formation of relationships of domination and subordination thus cannot be viewed entirely as the superimposition of extraneous elements upon a community; nor is stratification simply a dichotomous relationship between such elements and a pristine community.[44] In other words it is sharp fissions within communities and regions and the emergence of a complex of relations of domination and subordination which characterize a regional state society; this is irrespective of whether the polities representing such societies remained autonomous or semi-autonomous from, or became parts of, large state structures.[45]

In Rajasthan—the region from which I have analysed some of the empirical material[46]—the period approximately after the seventh century witnessed significant changes. The proliferation of ruling lineages,

[43] The volume of literature on early state formation is enormous. But the relevance of much of this literature for analysis of evidence from societies in which states had long been in existence is somewhat limited. However, the following works offer varied viewpoints on the implications of the emergence of the state in early societies: H.J.M. Claessen and Peter Skalnik, eds, *The Early State* (Mouton Publishers, 1978); Idem, *The Study of the State* (Mouton Publishers, 1981); Morton Fried, *The Evolution of Political Society* (New York, 1967); R. Cohen and E.R. Service, *Origins of the State: The Anthropology of Political Evolution* (Philadelphia, 1978); and H.J.M. Claessen and P. Van de Velde, eds, *Early State Dynamics* (Leiden, 1987).

[44] The use of terms such as 'village community' when applied to residents of a settled village which constituted a basic unit in a state, thus stands in the way of a proper understanding of rural social structure in the context of state society. If the residents of a village were differentiated in various ways, then constructing them into a 'community' would serve little purpose: intra-village as well as inter-village and trans-village networks would depend on how sections of rural residents were aligned across village boundaries. For relevant discussions, see B.D. Chattopadhyaya, *Aspects of Rural Settlements and Rural Society in Early Medieval India*, particularly, pp. 125–31.

[45] This is why the concept 'segmentary state', when applied to such large territorial kingdoms as the Cola, makes no sense. That concept is concerned merely with a superficial appraisal of how political powers representing different scales may have related to one another, not with the more vital dimension of their vertical structures. For bibliography and discussion, see B.D. Chattopadhyaya, 'Political Processes and Structure of Polity in Early Medieval India: Problems of Perspective'.

[46] See the relevant essays included in this collection and in *Aspects of Rural Settlements and Rural Society in Early Medieval India*, ch. 3.

which over time came to constitute the social category called 'Rajput', was initially spread over the period from the seventh to the tenth centuries. The process which crystallized in the formation of this social category drew in non-indigenous communities like the Hūṇas, as well as indigenous lineages like the Guhilas and the Caulukyas. In some cases, the integration of lineages bearing the same clan name laid the foundation of a stable state structure. This happened in the case of the Guhilas, several lineages of which were initially distributed over Gujarat and Rajasthan. By the twelfth-thirteenth centuries the Nagda-Ahar lineage of the Guhilas, which controlled the nuclear area of Mewar, had emerged as the most important lineage, preparing a stable base for the medieval state of Mewar.[47] In other parts of Rajasthan land grants as well as other varieties of grants after the seventh-eighth centuries point to the emergence of agrarian bases, supported in some areas by well irrigation. This was also the period when tribal and pastoral groups started getting either marginalized or began figuring, at least in epigraphic records, as cultivators. One specific case was the Gurjaras, who are mentioned as cultivators. But it should be noted that several ruling families of western India were likely to have emerged out of Gurjara stock.

The simultaneous operation of several processes of change in situations of regional state formation can be seen by making cross-regional references. The pattern was obviously not identical everywhere. For example, if one refers to the Orissa of the period between the fourth century and the mid-twelfth century in terms of three sub-phases (fourth-seventh centuries, seventh-tenth centuries and tenth-mid-twelfth centuries), one notices constant shifts in centres of power and the formation of new lineages side by side with the existence of some stable lineages. This goes on till the establishment of the major power of the Coḍa-Gaṅgas in the eleventh century.[48] The implication

[47] The history of the Guhila lineages of this phase and of the ascendancy of the Nagda-Ahar lineage has been worked out by Nandini Sinha, 'The Guhila Lineages and the Emergence of State in Early Medieval Mewar', unpublished M. Phil dissertation, Centre for Historical Studies, Jawaharlal Nehru University (New Delhi, 1988).

[48] The history and geographical distribution pattern of the ruling families of Orissa in this period are available in Upinder Singh, 'Kings, Brahmanas and Temples

of this political geography of Orissa between the fourth century and the mid-twelfth century is that the various loci of the ruling families which emerged were also, as the land grants tell us, the agrarian resource bases of such families. One can go further south and note how the formation of agrarian regions, in the context of the regional political structure, was taking place. It has been contended quite correctly that although the origins of the various sub-regions of Tamil Nadu go back to the early centuries,

> their development as agrarian regions, resource bases and cultural subregions took place over several centuries (seventh-thirteenth centuries). The earlier period was that of the Pallavas and Pāṇḍyas (seventh to ninth centuries) followed by the Colas (ninth to thirteenth centuries), particularly the last of them . . . In a sense, the macro-region evolved with the distinctive socio-political culture which developed under the Colas.[49]

As in the case of some areas of Rajasthan, the expansion of agrarian base and rural settlement region in Tamil Nadu too was linked with the expansion of irrigation networks. 'There is a general correspondence between the steady increase in irrigation works and the increase in the nāḍus under the Pallavas and early Colas'.[50] In fact one would suspect that the generalization made about Tamil Nadu would be applicable to other parts of peninsular India, though the pace and chronology of the formation of agrarian regions in such parts may have been somewhat different.

If we are willing to accept—and this will depend on how intent we are on departing from the overwhelmingly dominant notion—that

---

in Orissa: An Epigraphic Study (300–1147 C.E)', unpublished Ph.D dissertation (McGill University, 1990).

[49] R. Champakalakshmi, 'The Study of Settlement Patterns in the Cola Period: Some Perspectives', *Man and Environment*, vol. 14, no. 1 (1989), p. 92.

[50] Ibid., p. 97. This seems to correspond to Burton Stein's formulation regarding the expansion of settled agriculture and the acceleration in the pace of *nāḍu* formation in the Pallava-Cola periods. See *Peasant State and Society in Medieval South India*, ch. 2. For the importance of the Pallava-Pāṇḍya phase as marking a major beginning in irrigation works, see V. Venkayya, 'Irrigation in Southern India in Pallava Times', *Archaeological Survey of India: Annual Report 1903–04*, pp. 202–11; and Rajan Gurukkal, 'Aspects of the Reservoir System of Irrigation in the Early Pāṇḍya State', *Studies in History*, new series, vol. 2, no. 2 (1986), pp. 155–64.

local/sub-regional or regional state formation did not necessarily derive from the fragmentation of a given state structure, and that the stabilization of a state structure at local and regional levels implied changes of various dimensions, then it will be possible to turn to the other major societal process mentioned earlier, namely the peasantization of tribes and their absorption into the dominant social order as caste categories. Our readiness to accept an alternative perspective may also help us resolve certain anomalies which exist in our understanding of the conditions of the peasantry.

The anomaly can be stated in the following terms. It is often believed that the position of the Vaiśya *varṇa*, traditionally associated with cattle-keeping, agriculture and commerce, declined gradually as a result of the decline of long-distance commerce, and that the position of the Śūdras, whose ranks swelled through the assimilation of 'numerous aboriginal tribes and foreign elements' improved. In one formulation 'the new Śūdras do not seem to have been recruited as slaves and hired labourers like their older counterparts. They pursued their old occupations and were possibly taught new methods of agriculture, which gradually turned them into tax-paying peasants'.[51] At the same time it has been repeatedly stressed that the early medieval peasantry was a 'subject peasantry', their condition having undergone radical and adverse changes through the practice of land grants which introduced a layer of intermediaries between the state and the peasants.[52] The formulations in fact envisage two contradictory positions: (i) the 'subjection of the peasantry', their subjection having been generated by the practice of land grants.[53] This formulation thus does not seem

[51] R.S. Sharma, *Śūdras in Ancient India* (A Social History of the lower order down to *c.* AD 600), revised second edition (Delhi, 1980), pp. 240–41.

[52] The view that landed intermediaries undermined the cultivators through the practice of land grants has been most emphatically presented in R.S. Sharma, *Indian Feudalism*; and Idem, 'How Feudal was Indian Feudalism?', in *The Journal of Peasant Studies*, vol. 12, nos. 2–3, special issue edited by T.J. Byres and H. Mukhia (1985), pp. 19–43. See, for the use of the term 'subject peasantry', B.N.S. Yadava, 'Immobility and Subjection of Indian Peasantry in Early Medieval Complex', *The Indian Historical Review*, vol. I, no. I (1974), pp. 18–27.

[53] In addition to the references cited in note 52, see bibliography in B.D. Chattopadhyaya, 'State and Economy in Northern India: 4th century to 12th century' (forthcoming).

to relate to the Vaiśya peasants of the early historical period, whose economic and social status is believed to have declined because of the decline of commerce;[54] and (ii) the majority of the cultivators were by now tribes turned into tax-paying Śūdra peasants; these were no longer recruited as slaves and hired labourers, as were their older counterparts.[55]

This anomaly may be resolved if we get away from the *Dharmaśāstra* category of the Śūdra *varṇa.* This latter, when it related to the context of assimilated tribes and other ethnic elements, was in any case a product of the 'fiction of *varṇa-saṁkara*' (intermixture of *varṇas*).[56] Instead, we should examine the actual cultivating categories in different regional contexts. In fact, when I refer to cultivating groups in the post-Gupta period, I do not refer to them simply as Śūdras. I either use the status in terms of which they were known, or I use the specific names given to them in the sources. In Bengal, for example, the evidence from the Gupta period onwards refers to *kuṭumbins*, *mahattaras*, *mahāmahattaras* and to other categories who must have corresponded to different land-owning groups, including Brāhmaṇas.[57] Parallel references would be to the Kaivarttas who, in the context of the Pāla period, must have constituted a formidable community of cultivators. In addition to other types of evidence, the sustained (and for a period successful) peasant resistance put up by the Kaivarttas against Pāla rule bears adequate witness to this.[58] There

[54] R.S. Sharma, *Śūdras in Ancient India*, ch. 8.

[55] Ibid., pp. 240–1.

[56] Ibid. As R.S. Sharma correctly points out: 'The non-Sanskritic names of many of these mixed castes and their description as tribes or occupations at different places suggest that these were older tribes or occupations improvised into castes . . . ' (*Śūdras in Ancient India*, p. 336). And yet, by underlining conquests, territorial expansions and the 'practice of planting brāhmaṇas in the tribal areas through land grants' (ibid., pp. 337, 339) as the only mechanism through which transformation of tribes took place, he misses out on the process of change from below. In the period identified as early medieval, it was, as it has been shown in this essay, the changes from within localities and regions which alone can point to the ways in which not only were regional communities transformed but were hierarchized as well.

[57] For the implications of these references, see B.D Chattopadhyaya, *Aspects of Rural Settlements and Rural Society in Early Medieval India*, pp. 47–53 and 128–29.

[58] See R.S. Sharma, 'Problems of Peasant Protest in Early Medieval India', *Social*

is the occasional mention of groups of like *vardhakis* (carpenters)[59] or *carmakāras* (leather workers) either owning plots of land or having received land from the king to provide services to a newly established temple.[60] Attempts at systematization are evident from the Purāṇic literature. This not only relates diverse groups to the *varṇa* category but also makes distinctions between different tiers of a single *varṇa* such as Śūdra.[61]

The correlation between peasant economy based on wet-rice cultivation, and rural caste structure which derived essentially from a gradual transformation of a tribal region, is more evident from the inscriptions of Assam, which can be dated between the fifth and the thirteenth centuries. Several points which emerge from these inscriptions are worth noting. First, the language of the inscriptions, which is Sanskrit, 'is interspersed with a number of Khasi, Bodo and other non-Sanskritic tribal word formations which are indicative of the substratum of the region'.[62] For example, the occurrence of Bodo words used by the Kacharis living in the plains in the inscriptions is significant, since canal irrigation and other irrigational methods—through which the extension of cultivation took place—are also associated with the Kacharis. Second, it has been correctly stressed that 'the peasantry of pre-Ahom Assam is multi-ethnic in character'[63] and

Scientist, vol. 16, no. 9 (184) (1988), pp. 3–16. However, the nature of Kaivartta rebellion which brought Pāla rule to a close (for some time) would hardly suggest that they were 'subject peasants'; from all accounts they would appear to have been a formidable peasant community of eastern India.

[59] For references to individual carpenters owning plots of cultivated land in the late Gupta period, see D.C. Bhattacharyya, 'A Newly Discovered Copper Plate from Tippera', *The Indian Historical Quarterly*, vol. 6 (1930), pp. 54–60; and D.C. Sircar, *Select Inscriptions Bearing on Indian History and Civilization*, vol. I (University of Calcutta, second revised edition, 1965), pp. 340–5.

[60] See the evidence of the Paschimbhag copper plates of the Candra King Śrīcandra; D.C. Sircar, *Epigraphic Discoveries in East Pakistan* (Calcutta, 1973), pp. 31–6; 63–9.

[61] Niharranjan Ray, *Bāṅgālir Itihās (Ādi Parva)*, (in Bengali) (Calcutta, third edition, 1980), ch. 7; also B.N.S. Yadava, *Society and Culture in Northern India in the Twelfth Century*, ch. I.

[62] N. Lahiri, 'Landholding and Peasantry in the Brahmaputra Valley, *c.* 5th–13th centuries AD', *Journal of the Economic and Social History of the Orient*, vol. 33 (1990), pp. 157–68.

[63] Ibid.

that 'the dominant impression is of a number of tribal groups such as the Mikirs, Khasis, Kukis and Kacharis having taken to cultivation on a permanent basis at some point in the past before the creation of a dominant class of brahmin landholders'.[64] Assam inscriptions too refer to the Kaivarttas, and in fact one comes across at least two groups of Kaivarttas, the Abanchi Kaivarttas and the Svalpadyuti Kaivarttas.[65]

The point then is that, in the context of the post-Gupta period, the use of the category Śūdra is entirely insufficient when explaining the composition and status of the peasantry and the agricultural labour which constituted the base of an internally and highly hierarchized society—i.e. the problem of regional social stratification. To continue with the point which was being made above, it we turn to a region like Tamil Nadu, there would be an extensive continuum from such groups as the Paraiyar to the upper echelons of the dominant Vellāla.[66] In Karnataka too, epigraphs make clear distinctions with specific references to *prabhugāvuṇḍas, prajāgāvuṇḍas, bhūmiputrakas* and many other categories.[67] A detailed examination of the condition of the peasantry in the post-Gupta period is not intended here; we only need to note, by making a few cross-regional references, that the majority of regionally recognizable cultivating groups, such as the Gurjaras,

[64] Ibid.

[65] Ibid. For the situation is Assam, also see N. Lahiri, *Pre-Ahom Assam (Studies in the Inscriptions of Assam Between the Fifth and the Thirteenth Centuries AD)* (Delhi, 1991), ch. 4.

[66] Historical studies on stratification at the level of cultivating groups in individual villages have hardly been undertaken. A major reason for this may be that historians of pre-modern India have generally accepted the notion of a village community without considering the range of differentiation existing within it. For south India of the Pallava or the Cola periods, no systematic study of such stratification is therefore available. The major concern of historians has so far been to underline distinctions between peasant-dominated *urs* and brahmin-dominated *brahmadeyas.* However, the following publications may be consulted for a general impression of the agrarian situation in early medieval south India: K.A. Nilakanta Sastri, *The Colas* (University of Madras, reprint of second edition, 1975), ch. 21; N. Karashima, *South Indian History and Society: Studies from Inscriptions, AD 850–1800* (Delhi, 1984), chs 1 and 2.

[67] For a brief discussion of the evidence from Karnataka, see B.D. Chattopadhyaya, *Aspects of Rural Settlements and Rural Society in Early Medieval India*, pp. 93–114.

Kaivarttas, Gāvuṇḍas, Reḍḍis, Kalitas[68]—a bewildering multiplicity of which constitute the Indian peasantry—started figuring in historical records only from the Gupta, and more perceptibly from the post-Gupta period. The time span, which is the sixth-seventh centuries to the twelfth-thirteenth centuries, thus represents a crucial phase in the evolution of regional agrarian structures. This was, as pointed out already, the time span significant in the history of the regional political structures as well. Second, the use of *Dharmaśāstra* categories to posit the decline of the Vaiśya *varṇa* and the ascendancy of the Śūdra (which in any case creates a curious epistemological anomaly) has little relevance for explaining post-Gupta historical developments. The new Śūdras, if they represented tribal communities turned into castes, could hardly be taken to illustrate the process of upward social mobility of the early historical Śūdra *varṇa*.

IV

The ideological and religious dimensions of the society which was going through these processes of transition were, to say the least, complex. Indeed, if one were to consider that even such mutually incompatible situations as—(i) ritual power generated by the monopoly over the Vedas; (ii) the anti-Vedic Siddha or Somasiddhāntika protestations; and (iii) other levels in between these—were all ideological manifestations related to the period,[69] then it is difficult to envisage

[68] In addition to the references cited above, see S. Jaiswal, 'Varna Ideology and Social Change', *Social Scientist*, vol. 19, nos. 3–4 (1991), pp. 41–8.

[69] The ideological dimensions of the society identified as early medieval were indeed complex. Despite the fact that Brāhmaṇism—both in the spread and perpetuation of Vedism as well as in the crystallization of Purāṇism—figures prominently in records as projecting the widest range of recognized and revered symbols, it was not in itself homogeneous, and certainly not the only point of reference. The geographical spread of *brahmadeyas, agrahāras* and other types of Brāhmaṇic settlements was extensive. Repeated references to branches of Vedic and affiliated learning and to impressive Purāṇic compilations point to the general dominance of Brāhmaṇism. Yet movements against the norms and the order which Brāhmaṇism stood for, as well as tensions within Brāhmaṇism itself, are evident. There is no systematic study of this as yet, but for some samples, see A.V. Subramania Aiyar, *The Poetry and the Philosophy of the Tamil Siddhars—An Essay in Criticism* (Chidambaram, 1969); Kamil V. Zvelebil, *The Poets of the Powers* (London, 1973); David Shulman,

a homogeneous strand in the ideological evolution of the period. Yet meaningful attempts to understand the making of the early medieval phase of Indian history must relate to all these dimensions. It is generally believed that Bhakti and the worship through Bhakti of God as a Lord located in a temple, was the key ideological strand of the period. Evidence of the extensive spread of Bhakti is certainly available in south India. One form of this is the devotional hymns of the Vaiṣṇava Ālvārs and Śaiva Nayanars; a second is the records of their extensive itineraries at proliferating temple centres.[70] In south India the term for the temple (*kovil*) was the same as that for the king's residence. God was the Lord, and the relationship between God and his devotee was seen as parallel to an all-pervasive feudal ideology. Similarly, the pervasiveness of Tantra and its penetration into all religious systems and practices were seen as proceeding from and contributing to the degeneration into which Indian feudal society had sunk.[71]

'The Enemy Within: Idealism and Dissent in South Indian Hinduism' in S.N. Eisenstadt, Reuven Kahane and David Shulman, eds, *Orthodoxy, Heterodoxy and Dissent in India* (Mouton Publishers: Berlin, New York, Amsterdam, 1984), pp. 11–55.

[70] The literature on Bhakti is extensive and need not be cited in detail. For a treatment of Bhakti as an ideology from an historical perspective (in the context of early medieval south India), see M.G.S. Narayanan and Veluthat Kesavan, 'Bhakti Movement in South India', reprinted in D.N. Jha, ed., *Feudal Social Formation in Early India*, pp. 348–75; also R. Champakalakshmi, 'Religion and Social Change in Tamil Nadu (*c*. AD 600–1300)', in N.N. Bhattacharyya, ed., *Medieval Bhakti Movements in India*, Sri Caitanya Quincentenary Commemoration Volume (New Delhi, 1989), pp. 162–73. For extensive treatment of Kṛṣṇa-*bhakti*, oriented towards the institution of temples, see F. Hardy, *Viraha-Bhakti: The Early History of Kṛṣṇa Devotion in South India* (New Delhi, 1983), *passim*. Two points which Hardy makes and which bear vitally upon the concerns of this essay are: (i) Kṛṣṇa-*bhakti*, expressed in the hymns of the Ālvārs, represents increasing brāhmaṇization. Despite 'increasing popularization' it was at the same time showing increasing reorientation according to 'normative ideology'; and (ii) Kṛṣṇa-*bhakti* may be seen, apart from other things, in the light of its contribution towards a 'reconsolidated Tamil awareness'.

[71] The degeneration of Indian society in the post-Gupta or post-Harṣa period seems firmly rooted in the historians' perspective of the period. A sample of this perspective is K.M. Panikkar's remarks during his Presidential Address to the Indian History Congress: 'Another problem that faces the student is the decadence which seems to have overtaken Hindu society in the period between the 8th and the 12th centuries', Presidential Address, Indian History Congress, 18th session (Calcutta, 1955), p. 17. In recent years, strong statements on early medieval degeneration have

It is not possible here to examine the voluminous writings on these aspects nor even to attempt a synthesis of views. We can at the most turn now to the last major historical/societal process, i.e. the appropriation and integration of cults. It is necessary to briefly consider the operation of this process in order to understand how it relates to the problem of transition. Cult assimilation does not necessarily imply a harmonious syncretism, but it does imply the formation of a structure which combines heterogeneous beliefs and rituals into a whole even while making (or transforming) specific elements dominant.[72] In many significant ways the crystallization of a major cult illustrates the ideological dimensions of that phase of Indian history. First, the fact that the Brahmins came to control the major cults and cult centres was the mechanism which transformed the character of earlier 'local and tribal cults'. It has been aptly remarked:

> This new Hindu cult comprised, on the one hand, a *regular* sequence of daily rites, and was directed, on the other hand, to a permanently 'present' god who was worshipped either in the form of an *anthropomorphic* divine idol or as a Saivite liṅgam. This god, who was always present and visible, required also regular offerings. In contrast, the local tribal deities manifested themselves just now and then in their non-iconic symbols or in a priestly medium and received offerings only on these definite occasions. This comparison between the Hindu temple cults and the cults of the autochthonous local deities . . . might certainly have induced the people to draw comparisons between the status of their earlier tribal chiefs and that of a new Hindu rājā. In the basically egalitarian tribal societies of India the chiefs

---

come from Devangana Desai in her analyses of art activities of the period: 'Art under Feudalism in India: c. AD 500–1300', *The Indian Historical Review*, vol. I (1974), pp. 10–17; Idem, *Erotic Sculpture of India*, Delhi, 1975, *passim*.

[72] The implication of this crucial historical process in the structural formation of important cults has not been satisfactorily worked out. This is primarily because material on the historical stages through which different elements coalesced, as also on the general brāhmaṇization of these cults, is inadequate. The dimensions of appropriation, brāhmaṇization and politicization of a cult—and in some cases the growth of a cult to regional as well as trans-regional importance—are sufficiently evident in the history of the cult of Jagannātha; A. Eschmann, H. Kulke and G.C. Tripathi, eds, *The Cult of Jagannath and the Regional Tradition of Orissa* (Delhi, 1978), *passim*. That the process of appropriation is a continuing one emerges from the detailed study on the cult of Pattinī; see G. Obeyesekere, *The Cult of the Goddess Pattini*.

could assume a more elevated position only temporarily and in certain functions (as for example while waging war). Only in this functional position could they expect some regular presentations and services from people outside their own clan (villages?). The Hindu rājā claimed an altogether different position. In the Brahmanical theory of society he occupied an elevated rank which towered continuously above that of his former tribal brethren . . . In this new 'representation' he demanded regular tributes—as the ever present 'new' Hindu god in the temple nearby demanded worship continuously.[73]

The symbiosis which developed between royal power and the perception of divinity, as well as the nexus involving different social groups which operated around a major cult centre are very well illustrated by the detailed empirical work which has been done on the cult of Puruṣottama-Jagannātha at Puri in Orissa.[74] Another dimension of the historical process, perhaps territorially more pervasive during the period, was the spread of Śakti, signifying a coming to the fore of an hitherto dormant religious force. To demonstrate further how an understanding of the regional context as an arena for the interplay of societal processes is important, I shall refer briefly to the emergence of Śakti, principally by considering how this phenomenon has been viewed.

Dwelling on the impact of Tāntrism (including Tāntric Śāktism), B.N.S. Yadava, who has done extensive work which advocates the feudal character of early medieval India, writes: 'The *Bṛhaddharma Purāṇa* clearly reveals that Tāntric Buddhism, Tāntric Śaivism and Tāntric Śāktism had made the position of *varṇāśramadharma* critical in Bengal and the adjoining regions.'[75] Even without going into the question of which specific period is being talked about, significant in the statement is the assumption that the position of *varṇāśrama-dharma* was likely to have been 'critical' in 'Bengal and the adjoining areas'. This assumption proceeds from what I would call an 'epicentric, Dharmaśāstric' view of Indian society. It would see deviations from the Dharmaśāstric schema as social aberrations, not as a concrete

[73] H. Kulke, 'The Early and the Imperial Kingdom in Early Medieval India' (manuscript).

[74] A. Eschmann, *et al.*, *The Cult of Jagannath*, *passim.*

[75] B.N.S. Yadava, *Society and Culture in Northern India in the Twelfth Century*, p. 380.

regional reality. In other words, instead of assuming that Tāntric Śāktism made the position of *varṇāśramadharma* critical in eastern India, a more contingent query would have been to understand the reason for the reappearance and pervasiveness of Śakti in eastern India. To understand the reappearance of Śakti or the Goddess on the Indian religious scene, Daniel Ingalls notes:

What is strange about [the] Indian record is not so much the replacement of female by male hierophanies, a phenomenon which has occurred over most of the civilized world, as the fact that in India the Goddess reappears . . . why should the Indian record have differed? To such large questions there are no certain answers . . . I suspect that within India's diversified culture the worship of the Goddess never ceased. The two thousand year silence of the record may be explained by the fact that all our texts from that period are either in Sanskrit or closely related languages. Our earliest hymns to the Goddess, according to this view, are the continuation of an old religion, not an innovation. These first appear at the conjunction of two historical processes. On the one hand Sanskrit, by the third century, had become the nearly universal language of letters in India. On the other hand, the pre-Aryan worship of the Indians had spread by that time very widely among the Aryans. From the third or fourth century, at any rate, the religion of the Goddess becomes as much part of the Hindu written record as the religion of God.[76]

Once this conjunction takes place—and it does not necessarily have to be expressed in terms of Aryan and non-Aryan categories—regional elements begin to take shape through local assimilation as well as through the adoption of trans-regional idioms. On the eastern Indian regional Mother Goddess cult, the central theme of the *Kālikā Purāṇa*, B.K. Kakati makes the following generalization:

Once her existence was recognized and her worship formulated, all local and independent deities began to be identified with her as her local manifestations . . . The process of assimilation went on until in the Devī-Bhāgavata it came to be declared that all village goddesses should be regarded as partial manifestations of the goddess . . . Thus the concept of the Mother Goddess

[76] Daniel H.H. Ingalls, 'Foreword' in C. Mackenzie Brown, *God as Mother (A Feminine Theology of India)* (Vermont, 1974), pp. xiv–xv.

assumed a cosmic proportion and all unconnected local numina were affiliated to her.[77]

This seems to be substantially the opinion of K.R. Van Kooij too, when he refers to the division, or rather multiple manifestations, of one goddess as five separate goddesses: Kāmākhyā, Mahotsahā, Tripurā, Kāmeśvarī and Śāradā; also to the mode of worship adapted to each particular goddess who has her own magic formula (*mantra*), a geometrical figure (*yantra*) and her own iconography; and to secondary deities such as Śaktis, yoginīs, doorkeepers, etc. The 'common ritual covers by far the greater part of the fragment on devī-worship' in the text of the *Kālikā-Purāṇa*, and 'this fact is . . . a clear indication of the author's concern to have the deities of *his country* propitiated by a cult form closely corresponding to the ones usual in other parts of India of his time, and to draw in this way the borderland of Kāmarūpa in the fold of Hinduism'.[78]

The merger of diverse elements in the formation of a cult in Purāṇic Hinduism was nothing new. The composition of major divinities like Śiva, Viṣṇu and Umā derived from the same process. What becomes significant in the context of the shaping of regional society and culture is when we come across recorded references—for the first time and more or less within the same time-frame—to local and peripheral deities such as Araṇyavāsinī, Bahughṛṇādevī and Vaṭayakṣiṇīdevī in Rajasthan,[79] to Virajā in Orissa[80] and Kāmākhyā in Assam,[81] to cite a few cases. Juxtaposed with evidence of other kinds, they too become indicators of an overall process of change in these

[77] Banikanta Kakati, *The Mother Goddess Kamakhya (or Studies in the Fusion of Aryan and Primitive Beliefs of Assam)* (Gauhati, third impression, 1967), p. 65.

[78] K.R. Van Kooij, *Worship of the Goddess According to the Kālikā Purāṇa*, part I. (A Translation with an introduction and notes of chs 54–69) (Leiden, 1972), pp. 7–8.

[79] See *Epigraphica Indica*, vol. 20, pp. 97–9; ibid., vol. II, pp. 26–79.

[80] For Virajā of Jajpur, who was considered a form of Durgā and became a member of the group of *pañcadevatās* or five deities, see A. Eschmann, *et al.*, ed., *The Cult of Jagannath and the Regional Tradition of Orissa*, *passim*; also H. Kulke, 'Fragmentation and Segmentation versus Integration? Reflections on the Concepts of Indian Feudalism and the Segmentary State in Indian History', *Studies in History*, vol. 4, no. 2 (1982), pp. 237–64.

[81] Banikanta Kakati, *The Mother Goddess . . .*

regions. They do not all develop into major cults, but some do. They function towards the integration of other local cults and become one of the recognizable symbols of the region.[82] The religious and ideological expressions of a region in their varied forms thus become enmeshed in the web of its polity, economy and society. The interrelated vehicle of their expression is naturally language.[83]

V

The argument that I have been trying to develop, starting with a statement on historiography, can now be rounded off. Two points, in particular, need to be underlined. First, although an overview of Indian society of, say, the period between the sixth-seventh and the twelfth-thirteenth centuries would show it to be vastly different from Indian society of the early historical period, the change does not necessarily have to be envisaged in terms of a collapse of the early historical social order. In trying to decipher the dominant pattern from among apparently irreconciliable sets of evidence (alleged 'urban decay'[84] and the large-scale formation of states, for example), the most dominant pattern seemes to be the shaping of regional societies. The period indicated above was most crucial in so far as the majority of the territorial segments of the Indian subcontinent were concerned.

[82] In some regions, for instance Orissa, the integration of different cults came about by combining the worship of deities at different centres through concepts such as *pañcadevatā* or five deities. The five gods were Viṣṇu/Jagannātha of Purī, Śiva/Lingarāja of Bhuvaneswar, Durgā/Virajā of Jajpur, Sūrya of Konarak, and Gaṇeśa or Mahāvināyaka; cf. H. Kulke, 'The Early and the Imperial Kingdom in Early Medieval India' (manuscript).

[83] In addition to other evidence bearing on the increasing visibility of regional languages an important indicator would be the chronology of, and the manner in which, regional languages started figuring in the inscriptions. See D.C. Sircar, *Indian Epigraphy* (Delhi, 1965), ch. 2.

[84] R.S. Sharma, in his *Urban Decay in India* (pp. 177–81), envisages the decline of early Indian urban civilization in two stages. Curiously, he derives the ruralization of early Indian economy from this decline, thus making the implicit assumption that early Indian economy was not predominantly rural before this. In any case, his statement that 'the period *c.* 400–650 seems to have been particularly important for the rise of new states or kingdoms' (p. 168) obviously does not intend to suggest that there was any direct correlation between the decline of early historical urban civilization and the 'rise of new states or kingdoms'.

What I have called the shaping of regional societies was essentially a movement from within, following from the operation of several major historical/societal processes in regional contexts. This explains the relative long-range stability of regional social structures and identities.

Second, in the operation of the major historical/societal processes in regional contexts, the crucial agency of change was the phenomenon of state formation at diverse territorial levels, from local through supra-local to regional, at times expanding into supra-regional. It needs to be reiterated that the process of state formation was not a unique characteristic only of the time span discussed. However, the relationship between the process and region formation, considered from a pan-Indian perspective, was perhaps the closest in this period. Admittedly, in Indian history the crystallization of regions was, like the formation of states, a continuing process. Our period marked in a perceptible way the coming together of ingredients which go into the making of regions. State formation was a crucial agent of change in this respect, in the sense that it brought a measure of cohesion among local elements of culture by providing them a focus. At the same time it mediated in the assimilation of ideas, symbols and rituals which had a much wider territorial spread and acceptability. Common modes of royal legitimation and interrelated phenomena such as the practice of land grants, the creation of *agrahāras*, the emergence of major cult centres and temple complexes, social stratification subscribing to the *varṇa* order (even when the order in the strict sense of the term was absent)—all these were manifestations of the manner in which local-level states mediated in the absorption of ideas and practices which had been taking shape as a wider temporal and ideological process. The taking root of these ideas and practices was not a simple fact of diffusion from some elusive centre. It was an indication essentially of where and in what forms state society was taking shape.

This perspective leaves us pondering a few last points. If the transformation of early historical society took the form of the gradual shaping of regional societies, and if this transformation is seen as having essentially derived from the major ingredients of early historical society, then how do we respond to the schema of periodization which envisages an early medieval phase in the Indian context; also, what is our response to the notion of an Indian feudal society as characterizing that phase? Since the main concerns of the present exercise have been with historiography, and with delineating the directions taken by the transformation of early historical society, these problems seem marginal to this exercise. However, a brief response is in order, keeping in view the issues raised. Even in stereotypes which assert the changelessness of pre-modern Indian society, such markers of periodization as Hindu, Muslim and British, or Ancient, Medieval and Modern have been in use for very long. Despite the possible existence of sharply different notions of social change, markers differentiating broad historical phases need to continue in Indian history. Our perception of how the nature of early historical society changed may differ from the perceptions which are currently dominant, but continuing with the term 'early medieval', rather than using terms such as 'late Hindu' or 'late classical', has an advantage.[85] This term goes beyond the narrowly political and cultural dimensions of history, and, further, it clearly projects continuities in the operation of major societal processes well into later phases of Indian history. As argued earlier, the major thrust in the process of region formation may be located five or six centuries preceding the establishment of Turkish rule. It should be reiterated, simultaneously, that the process had neither its beginning nor its end during these centuries.

Whether this early medieval society was feudal is an altogether different issue. Even those who believe in feudalism as a typical and exclusively European social formation make exceptions by relating this concept to other societies.[86] So the issue of whether Indian history is entitled to a feudal phase or not can hardly ever be considered closed. The point I have tried to make is that the historiography on the transition to what is considered the feudal phase has been ever-shifting and essentially dependent on the directions of European historiography;[87] it therefore suffers from internal inconsistencies. Unless this

[85] The term is used in the title of a general survey of the period: M.K. Bose, *Late Classical India* (Calcutta, 1988).

[86] For example, Perry Anderson who is apparently critical of the particular 'version of materialist historiography' which views feudalism as 'an absolving ocean in which virtually any society may receive its baptism', is nevertheless prepared to discuss in detail 'Japanese feudalism'. Perry Anderson, *Lineages of the Absolutist State* (London, Verso edition, 1974), pp. 402, 435–61.

[87] B.D. Chattopadhyaya, 'State and Economy in North India: 4th century to

historiography reconciles itself to certain empirically validated major societal processes in Indian history, the current construct of Indian feudalism will continue with its Eurocentric orientation,[88] from a persistent refusal to consider alternative modes of social change. This paper outlines what I perceive, tentatively, as an alternative mode.

12th century' (forthcoming).

[88] Despite the fact that the term 'Indian feudalism' has been coined to stress the Indianness of what is perceived as the Indian feudal formation, the range of variables which have been chosen to construct 'Indian feudalism' still largely conforms to shifts in European historiography. It seems clear, from a recent restatement of the 'Marxist position in support of Indian Feudalism' (see Preface in D.N. Jha, ed., *Feudal Social Formation in Early India*), that both among 'antiquarians' and among other categories of historians, no satisfactory model of social change which works as an alternative to the Feudal mode, has been available so far.

2

*Irrigation in Early Medieval Rajasthan**

Although the two broad regions of Rajasthan, demarcated into east and west by the regular stretch of the Aravalli in a north-east-southeast direction, have distinct geographical characteristics,[1] yet perhaps neither of them can be justifiably called, to use two archaic expressions, *nadīmātṛka* (i.e. river-fed) or *devamātṛka* (i.e. rain-fed).[2] As such, any attempt to reconstruct the agrarian history of these areas will have to take into account the patterns of their irrigation system. The present paper seeks to examine available data on irrigation relating to the early medieval period, its emphasis being on methods of artificial irrigation. Apart from the nature of the relevant contents of inscriptions—the major source-material for this period—the impression that settlement areas proliferated in early medieval Rajasthan[3] while climatic conditions or natural drainage conditions either remained unaltered or deteriorated,[4] provides the only other rationale

* Reprinted from *Journal of the Economic and Social History of the Orient*, vol. XVI, parts II–III (1973).

[1] For the geography of Rajasthan I have largely depended upon V.C. Misra, *Geography of Rajasthan* (New Delhi, 1967).

[2] For the use and sources of these expressions, see S.K. Maity, *Economic Life of Northern India in the Gupta Period*, second edition (Delhi-Patna-Varanasi, 1970), p. 33; also A.K. Chaudhary, *Early Medieval Village in North-eastern India (AD 600–1200)* (Calcutta, 1971), pp. 113, 139, fn. 4.

[3] It is not possible to fully substantiate this supposition within the compass of this paper except by underlining that its main focus is on western Rajasthan where archaeological material on early historical settlements is almost totally absent.

[4] The only relevant evidence so far comes from Rang Mahal in north Rajasthan. See Hanna Rydh, *Rang Mahal* (The Swedish archaeological expedition to India 1952–54) (Lund-Bonn-Bombay, 1959); see also n. 8. For general impressions regarding increasing aridity, see P.C. Raheja, 'Influence of Climatic Changes on the Vegetation of the Arid Zone in India', *Annals of Arid Zone* (published by the Arid Zone Research Association of India), vol. IV, no. I, 1965, pp. 64–8; also, 'Proceedings of the Symposium on the Rajputana Desert' (*Bulletin of the National Institute of Sciences of India*), vol. I, *passim.*

for such an emphasis. The material examined here is confined to inscriptions of the early medieval period, but it is done in the hope that an initial brief survey may eventually lead to a more detailed and meaningful research. The first part of the paper deals with the territorial distribution of different devices of artificial irrigation; the second attempts to study, albeit sketchily, the relationship between irrigation and whatever imperfect knowledge we have about crop production in early medieval Rajasthan, and the final part seeks to view irrigation organization as part of the agrarian structure.

Although the paper refers roughly to *c.* 700–*c.* 1300, it also considers the pattern of crop production and irrigation in the earlier period to see whether any change in this pattern is perceptible. Quite naturally, the data for ancient times have so far been very meagre. Early excavation reports refer only perfunctorily to evidence relating to cultivation. Rairh, in the former Jaipur state—a site believed to have been under occupation between the third century BC and second century AD, with traces of partial occupation till the Gupta period—has yielded, from its ringwell or soakpit deposits, nondescript 'corn', and the finding of millet has been reported once.[5] The first century AD remains from Bairat, also in the former Jaipur state, include a fragment of cloth that may indicate local production of cotton.[6] Excavations at Nagari in Chitorgarh district do not seem to have yielded any corresponding specimen, and Bhandarkar's find of six alleged oilmills has no significance in this respect as there is no indication whatsoever regarding the dates of these finds.[7]

[5] K.N. Puri, *Excavations at Rairh during 1938–39 and 1939–40* (Department of Archaeology and Historical Research, Jaipur, no date), pp. 58–61, nos. 81, 82, 103.

[6] D.R. Sahni, *Archaeological Remains and Excavations at Bairat* (Department of Archaeology and Historical Research, Jaipur, no date), p. 22.

It is believed that Hiuen Tsang's seventh century account of P'o-li-ye-ta-lo or Pāriyātra gives an idea of the agricultural products of the Bairat area. 'According to him Pāriyātra (Bairat?) yielded crops of spring wheat and other grains, including a peculiar kind of rice', D. Sharma (General ed.), *Rajasthan Through the Ages*, vol. I (published by Rajasthan State Archives) (Bikaner, 1966), p. 67; also T. Watters, *On Yuan Chwang's Travels in India* (Delhi reprint, 1961), p. 300. The chronology of this evidence falls more within the scope of the early medieval rather than of the early historical period.

[7] D.R. Bhandarkar, *The Archaeological Remains and Excavations at Nagari* (Memoirs of the Archaeological Survey of India, no. 4) (Calcutta, 1920), p. 127.

Comparatively recent excavations at two sites, widely distant from each other, have produced more detailed results. Evidence of rice cultivation over a lengthy stretch of time comes from Rang Mahal in Bikaner in north Rajasthan.[8] The late phases at Ahar in Udaipur district also correspond to some extent to the early historical period. Here the cultivation of rice of long-seeded strain is believed to go back to phase I, period I, to which is assigned a date earlier than the middle of the second millennium BC. The site attests to the cultivation also of millet or *jawar*, the period probably being '*c.* 100 BC-AD'. It is also hopefully postulated on the strength of contemporary remains from other areas of India that 'it is more than probable that the Aharians ate wheat'.[9]

This appears to be the sum total of the picture so far as the early historical period is concerned.[10] All these crops continue down to early medieval times, but no other meaningful comparison either in terms of regional distribution of crops or any substantial addition, in the later period, to the number of crops cultivated, appears plausible. As we shall see later, early medieval cultivation was not limited to millet, rice, *jawar*, wheat and cotton (though, it may be guessed, they must have been the major items even in those times); the list for the early historical as also for the early medieval period may at best be considered to be only partial. Secondly, any possible addition in later times may not have been related to artificial irrigation.

However, whatever relevant data we have on the probable sources

[8] Hanna Rydh, *Rang Mahal*; pp. 79, 183. From an examination of textile impressions on Rang Mahal pottery, it has been suggested that the fabric used was from a 'vegetable fibre': jute, cotton or even hemp (p. 202). The area of origin of such fibres is, however, not specified. At the time of the publication of the Report, the plant remains from Rang Mahal were being examined at Dehra Dun. I am not aware of whether or not the results have been published.

[9] H.D. Sankalia, S.B. Deo and Z.D. Ansari, *Excavations at Ahar (Tambavati)* (Poona, 1969), pp. 217, 236; also Appendix II, Vishnu-Mittre, 'Remains of Rice and Millet', pp. 229–35.

[10] This appears particularly paradoxical in view of the fact that the earliest evidence of plough cultivation in the Indian subcontinent comes from north Rajasthan (Kalibangan in Ganganagar district). See *Indian Archaeology 1968–69—A Review*, pp. 29–30; also B.B. Lal, 'Perhaps the Earliest Ploughed Field So Far Excavated Anywhere in the World', *Purātattva* (Bulletin of the Indian Archaeological Society, no. 4) (1970–71), pp. 1–3.

of irrigation in early historical areas make a comparison with the later period to some extent relevant, particularly in view of the already underlined impression that settlement areas expanded in early medieval times. The Rairh area, as K.N. Puri mentions, is intersected by the river Dhil.[11] The Bairat valley is drained by two rivulets, the Bairat *nālā* running northward to join the Banganga river, and the Bandrol *nālā* in the south.[12] Ahar too is located on the bank of the Ahar river, a tributary of the Banas.[13] While the location of these three sites indicates their possible sources of water supply, the evidence seems to be more specific at Rang Mahal, where in early times, a high rainfall rate and annual flooding of the Ghaggar probably facilitated rice cultivation.[14] If these instances are taken to form any generalization regarding the early historical period, then the organization of artificial irrigation in early medieval Rajasthan certainly constitutes a departure from the earlier pattern. However, as will emerge from our discussion, the change is perceptible mostly in southern and western Rajasthan, from where the bulk of our material comes.[15]

I

We may start with the rather obvious statement that artificial irrigation in early medieval Rajasthan was provided by (i) tanks; and (ii) wells. These must have been common modes elsewhere as well, and yet in view of a variety of other existing methods, the prevalence of only these two in Rajasthan may have had some significance. We have perhaps no reference here to such big projects as canal excavation, which was sponsored by rulers in other areas.[16] In terms of financial

[11] K.N. Puri, *Excavations at Rairh. . .*, p. 1 and map facing p. 1.

[12] D.R. Sahni, *Archaeological Remains . . .*, p. 12.

[13] Sankalia, *Excavations at Ahar . . .*, p. 1.

[14] Hanna Rydh, *Rang Mahal*, pp. 33, 44, 183. The desertion of the area in the late sixth century has been attributed to changes in climatic conditions and the drying up of the Ghaggar (p. 33).

[15] A study of the published material relating to early medieval Rajasthan gives one the impression that western Rajasthan has been more intensively explored than any other area.

[16] Cf. Hatun rock inscription of the time of Paṭolaṣāhideva which records the construction, by the chief of the army at Giligitta (Gilgit), of a tank and the

investment, labour mobilization, impact on cultivation and the nature of land revenue assessment, the absence of such large-scale projects may have made the Rajasthan pattern considerably different.

References to tanks and reservoirs excavated by and perhaps named after individuals are not uncommon in early medieval records. In the period immediately preceding AD 700 they must have constituted an important source of water supply, as did wells. The Guhila inscriptions issued from Kishkindhā near Kalyanpur in the Dungarpur-Udaipur area of Udaipur district give us some idea about the possible methods of irrigation. An inscription of AD 689, while specifying the boundaries of two plots of land in the village of Mitrapallikā, mentions a *pāhakataḍāgikā* (a small tank) as one of the boundaries.[17] Similarly a second plot lay around a well (*kūpa-kaccha* is the expression used to denote the nature of the land).[18] A contemporary record, of AD 644, refers to *karkka-taḍāga* in the context of irrigated fields in the Bhilwara district.[19] There are repeated references to tanks and reservoirs in later inscriptions. Reference to three reservoirs (*rāhudatraya*) is found in the Sevadi (Bali, Pali district, former Jodhpur state) copper plates of AD 1119,[20] and the context would associate them with the irrigation of that area. This relationship is also clear in an inscription of AD 1155 from Thakarda in the former Dungarpur state,[21] which records the

excavation of a canal of 32,000 *hastas* (?) called *Makaravāhinī* which 'was taken out' to a forest to the east of the village Hātuna (*EI*, XXX, pp. 226–31). Also, the Dewal praśasti of AD 992–3 of Lalla of the Chhinda line (*EI*, I pp. 75–85), who claims to have conducted the river Kaṭha and to have shown it the 'way to the town'. For evidence of a somewhat different nature, see the *Rājataraṅginī*, vol. V, pp. 73, 80–91, 110–12. The reasons for the absence of such large scale irrigation works in Rajasthan have been summed up by R.C. Sharma: 'The seasonal and feeble flow in rivers, the great depth of the underground water, and the arid and sandy character of landscape allow little chance for large-scale irrigation', *Settlement Geography of the Indian Desert* (New Delhi, 1972), p. 23. Cf. also his other remark (*Settlement Geography* . . . , p. 22): 'It (water) is important in the location of the settlements of the region, e.g. in the western areas, the wells are significant in deciding the location of most of the villages; in the southern part, the tanks or ponds control the site of the villages.'

[17] *EI*, XXXIV, pp. 173–6.

[18] Ibid.

[19] *EI*, XX, pp. 122–25. See ibid., XXXV, pp. 100–02 for the revised date of the record.

[20] *EI*, XI, pp. 304–13.

[21] *IA*, LVI, pp. 225ff.

gift of one *hala* of land and other plots near a *taṭākinī*. Yet another record (Kadmal plate of Guhila Vijayasiṁha),[22] referring to the village of Palli in the Jodhpur region, mentions, among other things, a share given to a brahman of the income from a *taḍāga* or a reservoir.

Besides tank irrigation, well irrigation was also in vogue. A somewhat visual idea of how water was drawn in a leather bucket is provided by one of the Partabgarh inscriptions of the Gurjara-Pratihāra period (AD 946).[23] In modern times the average depth of wells in areas such as Jodhpur is about 150 feet, and 'except when wells are unusually full it takes a long time to bring up the often saline water by 30–40 gallon sacks hauled by a pair of bullocks or a camel'.[24] Despite these drawbacks wells were in common use, and the epigraphs give a rough idea of the areas covered by them.

Before, however, I try to map the distribution of irrigational wells in early medieval Rajasthan, it is perhaps necessary to discuss another problem: Do the relevant epigraphic expressions refer to a single type of well irrigation or do they indicate variations in the operation of irrigational wells? In the absence of adequate technical data, I would not like to enter here, except marginally, into a controversy regarding whether or not Persian wheels were in use in early medieval Rajasthan,[25] but would rather seek to highlight whatever indirect evidence I have from inscriptions.

[22] *EI*, XXXI, pp. 237–38.

[23] *EI*, XIV, pp. 176ff. The inscription refers to a piece of cultivated land in the following manner: *Kosavāhe Chittulaka-kṣetram māṇivāpa 10* (i.e., the *chittulaka* field which was irrigated with *kosavāha* and in which 10 *māṇis* of seed could be sown).

[24] O.H.K. Spate and A.T.A. Learmonth, *India and Pakistan: A General and Regional Geography*, third edition (London, 1967), pp. 619ff.

[25] In the majority of the translations of early medieval Rajasthani inscriptions, the term *araghaṭṭa* has been translated as either 'machine-well' or 'Persian wheel' (*PRASWC*, 1916–17, p. 65). Literary data on early medieval Rajasthan have been taken to refer to the use of the Persian wheel in that and also in an earlier period. Such views and data as may bear upon the history of the Persian wheel in India and the effects of its introduction in agriculture have been admirably presented by I. Habib in 'Technological Changes and Society: 13th and 14th Centuries' (Presidential Address, Medieval India section, 31st session of the Indian History Congress, Varanasi, December 1969), pp. 12–19. Professor Habib argues that the alleged references to Persian wheels in early India relate more appropriately to the 'noria' which could be used for drawing water from 'near the surface, or from a river', and

in which there is no hint either of a chain carrying the pots, or of any gearing'. He would place the introduction of the Persian wheel proper in India in the 13th–14th centuries as part of its largescale diffusion from the Arab world.

Perhaps the history of the use of the Persian wheel outside India is controversial too (compare the date given by Professor Habib on the strength of A.P. Usher's findings in *A History of Mechanical Inventions* (Boston, 1959), pp. 168, 177–8, with C. Singer *et al*, eds, *A History of Technology*, vol. II (Oxford, 1957), p. 676. In India, while no satisfactory technical details relating to the *araghaṭṭa* or *ghaṭiyantra* are available as yet, it is not true that these devices were not set up on wells (Habib, 'Technological Changes. . .', pp. 12–13). Recently M.C. Joshi has reinterpreted a passage in a Mandasor inscription of 532 which, referring to a newly constructed well, eulogises its 'rotary motion (moving ring) resembling a garland of skulls' which would continue to discharge 'nectarlike pure water'. This date accords with that of *Amarakoṣa* which also defines *ghaṭiyantra* as a device for drawing water from a well (M.C. Joshi, 'An Early Inscriptional Reference to Persian wheel', reprinted from *Professor K.A. Nilakanta Sastri 80th Birthday Felicitation Vol.*, pp. 214–17). However, Joshi's contentions that there was an operational difference between an *araghaṭṭa* (which he takes to represent a 'noria') and a *ghaṭiyantra*, and that the Mandasor inscription of 532 refers to a Persian wheel proper may still be disputed. In connection with the first point reference may be made to two citations in the *Śabdakalpadruma* (Motilal Banarsidass 1961, vol. I, s. v. *araghaṭṭa*) where *araghaṭṭa* is defined as a *mahākūpaḥ* (*mahākūpaḥityamarajaṭādharau*). More explicit evidence that an *araghaṭṭa*, with its pots, was set up on a well (like the *ghaṭiyantra* of *Amarakoṣa*) comes from a passage in the *Pañcatantra* (*Sa kadācid—dāyādair-udvejito-raghaṭṭaghaṭikā-māruhya kūpāt krameṇa nishkrāntaḥ*, ibid.). See also R. Nath, 'Rehant versus the Persian wheel', *Journal of the Asiatic Society*, XII (1–4) (1970), pp. 81–4. Archaeological evidence in support of this is available in the form of two sculptures from the Jodhpur region showing a wheel with pots set on a well, R.C. Agrawala, 'Persian Wheel in Rajasthani Sculpture', *Man in India*, vol. 46 (1966), pp. 87–8. They are from Mandor near Jodhpur and Saladhi near Ranakpur in Pali district and are thus from areas where epigraphic references to *araghaṭṭas* are profuse. One of the sculptures is assigned to the 10th–11th century and 'here we have a complete view of the Persian wheel, i.e., the string of pots is touching the water inside the well as well. The pots are tied to a rope in a row hanging below'. While the above references definitely show that *araghaṭṭas* were, contrary to Professor Habib's suggestion, set up on wells, they still do not indicate the use of both chain and gearing. To be set on a *mahākūpa* (big well), the wheel carrying the pots required the mechanism of a chain but, as has been pointed out (Habib, 'Technological Changes . . . ', p. 14), the gearing mechanism, which facilitated the use of animal power, may have come at a later stage. For the probable use of human labour in *araghaṭṭa*-operation in early medieval Rajasthan, see the Nanana plates of the first half of the 12th century (*EI*, XXXIII, pp. 238–46); also R. Nath, 'Rehant versus . . . ', p. 83. Among other recent discussions on the problem, see Lallanji Gopal, 'Araghatta—the Persian Wheel' in his *Aspects of History of Agriculture in Ancient India* (Varanasi, 1980), pp. 114–68 and I. Habib, 'Pursuing the History of Indian Technology—Premodern Modes of Transmission of Power', The Rajiv Bambawale Memorial Lecture, Indian Institute of Technology (New Delhi, 1990), manuscript.

Inscriptions use three different terms in connection with wells: *ḍhimaḍa* or *ḍhivaḍa*,[26] *vāpi* (step-well) and *araghaṭṭa*, *araghaṭa* or *arahaṭa*. This fact in itself may perhaps indicate operational variations in well irrigation, although what the exact differences were is not clear from these names alone. Leaving aside *vāpi*, the distinction between a *ḍhimaḍa* and an *araghaṭṭa* may perhaps be made clear from an epigraph which refers, in more than one context, to both *ḍhiku* (a variant of *ḍhimaḍa*) and *araghaṭṭa*.[27] Secondly, while the assertion by some epigraphists that a *ḍhimaḍa* or ordinary well (or 'small *araghaṭṭa*') irrigated half as much land as did an *araghaṭṭa*,[28] has never before been substantiated, the evidence of an inscription of 1287 from Pattanarayana in Sirohi[29] may have some bearing on this question. While specifying a levy on the produce of some irrigated fields, it enjoins that 2 seers should be paid from the field irrigated by a *ḍhimaḍa* and 8 seers from the field irrigated by an *araghaṭṭa*. The distinction made between these areas would perhaps also suggest a distinction between the two in terms of the methods of operation and their relative capacity to irrigate. Thirdly, the relative importance of *araghaṭṭas* may also perhaps be deduced from the fact that almost invariably they bear separate names and from the social status of the people who seem to have transferred land irrigated by an *araghaṭṭa*. I shall come back later to this point.[30]

While the above discussion does not elucidate the mechanism of an *araghaṭṭa*, nevertheless the impression emerges that its operation was distinct from that of an ordinary well. There are a few indications

[26] Its variants are *ḍhimaḍu*, *ḍhikuau*, *ḍhika* or *ḍhiku*, *ḍhimbaḍau*, *ḍhimaka*, etc. See *EI*, XIII, pp. 208–220; *IA*, XLV, pp. 77ff.

[27] *EI*, XIII, pp. 208ff.

[28] *PRASWC*, 1916–17, p. 65.

[29] *IA*, XLV, pp. 77ff.

[30] A somewhat indirect and largely undependable method for ascertaining the mechanism of an *araghaṭṭa* would be to compare its distribution with the present day distribution of Persian wheels in Rajasthan. Apart from the enormous time gap, the implied assumption would also run the risk of viewing an *araghaṭṭa* as definitely identical with the Persian wheel. Even so it may be mentioned that in Berach basin where, besides the staple crop, maize, other crops such as wheat, rice, millet, sugarcane and cotton are cultivated 'irrigation is almost entirely from wells by Persian wheel method' (V.N. Misra, *Pre-and Proto-History of the Berach Basin: South Rajasthan*, Poona, 1967, p. 6).

regarding the probable location of *araghaṭṭas* which would suit I. Habib's hypothesis that they represent pre-Persian wheel technology and operated on the water surface. An inscription of 644 from Dabok, near Udaipur,[31] while specifying certain pieces of land, mentions in one case a boundary formed by an *arahaṭṭa* field in front of the tank Karkka (*Karkkataṭākasya cāgrata arahaṭṭakṣetram*). In another inscription the boundary is described as *Rājakīya arahaṭṭakulyā*. Considering that a *kulyā* represents 'a small river, canal, channel for irrigation, ditch, dyke or trench',[32] *Rājakīya arahaṭṭakulyā* would probably suggest an irrigation channel on which the royal *arahaṭṭa* was set (perhaps an alternative and equally acceptable meaning would be drainage for water drawn from the royal *arahaṭṭa*, in which case the *arahaṭṭa* would not necessarily be operating on a stream or channel). Another inscription, of 1165 from Bamnera, lists at least 4 *ḍhikus* and 1 *arahaṭṭa* in the village of Koraṁṭaka, and in specifying the boundaries of a piece of land mentions a river as its eastern and northern boundaries.[33] An examination of a Survey of India map (NG 43) shows Koraṁṭaka (modern Korta) to be situated on one of the tributaries of the Jawai and may indirectly suggest the possibility that the *arahaṭṭa* in the village of Koraṁṭaka was used to draw water from the river surface.

The two pieces of evidence cited are, however, indirect, and even if references to *arahaṭṭa* in these two specific cases do correspond to 'noria' we would not, in view of the definition of *araghaṭṭa* as 'well' in early literary sources,[34] like to restrict the meaning of *araghaṭṭa* to 'noria' in all the known contexts. In the other Rajasthani records there is probably no indication that it is 'noria' that is meant. It is hardly possible that in all the areas where *araghaṭṭas* were in use, water from a stream or a reservoir would be readily available, and the existing knowledge of setting a wheel of pots in a deep well with the mechanism of a chain would certainly be utilized in areas where such wells were excavated.

The areas covered, for purposes of irrigation, by *ḍhimaḍa*, *vāpi*

[31] *EI*, XX, pp. 122–25; also ibid., XXXV, pp. 100–02.
[32] M. Monier-Williams, *A Sanskrit-English Dictionary* (Oxford, 1964 reprint), see under *Kulyā*.
[33] *EI*, XIII, pp. 208ff.
[34] See above.

and *araghaṭṭa* can be shown in the form of a table which indicates the chronology of the references to such expressions and their geographical contexts:

644	Dhor, Bhilwara district	Land irrigated by *araghaṭṭa*	*EI*, XX, pp. 122–25; ibid., XXXV, pp. 100–02.
689	Kishkindha, near Kalyanpur (Dungar-pur-Udaipur area, Udaipur district)	*kūpa*	*EI*, XXXIV, pp. 173–6.
827	Dholpur	*vāpi*	*ZDMG*, XL, pp. 38ff.
835	Kaman tahsil, Bharatpur district	small well	*EI*, XXIV, pp. 329ff.
946	Partabgarh, Chitorgarh district	*kosavāha*	*EI*, XIV, pp. 176ff.
946	Dharyavad, near Partabgarh	*arahaṭa*	*EI*, XIV, pp. 176ff.
994	Bolera, Sanchor	*kūpa*	*EI*, X, pp. 76–9.
1045	Bhadund, Pali district	*vāpi*	*JBBRAS*, 1914, p. 75ff.
1059	Panahera, Banswara district	*arahaṭṭa*	*EI*, XXI, pp. 42–50.
1083	Pali, Pali district	*arahaṭṭa*	*EI*, XXXI, pp. 237–48.
1086	Jhalrapatan, Jhalawar district	*vāpi*	JPASB, X (1914), pp. 241–3
1110	Sevadi, Pali district	*arahaṭṭa*	*EI*, XI, pp. 28–30.
1st half of the 12th century	Nanana, Pali district	*arahaṭṭa*	*EI*, XXXIII, pp. 238–46.
1143	Bali, Pali district	*arahaṭṭa*	*EI*, XI, pp. 32–3.
1143	Kekind, Jodhpur district	*arahaṭṭa*	*PRASWC*, 1910–11
1163	Bamnera, Jodhpur district	*ḍhiku*	*PRASWC*, 1908–9, p. 53.
1165	Bamnera, Jodhpur district	*arahaṭṭa*	*EI*, XXIII, pp. 208ff.
1165	Bamnera, Jodhpur district	*ḍhiku*	ibid., pp. 208–10.
1166	Ajahari, Jodhpur district	*ḍhiku*	*PRASWC*, 1910–11, pp. 38–9.

1166	Bamnera	*ḍhiku*	*PRASWC*, 1908–9, p. 53.
1176	Lalrai, Jodhpur district	*arahaṭṭa*	*EI*, XI, pp. 49–51.
1183	Ajahari	*arahaṭṭa*	PRASWC, 1910–11, pp. 38–9.
1185	Virapura, Chhappana (Udaipur district)	well (*araghaṭṭa*?)	*ARRM*, 1930, pp. 2–3.
1207	Ahada, Udaipur	*araghaṭṭa*	*ARRM*, 1931, p. 4.
1214	Arthuna, Banswara district	*araghaṭṭa*	*EI*, XXIV, 295–310.
1215	Manglana, Jodhpur district	*vāpi*	*IA*, XLI, pp. 85–8.
1265	Ghagsa, Chitorgarh district	*vāpi*	*ARRM*, 1927, p. 3.
1283	Burta, Jodhpur district	*vāpi*	*EI*, IV, pp. 312–14.
1287	Patanarayana, Sirohi district	*ḍhimaḍa*	*IA*, XLV, pp. 77ff.
1287	Patanarayana, Sirohi district	*arahaṭṭa*	ibid.
1287	Mala, Dungarpur district	*arahaṭṭa*	*EI*, XXI, pp. 192–6.
1290–91	Bamnera, Jodhpur district	*arahaṭṭa*	*PRASWC*, 1908–9, pp. 52–3.
1302	Vagin, Sirohi district	*ḍhivaḍa*	*PRASWC*, 1916–17, p. 65.

Briefly, the above list indicates two things: first, the majority of the references occur in inscriptions of the twelfth-thirteenth centuries, and second, the geographical context of many of them is west Rajasthan, a land of relatively higher water scarcity.

II

Having established artificial irrigation as a part of the system of cultivation, at least in some areas of early medieval Rajasthan, it is natural to now seek to examine what relationship, if any, it had with a supposed change in crop production and the development of agriculture in general. However, any idea of progress can be empirically substantiated only if sufficient comparable material is available for the early period, which, as we have seen, is not the case. Evidence of crop production in early medieval period has also to be strenuously culled from the mostly indirect information that the inscriptions offer. Hence, only a sketchy and descriptive presentation can be made here.

To start with I would like to go back to the Dabok inscription of 644;[35] the evidence conatined in it may be broadly applied to the Udaipur area. It specifies the boundaries of three plots of land and mentions therein *arahaṭṭas*, *puṣkariṇī* and *taṭākas.* The impression one thus gets is that the cultivated areas referred to were thoroughly irrigated. While no crop is mentioned, some of the areas are specified as *śāradya-graiṣmikakṣetram* suggesting, in all likelihood, that artificial irrigation facilitated double-cropping and the production of *kharif* and *rabi* crops in these areas. Unfortunately no such information is available from records of the few following centuries and it is only from the eleventh century onward that an idea of the crops cultivated emerges. An inscription of 1059 from Panahera (Banswara)[36] may refer to rice-fields irrigated by *araghaṭṭas.* Cultivation of *godhūma* (wheat) appears to have been on a larger scale and is attested by a number of inscriptions. Many of the Nanana (Marwar) inscriptions of the first half of the twelfth century[37] mention cesses and rents in the form of a certain measure of *godhūma* from *araghaṭṭa* fields. Identical evidence is obtainable from the Kekind (Jodhpur) inscription of 1143.[38] The Vagin (Sirohi district) inscription of 1302[39] also records the gift of a certain quantity of *godhūma* to a temple from land irrigated by a *ḍhivaḍa. Yava* (barley) was another cereal which was cultivated on a large scale by artificial irrigation. The Lalrai inscriptions of 1176[40] specify the amount of barley to be levied from different fields irrigated by *araghaṭṭa.* The Arthuna (Banswara) record of 1214[41] also mentions *arahaṭṭe yava-hāraka* (one *hāraka* of barley per *arahaṭṭa*) as one of the

[35] *EI*, XX, pp. 122–125.
[36] Ibid., XXI, pp. 42–50.
[37] Ibid., XXXIII, pp. 238ff.
[38] *PRASWC*, 1910–11, p. 35.
[39] Ibid., 1916–17, p. 65.
[40] *EI*, XI, pp. 49–51.
[41] Ibid., XXIV, pp. 295–310.

levies. Among others cereals *yugandharī* (*jawār* or millet) is mentioned as the produce of a royal holding (*rājakīyabhoga*) in the Sanderav inscription of 1164,[42] but the record does not indicate the effect on production of artificial irrigation. Pulses were another item of produce mentioned in the records. The Manglana (Jodhpur) inscription of 1215,[43] which refers to the construction of a *vāpi* in an area of water scarcity, fixes *dhānyakoraḍa se I* as the levy per plough. *Koraḍa*, according to the editor of the epigraph, represents, in local usage, such varieties as *muṅg, cānā, jawār*, etc., and *dhānya* is here certainly used in the sense of 'grain'. Among the items listed in the Bhinmal inscription of 1249[44] are *godhūma* (wheat), *cokhā* (rice) and *muṅga* (pulses); the list, however, relates to the stock of food grains in a *bhāṇḍāgāra*, and there is no way of ascertaining whether they were locally produced on irrigated fields. There is also little evidence of the cultivation of commercial crops and the benefits of artificial irrigation are not too explicit in epigraphic sources. Reference may, however, be made in this connection to the Sevadi (Bali district) inscription of 1119[45] which mentions *tila* (sesame) produced in an area which seems to have been under irrigation from reservoirs. Cultivation of oilseeds, perhaps making possible the operation of local *ghāṇakas* (oilmills), is attested to by the Manglana inscription of 1215,[46] cited above. The list of items brought to the market at Arthuna in Banswara[47] includes *ājyataila* (sesame oil), *taila* (oil) and *tavani* (sugar cane). As has been shown before, in both these areas barley and other varieties of grains were produced in fields irrigated by a *vāpi* and *araghaṭṭa*.

The above survey is not an exhaustive one and it certainly is not intended to cover the total area under cultivation, the extent of which is, in any case, beyond any method of computation at present. From a number of inscriptions only those that bear, directly or indirectly, upon the relationship between artificial irrigation and the production

[42] Ibid., XI, pp. 46–7.

[43] *IA*, XLI, pp. 85–8.

[44] *EI*, XI, pp. 53–7; also D. Sharma, *Early Chauhan Dynasties* (Delhi-Jullundur-Lucknow, 1959), pp. 300–01.

[45] *EI*, XI, pp. 304–13.

[46] See above. Cf. Nadlai (Desuri) inscription of 1143 which refers to oil from *ātmīyaghāṇaka* (*EI*, XI, pp. 41–2).

[47] See above.

of certain crops have been selected here. Even so it is perhaps significant that evidence relating to crop production and the emergence of settlements in water scarcity areas like Marwar does not date back to a period much earlier than the early medieval. This leaves some room for postulating a connection between territorial expansion of agriculture and artificial irrigation. Secondly, the reference to double-cropping,[48] although it is the only one of its kind, would establish that a certain growth in production could be achieved through the organization of artificial irrigation.

III

How was artificial irrigation socially organized? This question is particularly pertinent to western Rajasthan where water was scarce, so much so that in 994 when a land-grant was made at Bolera[49] in the kingdom of the Caulukya ruler, Mūlarāja I, to brahman Śrī Dīrghācāryya it consisted of a piece of land with a share of only one third of the water from a well (*Ghāghalikūpa-tribhāgodakena saha*). It is significant that the land lay in the *maṇḍala* of Satyapura (Sanchor) enjoyed by Mūlarāja I himself (*svabhujyamāna*) and its gift was executed by his *mahattama* Śivarāja. That water was an important administrative concern in this area is revealed by royal initiative in the necessary work of construction and the nature of gift specifications. The Manglana inscription of 1215[50] indicates Cāhamāna initiative in the construction of a *vāpi* in an area defined as a *daumārabhūmi* (land of water scarcity). The Kadmal plate of Guhila Vijayasiṁha (1083),[51] while giving away to the donee 'full right over the fifth part of every item of produce of the donated village to the extent of its boundaries', mentions as an exception 'the income of taxes and drainage, in which he received only half (i.e. one tenth part), the other half going to the donor himself'. Along with these may be grouped the evidence of a Bamnera plate which records that in 1165[52] when a well (*ḍhikuaḍa*)

48 See above.
49 *EI*, X, pp. 76–9.
50 See above.
51 *EI*, XXXI, pp. 237–48.
52 Ibid., XIII, pp. 208–10.

at the village of Koraṁṭaka was given to a brahman by the Nadol Cāhamāna prince, Ajayarāja, the donee was enjoined not to disturb or destroy the channel (*nālabāu na lopya*).

Such meaningful information is rather sparsely available. We may, however, raise two questions. First, what are the major categories of people from whom grants of the facilities of artificial irrigation emanate? The answer to this may indicate the incidence of ownership and the financing of artificial irrigation facilities such as tanks, reservoirs and *araghaṭṭas*. Secondly, who are the major beneficiaries of such grants? The answers to the second question are usually found in the same records which yield answers to the first one.

There are obvious indications in the records that grants of irrigational facilities emanated largely from the rulers and their officials. This, however, is an observation based on the proportion of such grants to the total number of grants examined and is not intended to suggest a rigid generalization. Still, it is significant that while an early inscription—of the middle of the seventh century—records the grant of two plots of *arahaṭṭa*-land to a temple by an individual called Vaidya Giyaka of a Kāyastha family,[53] such an example is seldom repeated in later times, although epigraphic references to *arahaṭṭas* are far more numerous in that period.

The majority of early medieval grants may, for our purpose, thus be arranged dynasty-wise, and some of the representative ones may be cited here. In 946 two plots of land were given out of the *bhoga* of Śrīvidagdha (his signature appears on the plate along with that of *mahāsāmanta daṇḍanāyaka* Śrī Mādhava, an official of the Gurjara-Pratihāras) for performance of different rites of the god Śrīmadindrādityadeva at the village of Dhārāpadraka ('Dharyavad in Mewar near the boundary of Partabgarh').[54] One of these plots was given along with an *araghaṭṭa* (*sādharaṁ Kacchakannāma arahaṭena tu saṁyutaṁ dattam*). No other comparable record of the Gurjara-Pratihāra period has been found[55] and it appears that the number of such grants increased in the period of the later Rajput dynasties. The evidence of

[53] See above.
[54] *EI*, XIV, pp. 176ff.
[55] Cf., however, the Dholpur inscription of 827 recording the construction of a *vāpi* by the Cāhamāna Caṇḍamahāsena (*ZDMG*, XL, pp. 38ff).

the Kadmal plate of the Guhila Vijayasiṁha has already been referred to.[56] The Virapura inscription of 1185 mentions Amṛtapāla Guhila of Vāgaḍa as having donated a well (an *araghaṭṭa*?) and two *halas* of land to a brahman at the village of Gatauda in Ṣaṭpañcāśata (Chappana in Udaipur district).[57] The inscriptions of the Paramāras of Vāgaḍa also record grants of different plots of land, including some irrigated by *araghaṭṭas*, to the god Maṇḍaleśvara at Panahera.[58]

It is, however, in the areas that belonged to the Nadol Cāhamāna family that certain aspects of agrarian economy, based on *araghaṭṭa*-irrigation, come into clearer focus. Here too we have a number of inscriptions recording straightforward grants of land. Thus several inscriptions of Bamnera, of 1163 and 1166, refer to the gift of *ḍoli* (i.e. land given to brāhmaṇas, *svāmis*, religious establishments and so on) irrigated by a *ḍhiku* and *araghaṭṭa* by the Nadol Cāhamāna rulers, Ajayasiṁha and Kelhana.[59] The Ajari record of 1183[60] mentions the grant of an *arahaṭṭa* by *kumāra* Pālhanadeva and *paṭṭarāṇī* Sigaradevī. A few other records specify gifts, not of *araghaṭṭas*, but of a share of the produce from *araghaṭṭa* fields, such gifts being, in fact, more common in the records of western Rajasthan. In 1110, in the reign of *mahārājādhirāja* Aśvarāja and the *yauvarājya* of Śrīkaṭukarāja, *mahāsāhanīya* Uppalarāja, along with his family members and relatives, made a gift of one *hāraka* of *yava* (barley) on each *arahaṭṭa* at three villages for the daily worship of Śrīdharmanātha at Samīpāṭīya Caitya (Sevadi, Bali district, Godwar).[61] The Lalrai inscription of 1176 mentions a local levy, apparently on the produce of an *araghaṭṭa*-field, for the festival of Śāntinātha fixed by prince Lāṣaṇapāla who enjoyed (the '*jāgīr*' of) Sinānava along with prince Abhayapāla and queen Mahibaladevī.[62] In 1291 at Korta, a *selahatha*[63] fixed 3 *drammas* (?) as

[56] See above.
[57] *ARRM*, 1930, pp. 2–3.
[58] See above, p. 309, note 1.
[59] *PRASWC*, 1908–9, p. 53.
[60] Ibid., 1910–11, pp. 38–9.
[61] *EI*, XI, pp. 28–30.
[62] Ibid., pp. 49–51.
[63] For *selahata* or *śailahasta*, see A.K. Majumdar, *Chaulukyas of Gujarat* (Bombay, 1956), p. 235.

payment to be collected from each *araghaṭṭa* for the fair festival of the sun-god Mahāsvāmī.[64]

It is not clear what such levies imply. The donors were obviously not transferring their entire revenue to the donees (as is usual in the case of land-grants) but only a part of it, and that too in connection with certain religious occasions. In the case of the royal and official holdings this may indicate that, apart from a fixed amount of revenue from tenants who were likely to have cultivated such holdings,[65] further and occasional redistribution of produce was in vogue—a process perhaps not unconnected with the provision of irrigational facilities in such lands.

This redistributional aspect is also clear from the Ahada grant of 1207[66] and the Nanana plates of the first half of the twelfth century.[67] The Ahada grant records the gift of the *araghaṭṭa* Māoḍa at Āhāḍa in Meḍāpaṭa (Mewar) to a brahman by the Caulukya, Bhīmadeva II, but 'the ninth part of the crops produced by irrigation from this well' was assigned to the local Bhāilasvāmī temple. According to the Nanana plates, the land and the *araghaṭṭa* apparently belonged to the temple of Śrīpuruṣa and several *maṭha* establishments at Nanana, but the king, Aśvarāja, probably intervened to make fresh allotments and reallotments. An *araghaṭṭa* called Naravāṭṭaka, located at the village of Devanandita, which was in the possession of the *maṭhapati*, was granted for the maintenance of the god Caṇḍaleśvara. Besides the retinue of songstresses and musicians allotted to the god were two individuals, Śilāpati and Śrīpāla, who were presumably engaged in the operation of the *araghaṭṭa*. Apart from the light this piece of evidence may throw

[64] *PRASWC*, 1908–9, pp. 52–3. There is one interesting record of 1143 from Bali (*EI*, XI, pp. 32–3) in which mention is made of contributions, not from *araghaṭṭas*, but for *araghaṭṭas*. In this period the village of Valahi (Bali) was being frequented by queen Śrī Tihunakā and on the occasion of the festival of goddess Bahughṛṇā of this village, one *dramma* each was granted by Bopanava-stambhana to the *araghaṭṭas* Sitka, Bhariya, Bohada, Hahiya, etc. It is not clear what such contributions imply.

[65] The tenant-stratum in the composition of agrarian classes is suggested by both the Dabok inscription of 644 (*EI*, XX, pp. 122–5) and the Nanana inscriptions of the first half of the twelfth century (ibid., XXXIII, pp. 238ff).

[66] *ARRM*, 1931, p. 4.

[67] *EI*, XXXIII, pp. 238ff.

on the possible existence of some form of temple slavery in early medieval Rajasthan, it also shows that on the strength of the ownership of *araghaṭṭa*-fields, a temple establishment could engage certain types of labour and assign to them fixed portions of produce from such fields. The second point is also clear from another Nanana plate which mentions an *araghaṭṭa* at the village of Bhiṇṭalavāḍa, which was probably leased out to one Kumāra whose annual rent to the temple—5 *droṇas* of wheat—was allotted to a *meharī* (songstress) named Śobhikā.[68]

Araghaṭṭas, where they existed, thus seem to have played an important role in rural economy and within the existing institutional framework of patronage. Apart from the kings, the *Pañcakulas*—apparently executive bodies mostly appointed by the king[69]—also transferred land and *araghaṭṭas* to brahman donees and religious establishments and were, in some cases, entrusted with the supervision of cesses from *araghaṭṭa*-fields.[70] In several cases a corporate body such as a *goṣṭhī* was instructed to look after the levy on agricultural produce imposed in an irrigated area.[71] A solitary record, from Lalrai, shows a group of *sīras* (cultivators) as transferring a share of their produce from an *araghaṭṭa* field to a temple, but here too the '*jāgīr*' of Saṁnānaka was held (*saṁnānakabhoktā*) by *rājaputra* Abhayapāla, and the cultivators were, in all likelihood, his tenants either individually or collectively.[72] Apart from the Dabok record of 644, to our knowledge the only other record which indicates the prevalence of individual ownership of *araghaṭṭa* fields is an inscription of 1143 from Kekind.[73] Here it is an individual, Copadeva, who makes a gift of 1 *hāraka* of wheat per *araghaṭṭa* to the god Guṇeśvara.

While the few records cited above may justifiably be taken to

[68] There are other records dealing with proprietary rights over lands and wells held by temple establishments. The Bamnera inscription of 1165 mentions a *ḍhiku* (well or field irrigated by a well) as the property of god Mahāsvamī (*PRASWC*, 1908–9, p. 53).

[69] For the composition and functions of the *Pañcakulas*, see A.K. Majumdar, *Chaulukyas of Gujarat*, pp. 236–42.

[70] *PRASWC*, 1910–11, pp. 38–9; *EI*, XXII, pp. 192–6.

[71] *IA*, XLI, pp. 85–8.

[72] *EI*, XI, pp. 50–1.

[73] *PRASWC*, 1910–11, p. 35.

imply that the organization of artificial irrigation was not an exclusive royal concern, the incidence of inscriptional references to official initiative in the construction of wells and reservoirs and of the ownership of *araghaṭṭas*, in twelfth-century Rajasthan in particular, still remains significant. In western Rajasthan this is understandable because of the naturally large size of the holdings[74] and the likelihood that the cost of tank excavation and well construction was very high.[75] If, on the basis of the discussion above, it is possible to suppose that there existed, in early medieval Rajasthan, a certain positive correlation between what may be called (to change the phraseology a little) 'induced' irrigation organization and a general growth in agricultural production, then irrigational efforts could and did to a certain extent generate economic and social power, albeit at microscopic political-spatial levels. This essay does not represent any attempt to revive the sensitive polemics on 'hydraulic society' *per se*,[76] but seeks merely to conclude, on the basis of some empirical data, that under certain geographical conditions and the initiatives taken by an emergent socio-political system the organizational aspects of irrigation could assume a significance which would perhaps be absent in a different historical context.

[74] See V.C. Misra, *Geography of Rajasthan*, p. 66.

[75] I have not been able so far to trace any contemporary Rajasthani evidence which would show what expenses were involved. There is, however, a sixteenth century inscription (Toda-Raising inscription of 1547, *EI*, XXX, pp. 192–3) from the Jaipur area which records that the construction of a *vāpi* cost *ṭaṁ* 1001 (i.e., *ṭaṅkā* identified with silver coins of Sher Shāh and Islām Shāh). Its equivalent in Mewar currency (*Mevāḍya nānā*) is also given, but the rate of exchange cannot be ascertained owing to the faulty nature of the evidence (I owe this reference to Professor D.C. Sircar). Another record, from Manda, Jhalawar, is dated 1485 AD and refers to the excavation of a tank at a cost of 7237¾ *ṭaṅkās* (*ARRM*, 1914, p. 6, no. 11). Contemporary evidence comes from Madhya Pradesh and also relates to the excavation of a tank. A Rewa inscription of samvat 944 (1192?) refers to the excavation of a tank by Malayasiṁha, a feudatory of the Cedis, at the cost of 1500 *ṭaṅkakas* with the figure of the Buddha on them (*PRASWC*, 1920–21, p. 52).

[76] Assaults on the application of this concept in an unqualified form to the Indian context will be found in: Irfan Habib, 'An examination of Wittfogel's Theory of Oriental Despotism', *Enquiry*, no. 6 (1961), 54–73; Romila Thapar, *The Past and Prejudice* (New Delhi, 1975), Lecture 3; and B. O'Leary, *The Asiatic Mode of Production: Oriental Despotism, Historical Materialism and Indian History* (Oxford, 1989), *passim*. See also P. Anderson, *Lineages of the Absolutist State* (London, 1979), note B.

3

Origin of the Rajputs: The Political, Economic and Social Processes in Early Medieval Rajasthan[*]

The origin of the Rajputs is a red herring much dragged about in historical writings on early-medieval and medieval India. These writings reveal an extreme polarity of opinions, extending in range from attempts to trace the Rajputs to foreign immigrant stocks of the post-Gupta period—explaining in the process a later origin myth, namely the *Agnikula* myth, as a purification myth—to contrived justifications for viewing the Rajputs as of pure kṣatriya origin.[1] The question of the indigenous origin of the Rajputs assumed symbolic overtones in the heyday of nationalist historiography, and in the historical and purely literary writings of various genres the military and chivalrous qualities of the Rajputs were repeatedly projected. At the level of historical writing, C.V. Vaidya may be cited as epitomizing an extreme stand in this viewpoint. He states:

> The Rajputs who now came to the front and who by their heroism diffuse such glory on the period of Medieval Indian history *cannot but have been* the descendants of Vedic Aryans. *None but Vedic Aryans* could have fought so valiantly in defence of the ancestral faith[2] (emphasis added).

Another facet of this viewpoint is revealed by the suggestion—repeated in recent writings—that the Rajputs rose to prominence in

[*] Reprinted from *The Indian Historical Review*, vol. III, no. 1 (1976).

[1] Theories about the origin of the Rajputs constitute a voluminous literature. The relevant bibliographical references are, however, available in some recent works on Rajasthan: D. Sharma, *Early Chauhan Dynasties* (*A Study of Chauhan Political History, Chauhan Political Institutions and Life in the Chauhan Dominions from c. 800 to 1316 AD*) (Delhi, 1959), *passim*; Idem, ed., *Rajasthan Through the Ages*, i (Bikaner, 1966), *passim*; and J.N. Asopa, *Origin of the Rajputs* (Delhi, 1976), *passim.*

[2] C.V. Vaidya, *History of Medieval Hindu India*, ii, *Early History of Rajputs* (*750 to 1000 AD*) (Poona, 1924), p. 7.

the process of resisting foreign invasions and that they 'shouldered willingly the Kṣatriyas' duty of fighting for the land as well as its people and culture'.[3]

At the level of narrative political history, the reconstruction of the early history of the Rajputs follows a pattern which has recently been characterized as a tendency to 'dynasticize'. This tendency is evident in most attempts to deal with genealogies found in epigraphs, and what such attempts manifest is 'the practice of rationalizing the inscriptions of a number of rulers of uncertain date and lineage into dynastic superstructures, thereby conferring both temporal and genetic relationships on them where the data provide neither', and further, the 'even more wide practice of juxtaposing and concatenating short genealogies and grafting them into an impressive whole which is truly greater than the sum of its parts'.[4]

The most recent writings on the early history of the Rajputs have not substantially deviated from these assumptions and methods. As a result, even in detailed studies on Rajasthan, the origin of the Rajputs in the early medieval period has hardly been examined as a process which may have had parallels or otherwise in early medieval developments outside the region. The study of the Rajputs in isolation, therefore, seldom refers to the factors, except in the form of facile generalizations, which are now known to have been in operation in early medieval India.[5] Admittedly, the pattern of the emergence of the Rajputs may show substantial deviations from developments outside western India, but the plea that the phenomenon should be examined as a total process still holds good. What is attempted in this paper, which is only an outline of an intended fuller study, is to view this process and to trace the early stages of the history of such clans as came to be recognized as Rajput.[6]

[3] D. Sharma, ed., *Rajasthan Through the Ages*, i, p. 106.

[4] David P. Henige, 'Some Phantom Dynasties of Early and Medieval India: Epigraphic Evidence and the Abhorrence of a Vacuum', *BSOAS*, xxxviii, pt. iii (1975), p. 526.

[5] What we have in mind here are such factors as the formation of numerous new castes, emergence of dynasties seeking kṣatriya status, accent on locality in social relations and so on. For a brief statement of some of the factors, see R.S. Sharma, *Social Changes in Early Medieval India* (*c.* AD *500–1200*) (Delhi, 1969).

[6] The existence of the Rajputs in the tenth-twelfth centuries has often been

The general framework for the paper is provided by the recent analyses of claims to traditional 'kṣatriya' status, which became widespread in the early medieval period.[7] Such claims were attempts to get away from, rather than reveal, the original ancestry, and they underline the nature of a polity in which new social groups continued to seek various symbols for the legitimization of their newly acquired power. Furthermore, 'Rajput', like the traditional *varna* categories, is known to have been assimilative in space and time and has, until recent times, been a recognizable channel of transition from tribal to state polity.[8] The processes of Rajputization, thus at work in different periods and different areas, may have been dissimilar, and the concept of Rajputization, which also has some bearing on the present problem, is taken here to be relevant only to the extent that it points to the necessity of viewing the Rajput phenomenon in the early medieval period in terms of a process, rather than in terms of the ancestry, genuine or concocted, of individual dynasties.

A preliminary idea of the processes involved may be formed by trying to define the term 'Rajput'. As in other periods, so in the early medieval period too, it may not be at all easy to distinguish the Rajputs from the non-Rajputs, despite the clear evidence regarding certain recognizable clans and frequent references to the *rājaputras* in inscriptions and literature. One way of recognizing the early Rajputs may be by extrapolating evidence from later literature. Statements regarding the lists of Rajput clans, traditionally numbering thirty-six, are avail-

---

doubted; see Norman P. Ziegler, 'Marvari Historical Chronicles: Sources for the Social and Cultural History of Rajasthan', *IESHR*, xiii, no. 2 (April–June 1976), p. 242. The doubt is, however, unfounded, since by the twelfth century the term *rājaputra* had come to acquire the later connotation of the term 'Rajput'. See the details that follow, particularly those in section IV.

[7] For relevant details regarding such claims, see D.C. Sircar, *The Guhilas of Kiṣkindhā* (Calcutta, 1965), pp. 1–23; also Romila Thapar, 'The Image of the Barbarian in Early India', *Comparative Studies in Society and History*, xiii, no. 4 (1971), pp. 427–9. For a few examples of how a standard *gotra* provided legimacy, see R.N. Nandi, '*Gotra* and Social Mobility in the Deccan', *PIHC*, XXXIInd session (1970), pp. 118–22. The *gotras* of the Rajput clans also require a fresh analysis.

[8] See Surajit Sinha, 'State Formation and Rajput Myth in Tribal Central India', *Man in India*, xlii, no. 1 (1962), pp. 35–80; also K. Suresh Singh, 'A Study in State-formation among Tribal Communities', in R.S. Sharma and V. Jha, ed., *Indian Society: Historical Probings* (*In Memory of D.D. Kosambi*) (Delhi, 1974), pp. 317–36.

able in relatively early works such as the *Kumārapālacarita*[9] and the *Varṇaratnākara*.[10] The *Rājataraṅgiṇī*[11] too refers to the number thirty-six. An analysis of the composition of various lists—for the lists never tally with one another[12]—suggests that the composition was not such as could be considered immutable by the contemporary compilers. If the early medieval and medieval references to the *rājaputras* in general are taken into account, they represented a 'mixed caste'[13] and 'constituted a fairly large section of petty chiefs holding estates'.[14] The criterion for inclusion in the list of Rajput clans was provided by the contemporary status of a clan at least in the early stages of the crystallization of Rajput power. However, the names of certain clans—such as the Cāhamānas or the Pratīhāras—occur regularly in the lists, possibly due to their political dominance. Sources relating to them are also voluminous, and as such references to these clans will be more frequent throughout this paper than to others.

There are two important pointers to the process of the emergence of the Rajputs in the early medieval records. As these records suggest, at one level the process may have to be juxtaposed with the spate of colonization of new areas. The evidence of such colonization has to be traced not only in the significant expansion of the number of settlements but also in some epigraphic references, suggesting an expansion of agrarian economy. Any assertion about an increase in the number of settlements is, in the absence of any detailed historical-geographical study, only impressionistic. But in view of the widespread distribution of archaeological remains[15] and epigraphs of the period as well as the appearance of numerous new place names, there cannot be any doubt about the validity of the assumption. A brief

[9] Cited in B.N.S. Yadava, *Society and Culture in Northern India in the Twelfth Century* (Allahabad, 1973), p. 37.

[10] Ibid.

[11] VII. 1617–8.

[12] Compare the lists given in Yadava, pp. 36–7.

[13] Cited in ibid., p. 34.

[14] *Aparājitapṛcchā*, a text of the twelfth century, cited in ibid., p. 34.

[15] Compare the lists of early historical sites with those of the early medieval period in K.C. Jain, *Ancient Cities and Towns of Rajasthan* (Delhi, 1972), *passim*. Archaeological reports covering sites, monuments and epigraphs of Rajasthan convey the same impression.

reference to the names of several places and territorial divisions may be meaningful in this context. The term *sapādalakṣa*, which was used to denote the territory of the Cāhamānas,[16] may indicate, like the territorial divisions of the Deccan suffixed with numbers, an expansion of village settlements.[17] In fact, some of the territorial divisions with suffixed numbers mentioned in the *Skanda Purāṇa* such as Vāgurī 80,000 or Virāṭa 36,000 have been located in Rajasthan.[18] The Nadol Cāhamāna kingdom was known as *saptaśata* and an inscription from Nanana, relating to this family, claims that it was made into *saptasāhasrika* by a Cāhamāna king who killed *sīmādhipas* (chiefs of the boundaries of his kingdom) and annexed their villages.[19] In the records of about the twelfth century, the Abu area was known as *aṣṭādaśaśata*.[20] If all this cumulatively suggests a proliferation of settlements, then the relationship of this process, through an expansion of agrarian economy, may be postulated with the emergence of the early Rajputs from about the seventh century. Apart from the inscriptions of the Guhilas of Kiṣkindhā[21] and of Dhavagartā,[22] which refer to irrigation-based agriculture,[23] a more specific connection is suggested by a few records of the Mandor Pratīhāras. A Ghatiyala inscription of Kakkuka, of AD 861,[24] credits him with cattle raids and the destruction by fire of villages in the inaccessible Vaṭanānaka. Kakkuka made the land 'fragrant with the leaves of blue lotuses and pleasant with groves of mango and madhuka trees, and covered it with leaves of excellent sugarcane'. Another Ghatiyala record, also of his time and dated AD

[16] D. Sharma, ed., *Rajasthan Through the Ages*, i, p. 18.

[17] See G.S. Diksit, *Local Self-government in Medieval Karnataka* (Dharwar, 1964), pp. 24–8; also T. Venkateswara Rao, 'Numerical Figures Affixed to the Names of Territorial Divisions in Medieval Andhra', *Itihas*, Journal of the Andhra Pradesh Archives, ii, no. 1 (January–June 1974), pp. 53–8.

[18] D. Sharma, ed., *Rajasthan Through the Ages*, i, p. 19.

[19] *hatvā sīmādhipān saṁkhye teṣāṁ grāmān pragṛhya ca, deśaḥ saptaśato yena saptasāhasrika kṛtaḥ*, Nadol fragmentary grant (V. 14), edited in D. Sharma, *Early Chauhan Dynasties*, p. 189.

[20] D. Sharma, ed., *Rajasthan Through the Ages*, i, pp. 18–19.

[21] Sircar, *The Guhilas . . .*, pp. 74–5.

[22] *EI*, xx, pp. 122–5.

[23] For an idea of the methods and spread of irrigation in early medieval Rajasthan, see 'Irrigation in Early Medieval Rajasthan' in this volume.

[24] *JRAS* (1895), pp. 519–20.

861,[25] mentions the resettlement of a place characterized as *Ābhīraja-nadāruṇaḥ*, 'terrible because of being inhabited by the Ābhīras'. The place was not only conquered, but a village, Rohinsakūpa, as well as Maddodara (identified with Mandor), were provided with markets. Kakkuka is repeatedly mentioned in the Ghatiyala inscriptions as having installed *haṭṭa* and *mahājana* in the area which, apparently unhabitable by good people (*asevyaḥ sādhujanānām*), now came to be crowded with brāhmaṇas, soldiers and merchants. When seen in the light of some other inscriptions of western and central India, which also speak of the suppression of the Śabaras, Bhillas and Pulindas,[26] this evidence from Rajasthan may reveal two important aspects of a process. First, the territorial expansion of what came to be known as Rajput power was achieved, at least in certain areas, at the expense of the erstwhile tribal settlements. Similar movements for expansion are found in the cases of the Guhilas and the Cāhamānas as well. Though the Guhila settlements in various parts of Rajasthan are found as early as in the seventh century AD, slightly later traditions recorded in the inscriptions of the Nagda-Ahar Guhilas trace their movement from Gujarat.[27] There is also a voluminous bardic tradition which suggests that the Guhila kingdoms in south Rajasthan succeeded the earlier tribal chiefdoms of the Bhils.[28] The Guhila connection with the Bhils, implied in the part that the latter played in the coronation ceremony of the Guhila kings,[29] is also suggested in an Ekaliṅgajī temple inscription of AD 1282:

> The enemies of king Allaṭa being impotent to show their contempt (towards him) in battlefield treat the Bhilla women disrespectfully who describe his actions with pleasure in each of the mountains.[30]

[25] *EI*, ix, p. 280.

[26] Ibid., i, p. 337, v. 22.

[27] *IA*, xxxix, pp. 186ff; *EI*, xxxi, pp. 237ff.

[28] Sircar, *The Guhilas . . .*, pp. 3–4.

[29] James Tod, *Annals and Antiquities of Rajasthan*, ed., William Crooke, Indian reprint (Delhi, 1971), p. 262.

[30] *A Collection of Prakrit and Sanskrit Inscriptions* (Bhavnagar Archaeological Department, Bhavnagar, n. d.), pp. 74ff. For further discussion, see also Nandini Sinha, 'Guhila Lineages and the Emergence of State in Early Medieval Mewar', M. Phil Dissertation (Centre for Historical Studies, Jawaharlal Nehru University, New Delhi, 1988).

The movement of the Cāhamānas, according to the tradition mentioned in their inscriptions, was from Ahicchatrapura to Śākambharī or Jāṅgaladeśa, which, one would assume from the name and topography of Jāṅgaladeśa,[31] led to the colonization of a generally uncharted area. The Nadol branch of the Cāhamāna family was founded in the Godwar region of southeast Marwar (Pali district) by Lakṣmaṇa, whose military adventurism, according to tradition recorded in the *Purātanaprabandhasaṁgraha* and *Nainsi's Khyat*,[32] led to the formation of a kingdom at the expense of the Medas of that area. Another example of the same process is available in the bardic legends of *Pallival Chand*, which narrate how Rāṭhoḍa Siha was brought in to keep away the Medas and Mīnās.[33] Secondly, as already mentioned in connection with the reference to Pratīhāra Kakkuka's inscriptions, the colonization of new areas appears to have been accompanied by what may be loosely termed a more advanced economy. In other words, Rajasthan, in the period when Rajput polity was beginning to emerge, was, in its various areas, undergoing a process of change from tribalism. Some facets of change that such a transition presented elsewhere in India may thus seem to have been present in early medieval Rajasthan as well.

As the second point suggests, to conceive of the emergence of the Rajputs only in terms of colonization would be to take a wrong view of the total process involved, and here we come to the second pointer provided by the records. The fact that the mobility to kṣatriya status was in operation elsewhere in the same period prompts one to look for its incidence also in Rajasthan. The cases of two groups who are included in the list of Rajput clans are significant in this context. One is that of the Medas who are considered to have reached the Rajput status from a tribal background.[34] The other is that of the Hūṇas.[35] The inclusion of these two groups in the Rajput clan structure is

[31] D. Sharma, ed., *Rajasthan Through the Ages*, i, p. 12, cites *Śabdārthacintāmani* to show the following characteristics of the region: 'the sky is generally clear, trees and water are scarce, and the land abounds in *śamī* (propis spicigena), *karira* (capprisaphylla), *pilu* (careya rborea) and *karkandhu* (ziziphus jujula) trees'.

[32] Cited by D. Sharma, *Early Chauhan Dynasties*, pp. 121–2.

[33] *IA*, xl, p. 183.

[34] Yadava, *Society and Culture in Northern India*, p. 34.

[35] Ibid.

sufficient to belie any assumption that the structure could be composed only of such groups as were initially closely linked by descent, 'foreign' or 'indigenous'.

II

Apart from the fact that the *rājaputras* are mentioned in certain sources as being of mixed caste, the evidence relating to the Medas and the Hūṇas cited above thus leads one to search not for the original ancestry of the clans but for the historical stages in which the Rajput clan structure came to be developed. This can initially be done with reference to some major clans which played a politically dominant role in early medieval Rajasthan. For the purpose of this paper, these clans are the Pratīhāras, the Guhilas and the Cāhamānas.

To start with the Pratīhāras, despite some laboured attempts to dissociate them from the Gurjaras on the plea that Gurjara, in the 'Gurjara-Pratīhāra' combine, represented the country and not the people[36] it would appear that the Pratīhāras who rose to prominence sometime in the eighth century were really from the Gurjara stock. In early India, *janapada* names were commonly interchangeable with tribal names.[37] Secondly, the argument that the Pratīhāras could not have emerged from the pastoral Gurjara stock is misplaced, because as early as in the seventh century, the Gurjaras of Nandīpurī represented a ruling family.[38] Thirdly, a branch of the Pratīhāras in the Alwar area is taken to represent the Bad Gujars.[39] Documents dating from the seventh century suggest a wide distribution of the Gurjaras as a political power in western India, and references to Gurjara commoners may indicate that the political dominance of certain families reflected a process of stratification that had developed within the stock. The *Pañcatantra* evidence which mentions the Gurjara country as providing camels for sale[40] may suggest, though inadequately, pas-

[36] D. Sharma, ed., *Rajasthan Through the Ages*, i, pp. 472ff.

[37] See H.C. Raychaudhuri, in *The Early History of the Deccan*, ed., G. Yazdani (Oxford University Press, 1960), ch. I.

[38] *IA*, xiii, pp. 70ff; *EI*, xxiii, pp. 147ff.

[39] K.C. Jain, *Ancient Cities and Towns . . .*, p. 195.

[40] *mayā gurjaradeśe gantavyaṃ karabhagrahaṇāya . . . tataśca gurjaradeśe gatvā*

toralism. The Gurjaras are mentioned as cultivators also in an inscription of a Gurjara-Pratīhāra king, Mathana, from Rajorgarh in Alwar.[41] It would seem that the Pratīhāras, like several other Gurjara lineages, branched off the Gurjara stock through the channel of political power, and the case probably offers a parallel to that of the Kuṣāṇas who, originally a sept of the Yüeh-chih, rose to political eminence and integrated five different *jabgous.*[42] Further, the fact that some Pratīhāras also became brāhmaṇas will find parallel in developments among the Ābhīras out of whom emerged Ābhīra brāhmaṇas, Ābhīra kṣatriyas, Ābhīra śūdras and so on.[43]

Admittedly, all this reconstruction is tenuous and, in the absence of evidence, even such reconstruction is not possible in the case of the Cāhamānas and the Guhilas. But a definite correlation did exist between the achievement of political eminence and a movement towards a corresponding social status. The pattern of this correlation may be indicated by the following few tables, prepared mostly on the basis of the epigraphs of the various families of the Pratīhāras, the Guhilas and the Cāhamānas.[44]

---

uṣṭrīṃ gṛhītvā svagṛhamāgataḥ, cited by Asopa, *Origin of the Rajputs* . . . , p. 81, fn. 1.

[41] *śrīgurjara vāhitasamastakṣetra*, *EI*, iii, pp. 263–7.

[42] Cf. the evidence of the *Hou Han-shu* cited in K.A. Nilakanta Sastri, *A Comprehensive History of India*, ii, *The Mauryas and Sātavāhanas* (Bombay, 1957), p. 226.

[43] B. Suryavansi, *The Abhiras: Their History and Culture* (Baroda, 1962), pp. 39–40.

[44] The inscriptional references from which these tables are drawn up are selective but not arbitrary. The column indicating 'political status' has often been left blank, as this status, not always defined in the records, has to be reconstructed. The status is mentioned in the column only when definite indications are available about it.

Gurjara-Pratīhāra

Locality	*Date*	*Family Name*	*Political Status*	*Nature of Claims about the Origin of the Family*
Gurjaras of Nandīpurī	Seventh century[45]	Gurjara-Nṛpati-vaṃśa	Feudatory, suggested by such titles as *mahāsāmanta*, etc., but special position suggested by the claim that they gave protection to the overlord	In some records claim made about descent from Mahārāja Karṇa, which substitutes the family name
Pratīhāras of Mandor	837[46]	Pratīhāra-vaṃśa	—	Descent traced from the kṣatriya wife of a brāhmaṇa, implying brahma-kṣatra status. Links established with Lakṣmaṇa who acted as the *pratīhāra* (doorkeeper) of Rāma
	861[47]	Pratīhāra	—	Similar, but name of the brāhmaṇa wife, mentioned in earlier record, dropped

[45] *IA*, xiii, pp. 70ff; *EI*, xxiii, pp. 147ff.
[46] *EI*, xviii, pp. 97–8.
[47] *JRAS* (1895), pp. 519–20.

Locality	*Date*	*Family Name*	*Political Status*	*Nature of Claims about the Origin of the Family*
Pratīhāras of Rajasthan and Kanauj	Ninth century[48]	Pratīhāra	Sovereign power	Descent traced from the Sun, suggesting claims to solar origin through Lakṣmaṇa who served as *pratīhāra* (doorkeeper) of Rāma
	Tenth century[49]	Indirectly referred to in the inscription of their Cāhamāna feudatories	Mentioned as the overlords of the Cāhamānas	Mentioned as the family of Raghu
Gurjara-Pratīhāras of Rajor in Alwar	960[50]	Gurjara-Pratīhārānvaya	Feudatories of the Pratīhāras of Rajasthan and Kanauj	—

[48] *EI*, xviii, p. 110.

[49] *IA*, xlii, p. 58. A contemporary text, Rājaśekhara's *Karpūramañjarī*, also refers to Mahendrapāla and Mahīpāla as *Raghukulatilaka*, cited by D.R. Bhandarkar, 'Foreign Elements in the Hindu Population', *IA* (1911), p. 83, fn. 80.

[50] *EI*, iii, pp. 263–7.

Guhila

Locality	*Date*	*Family Name*	*Political Status*	*Nature of Claims about the Origin of the Family*
Guhilas of Kiṣkindhā	Second quarter of the seventh century[51]	Guhilaputrānvaya	Feudatory, suggested by such titles as *sāmanta, samadhigatapañca-mahāśabda, mahārāja,* etc.	—
Guhilas of Chatsu	Middle of the tenth century[52]	Guhilavaṃśa	Originally feudatories of the Mauryas and Pratīhāras	*Brahma-kṣatrānvita*
Guhilas of Meẉar	661[53]	Guhilānvaya	—	—
	Late tenth to late eleventh century tradition[54]	—	—	Originator of the family described as *ānandapura vinirgata-viprakulānandaḥ mahīdevaḥ,* implying descent from a brāhmaṇa family of Ānandapura
	1285[55]	Guhilavaṃśa	—	Record implies claim to *brahmakṣatra* status

[51] Sircar, *The Guhilas . . .*, pp. 71–6.
[52] *EI,* xii, pp. 10ff.
[53] Ibid., iv, pp. 29ff.
[54] *IA,* xxxix, p. 191; *EI,* xxxi, pp. 237ff.
[55] *A Collection of Prakrit and Sanskrit Inscriptions* (Bhavnagar Archaeological Department, Bhavnagar), p. 89.

Locality	Date	Family Name	Political Status	Nature of Claims about the Origin of the Family
	1540[56]	Śilādityavaṃśa		Sūryavaṃśa, implying claim to solar origin

Cāhamāna

Locality	Date	Family Name	Political Status	Nature of Claims about the Origin of the Family
Early Cāhamānas of Gujarat	Middle of the eighth century[57]	Cāhamāna	Feudatory, as suggested by such titles as *mahāsāmantādhipati*, *samadhigatapañcamahāśabda*, etc.	—
Cāhamānas of Dholpur	827[58]	Cāhamāna	Possibly feudatories of the Pratihāras	—
Cāhamānas of Nadol	1119[59]	Cāhamāna	—	Ancestry traced to Indra through a person who came out of Indra's eyes

[56] Ibid., p. 141.
[57] *EI*, xii, pp. 197ff.
[58] *ZDMG*, xl, pp. 38ff.
[59] *EI*, xi, p. 304.

Locality	*Date*	*Family Name*	*Political Status*	*Nature of Claims about the Origin of the Family*
Cāhamānas of Śākambharī	946[60]	Cāhamāna	Feudatories of the Pratīhāras	—
	1169[61]	Cāhamāna *Kṣitirājavaṃśa*	Independent power	Vipraśrī Vatsagotra, implying claim to brāhmaṇical descent
	Twelfth century[62]	Cāhamāna	Similar	Ancestry traced to Sun-god, described as the right eye of Viṣṇu
	1191–3[63]	Cāhamāna	Similar	Origin traced to the Sun and the family related with the Ikṣvākus of the Kṛta age
Cāhamānas of Mt. Abu	1320[64]	Cāhamāna	—	Origin traced to the holy sage Vaccha who created the Cāhamāna as a new race of warriors when the solar and lunar races became extinct

[60] *IA*, xlii, pp. 57ff.
[61] *EI*, xxvi, pp. 84ff.
[62] Ibid., xxix, p. 179.
[63] *Pṛthvīrājavijaya* of Jāyanaka; the evidence of this text as also of other sources bearing on the changing claims regarding their ancestry made by the Cāhamānas has been extensively analysed by V.S. Pathak, *Ancient Historians of India: A Study in Historical Biographies* (Bombay, 1966), pp. 98–136.
[64] *EI*, ix, pp. 75ff.

The tables given in the previous pages seem to demonstrate a close correspondence between the different stages in the assumption of political power and the stages in which various claims to ancestral respectability were made, although the genealogies, having been drafted by different hands, did not always follow a uniform pattern. It would appear that feudatory status[65] was incompatible with the stage when detailed and fabricated reference to a respectable ancestry could be made. Apart from the evidence already cited, one further point should make this clear. In a period when detailed genealogies with a respectable ancestry were being put forward on behalf of sovereign families of a clan, another section of the same clan, placed in a feudatory position, did not advance any such claim at all. Thus a Guhila record of AD 1145 from Mangrol in south Gujarat[66] speaks of three generations of Guhila rulers of Maṅgalapura, who were feudatories of the Caulukyas, simply as Śrī Guhila, although in the same period claims to respectable ancestry were being made by the Guhilas elsewhere.

When one looks at the different stages in which the genealogies were being formulated, it further appears that for the majority of the newly emerging royal lines 'Brahma-kṣatra' was a transitional status, which once acquired was not, however, entirely given up, and explanations continued to be given for the supposedly authentic transition from the brāhmaṇa to the kṣatriya status. If it be accepted, on the strength of their relatively later records, that both the Guhilas and the Cāhamānas were originally of brāhmaṇical descent—although no claims to such descent have been made in their early records—then the status was being projected in order to legitimize their new kṣatriya role. It may also well be that the 'Brahma-kṣatra' was a relatively open status, as can be gathered from its wide currency in India in this period,[67] which was seized upon by the new royal families before they

[65] The term 'feudatory' is being used here, in the absence of a better alternative, simply to imply a subordinate position. For a recent critique of the indiscriminate use of this and such other terms, see B. Stein, 'The State and Agrarian Order in South India', in B. Stein, ed., *Essays on South India* (Hawaii, 1975), pp. 83–4.

[66] *A Collection of Prakrit and Sanskrit Inscriptions*, pp. 157ff.

[67] Sircar, *The Guhilas . . .*, pp. 6–11; also D.R. Bhandarkar, 'Foreign Elements . . .', pp. 85–6.

could formulate a claim to a pure kṣatriya origin. This gradual change is perhaps illustrated by a comparison between two Pratīhāra inscriptions of the ninth century from the Jodhpur area. While one, dated AD 837,[68] explains the origin of the Pratīhāra brāhmaṇas and Pratīhāra kṣatriyas in terms of the two wives, one kṣatriya and the other brāhmaṇa, of brāhmaṇa Haricandra, in the second, dated AD 861,[69] the brāhmaṇa wife is dropped from the genealogical list. The continuation of references to brāhmanical origin was as much related to a concern for pure descent as the need for finding a respectable source from which the kṣatriya status was derived. The genealogy of the Jodhpur Pratīhāras starts with Haricandra who is described in one record as *Pratīhāravaṃśaguru,*[70] but an elaborate statement of the connection with such a source is provided by a Guhila inscription of AD 1285 from Acaleswar (Mt. Abu):

> Assuredly from Brahmalike Hārīta (Hāritarāśi=sage) Bappaka obtained, in the shape of an anklet, the lustre of a Kṣatriya and gave the sage his own devotion, his own brāhmaṇical lustre. Thus even till now, the descendants of that line shine on this earth, like Kṣatriyahood in human form.[71]

Though not exactly identically, but in a largely similar way, the Ceros of Bihar, some of whom claimed Rajput status, claimed their descent from Cyavanarṣi.[72]

All this suggests that detailed genealogies of ruling clans, which came to be formulated only in the period of change from the feudatory to an independent status, can hardly be extrapolated for an assessment of actual origin, although some parts of such genealogies may have been based on a genuine tradition. The different stages in the formulation of genealogical claims also thus reveal a political process, it being that of upward mobility from an initial feudatory position. The Gujarat Gurjaras are stated, both in their titles and in the declaration of their allegiance to the Valabhī king, as feudatories. The early Guhilas of Kiṣkindhā and those of Dhavagartā were feudatories too, and Bappa

[68] *EI*, xviii, pp. 97–8.
[69] *JRAS* (1895), pp. 519–20.
[70] *EI*, ix, p. 279.
[71] *A Collection of Prakrit and Sanskrit Inscriptions*, p. 89.
[72] K. Suresh Singh, 'A Study in State-formation . . . '.

Rawala, the traditional founder of the Guhila line of Mewar, appears to have started with a feudatory status as the title *rawala* (identical with *rājakula* which was sometimes associated with a subordinate position) suggests. The Cāhamānas, both of Gujarat and Rajasthan, were clearly feudatories of the Gurjara-Pratīhāras, and it may be significant that the second name in the Cāhamāna genealogy is *sāmanta* (which indirectly suggests a feudatory status) which is in contrast with the next name *nṛpa* or *naradeva* (both meaning king).[73] The transition from feudatory to independent status was clearly through the growth of military strength. The Nandīpurī Gurjaras boast of the protection they gave to the lord of Valabhī who had been overpowered by Harṣa.[74] The Hansot plates of the Cāhamānas begin with the invocation, 'Victorious be the Cāhamāna family excelled with a large army'.[75] Similarly, inscriptions of the Cāhamāna and Pratīhāra feudatory families from Rajasthan highlight the part played by them in the military expeditions of their Gurjara-Pratīhāra overlords.[76]

The point just made should be interesting inasmuch as it shows that the emergence of the early Rajput clans took place within the existing hierarchical political structure. This point is often missed in efforts to build an image of the Rajputs as making a sudden and brilliant debut on the north Indian political scene. An understanding of this initial political stage is important on one more count. It provides us with a vantage point from which to examine further processes, namely how from their initial feudatory position the Rajput clans, in their bid for political ascendancy, moved towards creating economic and social bases for their interlocking interests.

III

The process of the emergence of the early Rajputs is associated, at the level of economy, with certain new features of land distribution and territorial system, which were perhaps present both in the large empires of the Pratīhāras and the Cāhamānas as also in the localized kingdoms

[73] The evidence of the Bijholi inscription of AD 1169, *EI*, xxvi, pp. 84ff.
[74] Ibid., xxiii, pp. 147ff.
[75] Ibid., xii, pp. 197ff.
[76] *IA*, xlii, p. 58.

such as those of the Guhilas. Such features have often been discussed before,[77] but in view of their continued association, in some form or other, with the Rajputs till later times, we shall only examine them in relation to the consolidation of clan networks among the early Rajputs. One feature, the incidence of which in this period appears to have been higher in Rajasthan than elsewhere, was the distribution of land among the royal kinsmen.[78] It must, however, be underlined—because it is not usually so done—that this feature appears to have represented a process which gradually developed and which was associated in particular with the spread of one clan, the Cāhamānas. The Pratīhāra empire being of a rather vast dimension, the composition of the assignees in the empire was varied,[79] although such expressions as *vaṃśapotakabhoga*[80] (this occurs in the Rajorgarh inscription of Gurjara-Pratīhāra Mathana of Alwar) have been understood in the sense of clan patrimony. A certain measure of clan exclusiveness, which could not have been very rigid in the system of land distribution, appeared in a nebulous form in Rajasthan in a slightly later context, and was, as mentioned earlier, associated in particular with the Cāhamānas. The Harṣa inscription of AD 973[81] from Jaipur area perhaps gives the earliest evidence of such distribution. Here are mentioned the *svabhogas* (personal estates) of king Siṃharāja, his two brothers, Vatsarāja and Vigraharāja, and his two sons, Caṇḍarāja and Govindarāja. The inscription also mentions another assignee, perhaps of the Guhila clan, holding a *bhoga*. A *duḥsādhya*, an official, had his own estate too within this kingdom, but his rights were obviously limited inasmuch as his authority to grant land depended on the approval of the king, whereas others needed no such sanction and made grants on their own. The process seems to have gone through further develop-

[77] See R.S. Sharma, *Indian Feudalism, c. 300–1200* (University of Calcutta, 1965), pp. 176ff; K.K. Gopal, 'Assignments to Officials and Royal Kinsmen in Early Medieval India (*c.* 700–1200 AD)' (*University of Allahabad Studies*, Ancient History section, 1963–4), pp. 75–103.

[78] For a general review of the evidence, see K. Gopal, 'Assignment to Officers . . .'.

[79] See B.N. Puri, *The History of the Gurjara-Pratiharas* (Bombay, 1957), pp. 109ff.

[80] *EI*, iii, p. 266f; cf. K. Gopal, p. 91.

[81] *EI*, ii, pp. 116–30.

ment till the twelfth century when in the areas held by the Nadol Cāhamānas, the assignments, termed variously as *grāsa*, *grāsabhūmi* or *bhukti*, came to be held by the king, the kumāra or the crown prince, *rājaputras* or sons of the king, the queens and, in one case, the maternal uncle of the king (who obviously was not a member of the same clan).[82]

To some extent tied up with this feature, but in actual operation distanced from it, was a new land unit which appears to have consisted of six villages and the multiples thereof.[83] The use of this land unit was by no means limited to Rajasthan; even so the incidence of its use in this period appears to have been higher in western India than elsewhere. The units were in many cases parts of such administrative divisions as *maṇḍala*, *bhukti* or *viṣaya*,[84] but the statements in inscriptions that villages were attached (*pratibaddha*) to such units may suggest that the units became the nuclei of some kind of local control. The earliest references to the units of eighty-four villages seem to be available in Saurashtra,[85] held, towards the close of the ninth century, by the Gurjara-Pratīhāras, and its spread to Rajasthan was perhaps intended to facilitate the distribution of land and political control among the ruling élites. The Harṣa inscription of AD 973, which we have cited earlier, mentions the Tṛṇakūpaka group of twelve as having been held by Cāhamāna Siṃharāja. In the eleventh century *radrahadvādaśa*, which was located within Cacchuriṇīmaṇḍala, was held by the Paramāras of Kota,[86] and in AD 1160 twelve villages attached to Naḍḍulai (*Naḍḍulai-pratibaddhadvādaśagrāmāṇi*) were assigned by Cāhamāna Ālhaṇa and his eldest son to Kīrttipāla, a younger son.[87] By the later part of the fourteenth century, the *caurāsia* or holders of eighty-four villages had become, as the evidence of the *Visaladeva Rāso* suggests, 'a well-known class of chiefs',[88] and, if the pieces of evidence cited above are any indication, such big holdings emanated

[82] Ibid., xi, pp. 32–3; cf. K. Gopal, pp. 92–4.
[83] U.N. Ghosal, *Contributions to the History of the Hindu Revenue System* (University of Calcutta, 1929), p. 260.
[84] *EI*, ix, pp. 2–6; ibid., iii, pp. 116–30.
[85] Ibid., ix, pp. 2–6.
[86] Ibid., xxiii, p. 135.
[87] Ibid., ix, pp. 62–6.
[88] Cited by K. Gopal, p. 96.

from the process of the distribution of land among the members of the ruling clans. The *caurāsia* arrangement was not always strictly adhered to in the territorial system of the Rajputs, but it did provide a 'theoretical frame' to that system in which the hierarchy of units and the linkages between clan members and units could be worked out fairly well.[89] Obviously, the details for identifying such linkages are absent in our records, but it is significant that, despite inadequate inscriptional evidence, the rudiments of the *caurāsia* arrangement and its connection with the distribution of land can be traced to the early phases of the crystallization of Rajput polity.

The early phase of Rajput ascendancy also coincided with the construction of fortresses, numerically on a large scale—a feature which appears to have been absent in the earlier kingdoms of Rajasthan,[90] but which came to be very much a part of the Rajput territorial system later on. Early medieval inscriptions suggest their location in different parts of Rajasthan: Kāmyakīyakoṭṭa in Bharatpur area,[91] Rājayapura at Rajor in Alwar,[92] Māṇḍavyapuradurga at Mandor near Jodhpur,[93] Citrakūṭamahādurga at Chitor,[94] Kośavardhanadurga at Shergarh in Kota,[95] Suvarṇagiridurga at Jalor,[96] Śrīmālīyakoṭṭa at Bhinmal,[97] Takṣakagaḍha[98] and other places. The fortresses served not only defence purposes but had, as the composition of population in some of them will show, wider functions.[99] They represented the numerous foci of power of the ascendant ruling families and appear to have had close links with landholdings in the neighbouring areas. The Ropi plates of Paramāra Devarāja, dated AD 1052, mention the grant of a

[89] C.U. Wills, 'The Territorial System of the Rajput Kingdoms of Medieval Chattisgarh', *Journal and Proceedings of the Asiatic Society of Bengal*, New Series, xv (1919), p. 199.

[90] See, for example, the early historical material in K.C. Jain, pp. 80–154.

[91] *EI*, xxiv, pp. 329ff.

[92] Ibid., iii, p. 263.

[93] Ibid., xvii, p. 98.

[94] H.C. Ray, *The Dynastic History of Northern India* (*Early Medieval Period*), ii, Reprint (Delhi, 1973), p. 1191.

[95] *EI*, xxiii, p. 132.

[96] Also mentioned as *Kāñcanagirigaḍha*, ibid., i, pp. 54–5.

[97] Ibid., xxii, pp. 196–8.

[98] K.C. Jain, pp. 256–8.

[99] *EI*, xxiv, pp. 329ff; ibid., xxiii, pp. 137–41; *IA*, xl, pp. 175–6.

piece of land in the *svabhujyamānaviṣaya* of Devarāja, the land having been located to the south of Śrīmālīyakoṭṭa.[100] Among its boundaries are mentioned lands belonging to two brāhmaṇas and a *mahāsāmantādhipati*. Another inscription, of the time of Paramāra Udayāditya, from Shergarh in Kota district, mentions the village Vilapadraka as belonging to a temple in the Kośavardhanadurga.[101]

References to *durgas* in the context of lands donated obviously suggest that the forts were foci of control for their rural surroundings—a point which may be further substantiated by a reference to the Gopagiri inscriptions of the time of the Gurjara-Pratīhāras,[102] which also suggest the same kind of control wielded by an early medieval fortress. Thus along with the assignment of land, occasionally in terms of units which could be made into administrative units as well, the construction of fortified settlements in large numbers could be seen as a part of a process of the consolidation of their position by the ruling clans.

At the level of social relations, the obvious pointer to this process would be the marriage network among the clans. The information available from inscriptions is unfortunately rather limited, and so when in the genealogical lists a few cases of marriage are mentioned, it may be assumed with certainty that they have been recorded because of their significant political implications for the family. Proceeding onward chronologically from the Pratīhāra family, one can see a change in the marriage network pattern in which not only does the supposed origin of a family play an unimportant part, but there is also a development towards an understandable pattern of interclan relationship. As mentioned earlier, in an inscription of AD 837 of the Pratīhāra family from the Jodhpur area, the originator of the family is mentioned as having married a brāhmaṇa and a kṣatriya wife. In another inscription, of AD 861, the brāhmaṇa wife is dropped from the account of the ancestry. Towards the end of the genealogy, Kakka, who is very close to the last and the current ruler in the genealogical list, is mentioned as having married Padminī of the Bhaṭṭi clan, considered

[100] *EI*, xxii, pp. 196–8.
[101] Ibid., xxiii, pp. 131–6.
[102] Ibid., i, pp. 154ff.

by some to be identical with the Bhaṭṭis of Jaisalmer area.[103] Records of other families suggest a similar development towards a network which involved mostly the ruling Rajput clans. In the inscriptions of the Cāhamānas there seems to have been a distinct preference for the Rāṣṭrakūṭas, Rāṭrauḍhas or Rathors. A *rāṇaka* Tribhuvaneśvara of this family was married to Rāṣṭrakūṭa Lakṣmīdevī.[104] Ālhaṇa of the Cāhamāna family of Nadol also married Annalladevī of the Rāṣṭrakūṭa family.[105] Among the Paramāras of Rajasthan, the marriages known to have been contracted were with the Cāhamānas. Paramāra Dhārāvarṣa of Mt. Abu married the daughter of Cāhamāna Kelhaṇadeva.[106] Paramāra Satyarāja of the Vāgaḍā family married Rājaśrī, apparently of another Cāhamāna family.[107] The network was, however, more varied and widespread with the Guhilas. Two records, respectively of AD 1000[108] and 1008,[109] mention two wives of Guhila *mahāsāmantādhipati* of Nāgahrada: one was *mahārājñī* Sarvadevī who was the daughter of a *mahāsāmantādhipati* of the solar family; the other was *mahārājñī* Jajukā who was similarly the daughter of a *mahāsāmantādhipati* of the solar family of Bharukaccha. Ālhaṇadevī, from a Guhila royal family, was married to Gayakarṇa of the Cedi family.[110]

Marriage relations, contracted by the Guhilas with specifically Rajput clans, extended to the Caulukyas,[111] the Paramāras,[112] the Rāṣṭrakūṭas,[113] the Cāhamānas[114] and the Hūṇas.[115] Interclan relationships in terms of marriages contracted could, at a certain point of time, be limited to two clans and any consistency in the pattern may have been due to the nature of political relations between such clans,

[103] *EI*, xviii, pp. 87–99; also D. Sharma, ed., *Rajasthan Through the Ages*, i, p. 124, fn. 2.

[104] *EI*, xxxvii, pp. 155–8.

[105] Ibid., ix, pp. 66ff.

[106] Ibid., xxxii, pp. 135–8.

[107] Ibid., xxi, pp. 42–50.

[108] *ARRM* (1936), p. 2.

[109] Ibid.

[110] *IA*, xvi, pp. 345–55.

[111] *PRASWC* (1905–6), p. 61.

[112] *EI*, xxxi, pp. 237–48.

[113] Ibid.

[114] *IA*, xxxix, pp. 188–9.

[115] Ibid.

or, as in the case of the Guhilas, it could be quite expansive. But the network operated mostly among such clans as came to constitute the Rajput category. The choice was essentially political, because the families cited here constituted the ruling elites of early medieval Rajasthan. Interclan relationships, however, revealed through cases of marriage, seem to have had wider social implications as well. It could provide social legitimacy to such groups as the Hūṇas who had acquired sufficient political power in western India by this period,[116] leading finally to their inclusion in the Rajput clan list. Secondly, interclan marriage relationships may have led to collaboration in wider areas of social and political activity. Thus Guhila Allaṭa, who was married to a Hūṇa princess, had a Hūṇa member in a *goṣṭhī* in the kingdom of his son, Naravāhana.[117] Similarly, Ana, belonging to the family of the Hastikuṇḍi Rāṣṭrakūṭas, was involved in activities concerning a religious institution in the kingdom of Paramāra Dhārāvarṣa who had entered into matrimonial relations with the Hastikuṇḍi family.[118] In an inscription of AD 1168 from Hansi, Hissar district, there is a reference to one Guhilauta Kilhaṇa, who was the maternal uncle of Pṛthvīrāja Cāhamāna and put in charge of the Āsika fort of the Cāhamānas.[119] These examples are obviously inadequate, but interclan relationships offer a key to an understanding of the processes through which Rajput polity evolved in the early medieval period.

IV

In our discussion of the processes leading to the emergence of the Rajputs in the early medieval period, we have focused so far on a few major ruling families. Although the term *rājaputra* continued to denote, along with *mahārājakumāra*, the 'son of a king', as in the inscriptions of the Nadol Cāhamānas,[120] there was certainly a gradual change in the connotation of the term which came to denote descent

[116] For the pockets of Hūṇa power in this period, see D.C. Sircar, *Some Problems of Kuṣāṇa and Rajput History* (University of Calcutta, 1969), pp. 83–7.
[117] *IA*, lviii, pp. 161ff.
[118] Ibid., lvi, pp. 50–1.
[119] Ibid., xli, pp. 17–9.
[120] *EI*, xi, pp. 49–51.

groups and not necessarily a particularly exalted political status. A Chitor inscription of AD 1301 mentions three generations of *rājaputras*,[121] perhaps suggesting that by the close of the thirteenth century the term *rājaputra* conveyed not merely a political status, but an element of heredity as well. The proliferation of the Rajputs in the early medieval period is suggested by a variety of sources. Hemacandra's *Triṣaṣṭiśalākāpuruṣacarita* refers to *rājaputrakāḥ* or numerous persons of *rājaputra* descent;[122] a Mt. Abu inscription of the late eleventh century speaks of 'all the *rājaputras* of the illustrious *Rājaputra* clan.'[123] Merutuṅga in his *Prabandhacintāmaṇi* mentions hundred *rājaputras* of the Paramāra clan.[124] It is understandable then that among the ruling élites, *rājaputra* covered a wide range, from the 'actual son of a king to the lowest ranking landholder'.[125] In terms of the actual clans recognized as Rajputs, it is clear from the evidence in the *Kumārapālacarita* and the *Rājataraṅgiṇī* that the number had become substantial, as mentioned earlier. However, the number given in these texts suggests not so much a rigid set of thirty-six clans as the idea of descent setting apart the *rājaputras* from the others. To quote a relevant passage from the *Rājataraṅgiṇī*, 'Even those Rājaputras Anantapāla and the rest, who claim descent from the thirty-six families and who in their pride would not concede a higher position to the sun himself . . .'.[126]

From about the twelfth century onward, one comes across a variety of expressions which are applied to the ruling élites and which are different from such ranks as *sāmanta* and *mahāsāmanta*, the use of which appears to have become less frequent now. The most common terms are *rājaputra*, *rāutta* or *rāuta*, *rājakula* or *rāvala*, *mahārājakula* or *mahārāvala*, *rāṇaka*, and so on, and to these are sometimes tagged

[121] Cited in Asopa, pp. 9–10.
[122] Ibid.
[123] Ibid.
[124] Ibid.
[125] Irfan Habib, 'The Social Distribution of Landed Property in Pre-British India (A Historical Survey)', in R.S. Sharma and V. Jha, ed., *Indian Society: Historical Probings*, p. 285.
[126] M.A. Stein, *Kalhaṇa's Rājataraṅgiṇī: A Chronicle of the Kings of Kashmir*, i, Reprint (Delhi, 1961), p. 593.

official titles like *sāmanta*, *mahāmaṇḍaleśvara*[127] or *mahāmāṇḍalika*,[128] indicating the ranks that the *rājaputras* and such others may have attained in an administrative arrangement. What is common to all such terms as *rājakula*, *rājaputra* or *rāṇaka* is suggested affiliation to royalty and although it is not always possible to trace a direct lineal connection between a *rājaputra* or *rāṇaka* and a royal family, an explanation for the use of such terms may be sought in the high incidence of their connection with the clans, families from which constituted the royalty in early medieval Rajasthan. Indeed, references to *rājakula* (AD 1208),[129] *mahārājakula* (AD 1186, 1292, 1302),[130] *mahārāvata* (AD 1302),[131] *rāṇā śrī rājakula* (AD 1167),[132] *ṭhakkura rāuta* (AD 1138),[133] etc., of the Guhila families; *rāṇaka* (son of a *māṇḍalika*),[134] *rājaputra* (AD 1287), etc., of the Cāhamāna families[135] and so on become frequent from the twelfth century onward. This evidence should certainly not be construed to mean that *rājaputra* and such other distinguished epithets were confined to a few select clans. In the inscriptions one comes across Śrī Vaṃśagottiya *rāuta* (AD 1156),[136] Gurjarajātīya *ṭhakkura* (AD 1283)[137] or a *rāṇaka* from the Karnāṭa country (AD 1143),[138] and these are a measure of the flexibility of the system in which new groups could be accommodated by virtue of their political initiative and power.

The proliferation of the Rajputs in the early medieval period, both among the established clans as well as those outside them, is a key indicator for an analysis of the structure of Rajput political dominance. There is no direct evidence regarding the changing status of the traditional 'ksatriya' groups or ruling élites of Rajasthan, and one can

127 *PRASWC* (1910–1), pp. 38–9.
128 Ibid., p. 35.
129 *ARRM* (1927), p. 3.
130 *PRASWC* (1914–15), p. 35.
131 Ibid.
132 Ibid. (1911–12), p. 52.
133 *EI*, xi, pp. 36–7.
134 Ibid., xxxvii, pp. 157–8.
135 *IA*, xlv, pp. 77ff.
136 P.C. Nahar, *Jaina Lekha Saṃgraha*, pt. i (Calcutta, 1918), p. 218.
137 Ibid., pt. ii (Calcutta, 1927), p. 25.
138 *PRASWC* (1908–9), p. 45.

even assume their incorporation into the Rajput structure if they survived in power, but the evidence of two inscriptions of the tenth century may suggest the possibility that some among the traditional 'kṣatriyas' were going through a process of change. A record of AD 956 from Mandkila Tal, near Jodhpur,[139] mentions the son of a learned kṣatriya, who engraved a *praśasti* and was a *sūtradhāra* by profession. Another inscription, of the tenth century, of the Gurjara-Pratīhāras from the Doab area in UP,[140] refers to a kṣatriya *vaṇik*. Though obviously inadequate, the examples may nevertheless be taken to indicate that the proliferation of the Rajputs contributed towards an undermining of the political status of the early kṣatriya groups which were taking to less potent occupations and also that the preferred term for the ruling stratum was now not so much 'kṣatriya' as 'Rajput'.

As a hypothesis, the substitution of the traditional 'kṣatriya' groups by the Rajputs and the consolidation of the Rajput structure may be viewed as a result of collaboration between the emerging clans, not only in terms of interclan marriage relationships but also in terms of participation at various levels of the polity and the circulation of clan members in different kingdoms and courts. Although the beginning of this process may be traced to the feudatory-overlord relationship between the Pratīhāras, Cāhamānas and others, a wider network of relationships appears to have spread to other levels of the polity only gradually. One may start here by pointing to the changing typology of the inscriptions of Rajasthan. Whereas the royal commands conveyed through epigraphs from about the seventh to tenth century—and in some cases to the twelfth century as well—were addressed to various categories of officials (in the Dungarpur inscription of AD 689,[141] for example, the list runs as: *nṛpa, nṛpasuta, sandhivigrahādhikṛta, senādhyakṣa, purodhā, pramātṛ, mantrī, pratīhāra, rājasthānīya, uparika, kumārāmātya, viṣayabhogapati, cauroddharaṇika, śaulkika, vyāpṛtaka, daṇḍapāśika, cāṭa, bhaṭa, pratisaraka, grāmādhipati, drāṅgika*, and so on), in later inscriptions lists of such officials are generally

[139] *EI*, xxxiv, pp. 77ff.
[140] Ibid., xix, pp. 52–4.
[141] Ibid., xxxiv, pp. 173–6. See also Rajor inscription of AD 960, ibid., iii, pp. 263–7; Bamnera plate of Paramāra Bhoja of AD 1019, *IA*, xli, pp. 201–2; a Nadol inscription of AD 1119, *EI*, xi, pp. 304ff.

absent. The change is perhaps best shown by the form of address in a Nadol Cāhamāna inscription of AD 1161: *deśāṃto rājaputrān janapadagaṇān bodhayatyeva.*[142] Here the *rājaputras* who are distinguished from the *janapadagaṇa* alone seem to stand for all the categories of officials mentioned in the earlier inscriptions. This is not to say that the earlier ranks had completely disappeared. In fact, according to traditions relating to the twelfth century,[143] there were one hundred *sāmantas* in the Cāhamāna court. But from a study of the inscriptions one is strongly tempted to assume that such ranks mostly circulated among those groups who were claiming to be *rājaputras* as well. Although there is an early reference to a Pratīhāra member of a *goṣṭhī* in the seventh century Vasantgarh inscription of Varmalāṭa,[144] it is only in a much later period that the *rājaputras*, or more generally the members of various clans, are found placed at various positions in the Rajput socio-political structure. It is in this period that the inscriptional evidence relating to the composition of élites suggests a distinct trend towards what we have earlier called collaboration between the clans.

Thus in the Ahada inscription of Guhila Allaṭa (AD 942)[145] a Hūṇa and a Pratīhāra are mentioned as members of a *goṣṭhī*; again, in the Paldi inscription of Guhila Arisiṃha (AD 1059)[146] a *Saulaṃkivaṃśīya rājaputra* figures as a member of a *goṣṭhika*. In the Mala plates of Vīrasiṃha (AD 1287),[147] a *rāuta* is among various witnesses mentioned. The Hansi stone inscription of Pṛthvīrāja Cāhamāna[148] contains some relevant information in this connection: (i) Āsikadurga, a fort, was given to a *Guhilautānvaya* or a person belonging to the Guhila clan; and (ii) a *Doḍānvaya* or a person belonging to the Doḍā subclan was a subordinate of Pṛthvīrāja's maternal uncle. Both these references, showing the inclusion of Guhila and Doḍā elements in the Cāhamāna polity, are by no means exceptional, because in the same kingdom

[142] Ibid., ix, pp. 62–6.
[143] D. Sharma, ed., *Rajasthan Through the Ages*, i, p. 359.
[144] *EI*, ix, pp. 187–92.
[145] *IA*, lviii, pp. 161ff.
[146] *EI*, xxx, pp. 8–12.
[147] Ibid., xxii, pp. 192–6.
[148] *IA*, xli, pp. 17–9.

one comes across references to *mahāmāṇḍalikas* of Boḍānā origin[149] and other categories of feudatories of Dadhica origin.[150] The presence of Guhila landowning élites in the Cāhamāna kingdom is revealed by the Bijholi inscription of AD 1169[151] which refers to grants of land made to a Jain temple by Guhilaputra Rāvala Dhādhara and Guhilaputra Rāvala Vyāharu. A *rājaputra*, Śrī Sallakṣaṇapāla, is mentioned as the *mahāmantrī* of Vigraharāja in the Delhi-Siwalik pillar inscription of AD 1163.[152] In the Nadol Cāhamāna kingdom a Raṣṭrakūṭa or member of the Rathor clan probably figures as a *talāra* in AD 1164.[153] This kind of information is available from other kingdoms as well. An inscription of AD 1287[154] mentions a Guhilaputra and also a member of the Devarā subclan as important landholders in the kingdom of the Sirohi Paramāras. Between the middle of the twelfth and the early part of the thirteenth century the Caulukya feudatories in southern Rajasthan comprised the Paramāras[155] and the Cāhamānas.[156] These few examples are likely to represent a wide range of similar information and may show that apart from kinship ties within a clan which have earlier been shown to have at least partly influenced the distribution of land, the interclan relationship governing the distribution of power helped consolidate the structure of Rajput polity in the early medieval period.

An extension of this argument would be to examine the nature and incidence of the participation, among the ascendant clans, in the military exploits of the period. There is practically no direct and detailed evidence about the composition of the warriors at various levels, but one can make use here of the evidence of a particular type of sculptured stone which, though originating elsewhere much earlier, became widespread in Rajasthan from the early medieval period onward.[157] These stones are memorial relics, usually known as *govardhana*

[149] Ibid., pp. 202–3.
[150] *EI*, xii, pp. 56–61.
[151] Ibid., xxvi, pp. 84ff.
[152] *IA*, xix, pp. 215–9.
[153] *EI*, xi, pp. 46–7.
[154] *IA*, xlv, pp. 77ff.
[155] Ibid., lxi, pp. 135–6.
[156] *PRASWC* (1907–8), p. 49, *IA*, lxii, p. 42.
[157] For useful details of the memorial stones of early medieval Rajasthan, see H.

dhvajas[158] and *paliyas* or *devali*, *deuli* or *devakulikā*[159] as they are called in inscriptions. They were installed to commemorate death, including death on the battlefield. The range of social groups which the memorial stones generally cover is quite extensive, but the memorials to violent deaths relate mostly to such groups as came to be recognized as Rajputs, and the incidence of memorial stones in general among them, at least in the early medieval period, seems to be higher than among others.[160] The names of various clans as can be collected from the memorial stones alone are: Pratīhāra,[161] Cāhamāna,[162] Guhila,[163] Paramāra,[164] Solāṅki,[165] Rāṭhoḍa,[166] Candela,[167] Mahāvarāha,[168] Māṅgaliya,[169] Boḍānā,[170] Mohila,[171] Devarā,[172] Doḍā,[173] Dahiya,[174] Pavāra,[175] Dohara,[176] Bhici,[177] Ghaṃgala,[178] Dharkaṭa[179] and so on. Further, in a number of cases, titles indicative of the political and social status of the commemorated occur in the same records, such titles being *rājā*,[180]

Goetz, *The Art and Architecture of Bikaner State* (Oxford, 1960), pp. 61ff; R.C. Agrawal, 'Paścimī Rājasthana ke kucha Prārambhika Smṛtistambha', *Varadā* [in Hindi], April 1963.

158 *ARIE* (1964–5), p. 102.

159 *PRASWC* (1911–12), p. 53.

160 I have discussed this elsewhere. See the article, 'Early Memorial Stones of Rajasthan: A Preliminary Analysis of their Inscriptions' in this collection.

161 *IAR* (1959–60), p. 60.

162 Ibid. (1962–3), p. 54.

163 *PRASWC* (1909–10), p. 61; ibid. (1911–2), p. 52.

164 Ibid. (1916–7), p. 70.

165 *IA*, xl, p. 183.

166 Ibid., pp. 181–3.

167 *ARRM* (1935), pp. 3–5.

168 *PRASWC* (1911–2), p. 53.

169 Ibid.

170 Ibid.

171 Ibid.

172 *ARRM* (1909), p. 10, Appendix D. For the Devaḍās, see also *IA*, xlv, pp. 77ff; *EI*, ix, p. 79.

173 *ARRM* (1922–3), p. 2.

174 *IA*, xlii, pp. 267–9.

175 *ARIE* (1964–5), p. 102.

176 Ibid. (1959–60), p. 113.

177 *JPASB* (1916), pp. 104–06.

178 Ibid.

179 Ibid.

180 *PṚASWC* (1909–10), p. 51.

mahāsāmanta,[181] *rāṇā*,[182] *rāuta* or *rājaputra*,[183] etc. The memorial stones may have been a borrowed concept, but the way they were fashioned and the contexts many of them represented in early medieval Rajasthan relate largely to the new 'kṣatriya' groups which together made up the political order of Rajasthan.

V

It should be clear from some references made in the preceding section that an important aspect of the proliferation of the Rajputs in the early medieval period was the emergence of various minor clans and subdivisions of the major clans. Mention has been made earlier of the *Prabandhacintāmaṇi* evidence which refers to hundred *rājaputras* of the Paramāra clan. Speaking of the Guhila family, the Acaleswar (Mt. Abu) inscription of AD 1285[184] describes it as full of branches and sub-branches which consist of good members (*suparvāḥ patravibhūṣitāṃśāḥ*). This development seems to apply to all the major clans. Further, the continuing process of the formation of Rajput clans, presumably through the acquisition of political power, is attested by a few inscriptions. A record of AD 1156[185] mentions a *mahārāja* who was a Boḍānā. Mahāvarāha, another clan, appears in a record of AD 1011.[186] The subdivisions of the major clans had become fairly numerous by this time, as will be clear from the following list: Doḍā, subdivision of Paramāra; Pipāḍiā[187] and Māṅgalya, subdivisions of Guhila; Devaḍā, Mohila and Soni or Sonigārā,[188] subdivisions of Cāhamāna; and Dadhica, subdivision of Rathor. That the new clans and what came to be recognized as subdivisions of earlier clans were being drawn into the Rajput network is suggested by a few cases of marriage of which records are available. In a record of AD 1180[189] a

[181] *ARIE* (1961–2), p. 115.
[182] *PRASWC* (1911–12), p. 53.
[183] *ARIE* (1954–5), p. 59.
[184] *A Collection of Prakrit and Sanskrit Inscriptions*, p. 88.
[185] *IA*, xli, pp. 202–3.
[186] *PRASWC* (1911–12), p. 53.
[187] Ibid., p. 52.
[188] *EI*, xi, pp. 60–2.
[189] *PRASWC* (1911–12), p. 53.

rāṇā of the Guhila family is mentioned as having married a Boḍāṇī, that is, a girl of the Boḍāna family. Another record, of AD 1191,[190] refers to a Guhila who married a girl from the Mohila subdivision of the Cāhamānas.

How did these subclans emerge? The process expected to explain this phenomenon would be the segmentation of clans, which sometimes resulted from their movements to new areas. But there is no actual evidence in our period of such segmentation leading to the formation of subclans. For example, the Cāhamānas of the Śākambharī line segmented to form the Cāhamāna family at Nadol, a splinter group from which again established itself at Jalor.[191] No subclan seems to have emerged from this process.[192] Similar events also took place in the royal family of the Paramāras, resulting in the starting of new lines at Vāgaḍā and Mt. Abu, which nevertheless continued as the Paramāras.[193] What may be useful to invoke in this context is the phenomenon of caste formation in the early medieval period in which the element of 'localism' was substantially involved.[194] In Rajasthan the working of 'localism' may be seen in the rise of Śrīmāla or Bhillamāla brāhmanas,[195] and the process may be further extended to analyse such groups as Dahiya brāhmaṇas as well as Dahiya Rajputs who, having originated in the same locality, had strong 'affinities' with each other.[196] Secondly, as has already been indicated, Rajputization was a process of social mobility which, in the wake of its formation into a structure, drew in such disparate groups as the Medas and the Hūṇas. From these perspectives, the formation of various subclans was not necessarily a result of the direct segmentation of clans, but perhaps a product of the mechanism of the absorption of local elements, when such elements came into contact with some already established clans. This element of 'localism' in the formation of Rajput

[190] Ibid., p. 53.

[191] D. Sharma, ed., *Rajasthan Through the Ages*, i, pp. 546–7.

[192] However, the segmentation of a major clan like Cāhamāna over a period of time may be suggested by the reference which D.R. Bhandarkar makes to Nādoliās, Sonigārās and Sancorās, all subdivisions of the Cāhamānas of Marwar, *EI*, xi, p. 26.

[193] Ibid., pp. 549–52.

[194] R.S. Sharma, *Social Changes in Early Medieval India.*

[195] D. Sharma, ed., *Rajasthan Through the Ages*, i, pp. 442–4.

[196] *EI*, xii, pp. 56–61; *IA*, xli, pp. 85–8.

subclans is suggested in the early medieval period by the Pipāḍiā Guhilas and the Sonigārā Cāhamānas, Pipāḍiā having been derived from the place name Pippalapāda and Sonigārā from Suvarṇagiri (Jalor). That one of the channels for rising to the status of a recognized clan was through marriage relationships is suggested by instances of such relationships between the Guhilas on the one hand and the Boḍāṇās and Mohilas (subdivision of the Cāhamānas) on the other.

In conclusion, two chronological stages of the emergence of the Rajputs in the early medieval period may be envisaged. In the first stage it was essentially a political process in which disparate groups seeking political power conformed to such norms as permeated the contemporary political ideology. As the entry into the Rajput fold basically continued to be through political power, the traditional norms or the need for legitimization remained. In this respect, the emergence of the Rajputs was similar to a pan-Indian phenomenon, namely the formation of dynasties, many of which sought legitimization through zealously claimed linkages with kṣatriya lines of the mythical past. But in the second stage, which we would roughly date from the eleventh-twelfth centuries, the rise of the Rajputs became a comprehensive social phenomenon as well. As such the multiplication of the *rājaputras* should not be viewed as merely reflecting the consolidation of a political power structure; its implication should be extended also to explain the growing phenomenon of minor clans and subclans. And if one were to venture a final hypothesis, it was in the expansion of mere 'dynastic' relations towards a wider arena of social relations that lay the future growth of the Rajput network.

4

*Markets and Merchants in Early Medieval Rajasthan**

'All enduring social relations', as Cyril Belshaw puts it, 'involve transactions, which have an exchange aspect',[1] but since the 'exchange aspect' of trade has specificities which cannot be identical at all times and places, the objective of a study on trade ought finally to locate it in the context of the society in which it takes place as an economic activity. The preliminary areas of investigation in such a study would be: (i) an assessment of the nature of goods that appear as regular items of exchange; (ii) an analysis of the process of mobilization of goods; and (iii) the nature of exchange centres and the nature of authority at such centres. The range of goods that figure as exchangeable items may be large, but it is the regularity or the irregularity with which the items appear at various centres in a region that ought to be taken as a crucial pointer to the nature of commerce in that region. An analysis of the process of the mobilization of goods will involve not only differentiation between the various categories of sources of goods and of the agents of exchange but also an understanding of the destinations to which the goods are required to be mobilized. One of the important points that ought to be considered here, depending on the availability of the data for the purpose, is the physical distance which the goods cover to arrive at the place of exchange. In so far as an examination of the nature of exchange centres

* The term 'market' is used here in the limited sense of a space where buying and selling of goods take place as a somewhat regular activity. This sense would be conveyed by the expression *kraya-vikraya* (i.e. buying and selling) which occurs in an inscription of the tenth century found at Bijapur, on the route from Udaipur to Sirohi, but traced to the Pali district of the former Godawad region in southeast Marwar, *EI*, vol. 10, p. 24, 1.27. This essay is reprinted from *Social Science Probings*, vol. 2, no. 4 (1985).

[1] Cyril S. Belshaw, *Traditional Exchange and Modern Markets* (Prentice Hall of India Private Limited, New Delhi, 1969), p. 4.

and of the nature of authority at such centres is concerned, detailed studies of individual centres, to the maximum extent possible, are necessary because the pattern of regional economy can become understandable in a large measure by analyzing how the centres integrate various economic activities through the processes of exchange.

The theme of this essay is the pattern of local commerce in early medieval Rajasthan. I may as well begin with the confession that the statement of objectives outlined above is rather ambitious, considering that the material available for the theme is both sporadic and sketchy. The material, derived mostly from the epigraphs of Rajasthan, is of a nature which is not commercial but religious. The inscriptions are concerned with specifying levies imposed by authorities on various heads, including items manufactured or exchanged at a locality. The levies which ought to be called 'prestations' were often of an *ad hoc* nature and were acts of patronage. The attempt to analyze the nature of commerce on the basis of such one-dimensional evidence may lead to very questionable generalizations. Secondly, epigraphic evidence, while it may not always exactly contradict the evidence of literary texts, often used for reconstructing the activities of traders in early medieval Rajasthan, does not happily blend with the evidence of such texts either. This point may be illustrated by presenting the major features of trade as they appear in two much-used texts, the *Samarāicca-Kahā* of Haribhadra Sūri[2] and the *Kuvalayamālā* of Udyotana Sūri.[3] The kind of trade they seem to portray had two major features: (i) long-distance trade, involving the organization of caravans as also of maritime voyages. Initiatives for this kind of trade possibly came from individual merchants of high standing and immense wealth. The distance covered not only extended to different traditional trading regions and centres such as Konkan, Ujjayinī, Tāmralipta and Tagara but also to such trans-oceanic centres as Kaṭāha, Ratnadvīpa, and so on; (ii) the trade was essentially in high-value goods. In one case, for

[2] The text has been dated to the middle of the eight century or later by H. Jacobi, *Samarāicca Kahā: A Jaina Prākṛita Work*, vol. I (Calcutta, 1926).

[3] This text was written in the last quarter of the eighth century. See A.N. Upadhye, *Kuvalayamālā*, pt. 2 (Bombay, 1970) and particularly the section titled 'A Cultural Note on the Kuvalayamālā' by V.S. Agrawala, pp. 113–29.

example, reference is made to goods worth five lakhs of *dīnāras*[4] (a term which incidentally does not occur in contemporary inscriptions of Rajasthan but is found in Gupta period inscriptions from other parts of India).[5]

High-value goods converged at princely courts which, as centres of exchange, were limited in number as was the circulation of goods traded. Big merchants and long-distance trade are phenomena not absent from western India since the tenth century, more particularly since the eleventh-twelfth centuries, but considering the period of the texts that we have cited, they seem to carry over a stereotype from the past[6] or to project an ideal for the leaders of merchant communities in the initial phase of the early medieval period. In the choice of sources, the verdict will thus be in favour of epigraphy which, because of the chronological and spatial specificities of its evidence, makes it possible to work out the stages of change.

I

In the context of early medieval Rajasthan, the first stage may be taken to correspond to the pre-Pratīhāra as well as the major part of the Pratīhāra period. The period witnessed what may be imperfectly labelled as the emergence of a new thrust which, intermingled with the existing pattern, gradually led to the crystallization of the early medieval pattern of commerce in Rajasthan. Merchant groups, with *praśastis* written for them, are found at several centres and their association with such centres may be derived from the brief genealogies which the records provide. For example, several records from the Sekhavati area, dating back to the early ninth century, refer to *goṣṭhikas* constituted by the *vaṇiks* and *śreṣṭhīs* of the Dhūsara and Dharkaṭa

[4] Jacobi, *Samarāicca Kahā* . . . .

[5] See *EI*, vol. 15, pp. 130ff. Also, Haribhadra Sūri uses the term *kārṣāpaṇa* in the sense of a coin, which is frequent in early historical records but not in early medieval India. See D. Sharma, ed., *Rajasthaṇ through the Ages*, i (Bikaner, 1966), p. 497.

[6] This impression is further conveyed by repeated references to such old place names as Hastināpura, Kusumapura and Kauśāmbī and the importance attached to them in the texts cited above.

families; the distribution of the early records of these families at Khandela, Sakrai, Mandikila Tal[7]—all in the former Jaipur state—points to an area of concentration which may have been an operational base of local but important merchant groups. (Such merchant groups and the proliferation of their bases will be discussed in detail later.) *Vaṇiks* also figure in the list of addressees which include officials and brāhmaṇas in the records of the Guhilas of Kiṣkindhā (Kalyaṇpur in the Udaipur district).[8] At the same time, one significant set of evidence relates to the movement of merchants, sometimes of well-established families, not only to old settled areas, but also to areas which were perhaps being effectively colonized for the first time. A Chitorgarh inscription of the early sixth century, assignable to the period of the Aulikaras of Mandasor, refers to the family of Viṣṇudatta who is described in the record as *Vaṇijāṃ śreṣṭho*, 'best among the merchants'.[9] Genealogically he appears to have been connected with the *naigama* or merchant family of Mandasor, referred to in a Mandasor record of 532.[10] A comparison of the two records may thus suggest the movement of a family of merchants, earlier settled in Mandasor, to a not too distant old settled area of Madhyamikā-Chitor in the early part of the sixth century. The Samoli record of 646, on the other hand, suggests movement away from a settled area, Vaṭanagara,[11] identified with Vasantgarh in Sirohi district, by a community of *mahājanas*, headed (two terms in the record, *pramukha* and *mahattaka*, imply this) by a person called Jentaka. The community started an *āgara*, possibly the operation of a mine, at a place called *Araṇya-kūpagiri*. That the terrain implied by the expression is significant is suggested also by the construction of a *devakula* for the deity Araṇya-vasinī by the community. The place name mentioned in the record which belongs to an early stage in the history of one of the Rajput

[7] See Sakrai stone inscription of AD 822, *EI*, vol. 27, pp. 27ff; Khandela stone inscription of AD 807, ibid., vol. 34, pp. 159–63; Mandkila Tal inscription of AD 986, ibid., vol. 34, pp. 77ff.

[8] See Dungarpur plates of Bābhaṭa, Harṣa era 83, in D.C. Sircar, *The Guhilas of Kiṣkindhā* (Calcutta, 1965), p. 74, *1. ii*; also *EI*, vol. 34, p. 175.

[9] Ibid., pp. 53–8.

[10] Ibid., pp. 54–5.

[11] Ibid., vol. 20, pp. 97–9. The record, incidentally, also refers to *nānādi-deśamāgatā aṣṭadaśavaitālika*, i.e., 'eighteen' bards coming from various countries.

lineages, the Guhilas, consists of three parts: *araṇya*, *kūpa* and *giri*. While *araṇya* (forest) and *giri* (hills) are self-explanatory, *kūpa* is not so, but it is significant that many early medieval records of western India contain place names with the suffix *kūpa* or *kūpaka* and sometimes end with *viṣaya*.[12] The significance of the Samoli record lies in the fact that it points to a movement leading to the exploration of a new area and its colonization, most probably providing a supply base for local manufacture.

The evidence of some early Pratīhāra records from the Jodhpur area will have to be seen in the light of this process. These records too imply extension into areas which were previously under the control of such communities as the Ābhīras, of the creation of bases of agriculture and settlements and of the establishment of exchange centres (*haṭṭa*) and of communities of merchants.[13] The village mentioned in one case is incidentally called Rohinsakūpaka. The emergence of exchange centres in different pockets appears to have been a continuous process. This is suggested by an earlier record from Dabok (located eight miles to the east of Udaipur), of AD 644, of the time of the Guhilas of Dhavagartā (Dhod in Bhilwara district), which, apart from containing a curious expression, *vaṇiksāmānyadevadāyatva*, refers to *haṭṭa* and *haṭṭamārga* within the spatial limits of Dhavagartā, close to which lay the fields donated to a religious establishment mentioned in the record.[14]

Several points seem to emerge from the meagre evidence presented so far. There indeed existed old settlement areas and centres of merchant activities in which the merchants as a significant social group are seen as undertaking works of religious benefactions and having *praśastis* composed in honour of their family and caste. But if one takes an overview of a long chronological span, it may be possible to note a new trend with which are associated, at least initially, move-

[12] Examples of such place names are Rohinsakūpa, Khaṭṭakūpa, Tṛṇakūpa, Īśānakūpa, Kolikūpaka, etc. See *EI*, vol. 9, p. 280; ibid., vol. 2, pp. 129–30. It has been suggested to me by several scholars of Rajasthan history that place names with the suffix *kūpa* or *kūpaka* would indicate the presence of a well (literally *kūpa*) in the area; I am still not satisfied with this explanation.

[13] Ibid., vol. 9, pp. 277–80.

[14] Ibiḍ., vol. 20, pp. 122–5; also ibid., vol. 35, pp. 100–02.

ments of individual merchants and merchant groups and establishments of new exchange centres. This process will have to be seen in the broader context of the history of Rajasthan in this period which was marked by a gradual agrarian expansion[15] and the proliferation of ruling lineages with their various centres of power.[16] The linkage between the proliferation of such centres and of centres of exchange is a possibility which may be kept in mind at this point. Finally, the records from roughly the tenth century present, in one very important respect, a contrast with those preceding it: the pre-tenth records generally lack in information regarding items of exchange. This contrast too may be taken to suggest certain possibilities which will have to be explored by taking into consideration, along with other factors, the spatial contexts of the exchange centres.

II

Although it may be facilely assumed that the power centres of the various ruling lineages of early medieval Rajasthan were all in some way nodes in the local network of exchange, it seems safer to start with references which are specific. The use of two terms—*haṭṭa* and *maṇḍapikā*[17]—was widespread in early medieval times as signifying centres of exchange; *maṇḍapikā* is especially understood to have denoted a centre where commercial cess was imposed and collected. Both terms occur in the records of Rajasthan, and a compilation of references to them in chronological order may help us understand the distribution pattern of the exchange centres in the region. There were, however, centres which are not clearly designated in the records as *haṭṭas* or *maṇḍapikās* but the fact that cesses were collected at these points may perhaps suggest that they too represented some types of exchange centres. Two separate lists of exchange centres, compiled from a variety of early medieval epigraphs from different parts of Rajasthan but by no means comprehensive, follow:

15 See 'Irrigation in Early Medieval Rajasthan', in this volume.

16 See my paper, 'The Origin of the Rajputs: Political, Economic and Social Processes in Early Medieval Rajasthan', in this volume.

17 For the significance of these terms, see my paper, 'Urban Centres in Early Medieval India: An Overview' in this volume.

TABLE 1

LIST OF EXCHANGE CENTRES

Date	*Location of the Centre of Exchange*	*Ruling Lineage*	*Term Used in the Record with Reference to the Centre of Exchange*
644	Dhod, Bhilwara district[18]	Guhila	*haṭṭa*
861	Ghatiyala, near Jodhpur[19]	Pratīhāra	*haṭṭa* at Rohinsakupaka *grama*
905	Kaman, Bayana[20]	Pratīhāra	Kambali-*haṭṭa* at Kāmyakīya *Koṭṭa*
916, 939, 997	Hastikuṇḍikā[21] Godwar area in southeast Marwar, (Pali district)	Rāṣṭrakūṭa	*rājadhānī*
953	Āhāḍa, part of Udaipur[22]	Guhila	*haṭṭa*
1278	Āhāḍa[23]	*maṇḍapikā* at Āghāṭapura	
955	Bayana, Bharatpur[24]	Pratīhāra, the feudatory local lineage being Śūrasena	i) *maṇḍapikā* at Vusāväṭa ii) *maṇḍapikā* at Śrīpatha
961	Rajor, Alwar[25]	Pratīhāra	*haṭṭa* at Rājyapura
1017–18	Shergarh, Kota[26]	Paramāra	*maṇḍapikā*
1080	Arthuna, Banswara[27]	Paramāra	*haṭṭa*

[18] *EI*, vol. 20, pp. 122–5.
[19] Ibid., vol. 9, pp. 277–80.
[20] Ibid., vol. 24, pp. 329–36.
[21] Ibid., vol. 10, pp. 17–24.
[22] *The Indian Antiquary*, vol. 58, pp. 161ff.
[23] G.H. Ojha, *Udaipur Rajya Ka Itihasa* (in Hindi), pt. I (Ajmer, 1928), p. 176.
[24] *EI*, vol. 22, pp. 120–27.
[25] Ibid., vol. 3, pp. 263–7.
[26] *The Indian Antiquary*, vol. 40, pp. 175–6; *EI*, vol. 23, pp. 137–41.
[27] *EI*, vol. 14, pp. 295–310; also H.V. Trivedi, *Inscriptions of the Paramāras, Chandellas, Kachchapaghātas and Two Minor Dynasties* (Corpus Inscriptionum Indicarum, vol. 7, pt. 2) (New Delhi, n.d.), pp. 286–96.

Date	*Location of the Centre of Exchange*	*Ruling Lineage*	*Term Used in the Record with Reference to the Centre of Exchange*
1109	Talabad, 12 miles south of Banswara[28]	Paramāra	*pattanavara*
1115 1278	Sevadi[29], Pali district	Cāhamāna	i) Śamīpāṭī-*pattana* ii) *Maṇḍapikā*
1156	Badari, near Nadol[30], Pali district	Cāhamāna	*Maṇḍapikā*
1161	Nadol[31]	Cāhamāna	Naḍḍūla-talapada-*śulka-Maṇḍapikā*
1178	Kirātakūpa (Kiradu)[32]	Caulukya, local lineage being Cāhamāna	*śulka-*(*maṇḍapikā*)
1184	Mandor, near Jodhpur[33], Jodhpur district	Cāhamāna	*māṇḍavya-purīya-maṇḍapikā*
1250	Khamnor, near Udaipur[34]	—	*māṇḍavi*
1276 1291	Ratanpur, near Jodhpur[35], Jodhpur district	Cāhamāna	*haṭṭa*
1278	Chitor[36], Chitorgarh district	—	*haṭṭa*
1288	Chandravati, Sirohi[37] district	Paramāra	Candrāvatī-*maṇḍapikā*
1296	Jalor[38], Jalor district	Cāhamāna	*niśrānikṣepa-haṭṭa*

[28] *EI*, vol. 21, p. 52.
[29] Ibid., vol. 11, pp. 30–32; *PRASWC*, 1907–8, p. 52.
[30] *The Indian Antiquary*, vol. 41, pp. 202–03.
[31] *EI*, vol. 9, pp. 62–66.
[32] *The Indian Antiquary*, vol. 62, p. 42.
[33] *JPASB*, vol. 10 (1914), pp. 405–7.
[34] *ARRM*, 1932, p. 3.
[35] P.C. Nahar, *Jaina Inscriptions*, vol. I, pp. 248–9. The ruler mentioned in the records is Sāmantasiṃha who can be identified with Cāhamāna Sāmantasiṃha of Jalor. See D. Sharma, *Early Chauhan Dynasties* (Delhi, 1959), pp. 159ff.
[36] G.H. Ojha, *Udaipur Rajya* . . . .
[37] H.V. Trivedi, *Inscriptions of the Paramāras* . . . , p. 277.
[38] *EI*, vol. 11, pp. 60–61. *Niśrānikṣepahaṭṭa* is taken to signify a part of a *haṭṭa*

TABLE 2

CENTRES NOT SPECIFICALLY SO DESIGNATED BUT PERHAPS SERVING AS CENTRES OF EXCHANGE

Date	*Location of the Centre of Exchange*	*Ruling Lineage*	*Nature of the Evidence*
1138 } 1145 }	Nāḍulaḍāgikā (Narlai)[39], Pali district	Cāhamāna	i) Presence of the *deśī* of Vanajārakas ii) Reference to levies on loaded bulls on transit
1141	Dhalopasthāna, near Nadol[40]	Cāhamāna	The document relates to the interception of goods from various categories of people, including traders; *samasta-mahājana*, including those from Aṇahilavāḍa, among witnesses mentioned in the document
1295	Vāhaḍameru, Juna-Vadmer, near Barmer[41]	Cāhamāna	Presence of a caravan (*sārtha*) of camels and bulls

The distribution pattern of the exchange centres may now be related to their individual spatial contexts. Without making a detailed survey of the areas in which they were located, reference to a few selected centres will serve the purpose of providing a general idea. To repeat the evidence already cited, Rohinsakūpaka where Pratīhāra Kakkuka installed, around 861, a *haṭṭa* with its various shops and established *mahājanas* was a *grāma* (village); his inscription also pos-

used for storing merchandise which was to be subsequently moved out for the purpose of exchange, ibid., p. 60. The term *nikṣepa* which occurs in the *Artha-śāstra* and the *Amarakośa* is taken also to refer to depositing some goods with an artisan or craftsman so that they could be manufactured into finished items, S.C. Mishra, 'An Inscriptional Approach to the Study of the Arthaśāstra of Kauṭilya', Ph.D. dissertation submitted to Delhi University, 1984, p. 142.

39 *EI*, vol. 11, pp. 36–7, 42–3.

40 Ibid., pp. 37–41.

41 Ibid., pp. 59–60.

sibly suggests the introduction of a few agricultural innovations in the area.[42] In 961, Pratīhāra Mathanadeva of Rājyapura (Rajor, Alwar) made several provisions for a temple, and the categories of people he addressed were headed by, among others, the *vaṇik* and *pravaṇi*, suggesting their substantial presence at the exchange centre at Rājyapura. Among the varieties of donations mentioned, the following may be underlined: (i) cultivated fields located in the *bhoga* of the donor and neighbouring fields cultivated by the Gurjaras (*samastaśrīgurjaravāhitasamastakṣetra*). The imposts on all crops are mentioned, including those termed in the record as *skandhaka* and *mārgaṇaka* (*samastaśasyānāṃbhāga-khalabhikṣā-prasthaka-skandhaka-mārgaṇaka*).[43] For the spatial context of the Rājyapura exchange centre the expressions are significant for they suggest a range of activities extending to movement of agricultural produce, *skandhaka* and *mārgaṇaka* being imposts on such movement; (ii) imposts, in cash, on loads of agricultural produce brought at the exchange centre for sale. The exchange centres were thus located in the context of the bases of agrarian production, and a close look at the records will yield the same spatial pattern for most exchange centres in other areas where clusters of rural settlements occur. An excellent example of this is further provided by two records of the second half of the twelfth century from Nadol, the seat of a Cāhamāna ruling lineage. One record of 1160 speaks of twelve villages with Naḍḍūlagrāma apparently as their centre, which were assessed in cash for the purpose of making a donation to the local shrine of Mahāvīra Jina.[44] The second record, of 1161, also mentions religious donations but out of the income accruing from *Naḍḍūlatalapada-śulka-maṇḍapikā*.[45]

Naḍḍūla, even though mentioned as a *grāma* in the earlier record (it is of course elsewhere designated as a *pura*),[46] was a node in a cluster of rural settlements and its emergence as a node and an exchange

[42] Ibid., vol. 9, p. 280; for reference to mango-groves and sugarcane plantations in this area, see *Journal of the Royal Asiatic Society of Great Britain and Ireland*, 1895, pp. 513–21.

[43] *EI*, vol. 3, pp. 263–7.

[44] Ibid., vol. 9, pp. 66–70.

[45] Ibid., pp. 62–6.

[46] Nadlai inscription of 1171, ibid., vol. 11, pp. 47ff.

centre at which commercial levies were collected was obviously related to its being a centre of Cāhamāna power. The integration of rural units of production and of commercial traffic through centres which in the early medieval period were, in many cases, also seats of ruling lineages, is the primary point from which we can start exploring two further aspects of the exchange centres. First, in a number of cases, the exchange centres, which could not all have been identical in structure, combined inflow of goods from outside with local manufacture. The second aspect concerns the reconstruction of a hierarchy of exchange centres. At Kāmyakīya or Kaman in Bharatpur a record of 905 refers to *Kambalī-haṭṭa* which has been taken to mean a cattle-market. It was, however, not a periodical market although it may have been so originally; *āvārikas* or enclosures with *vīthis* or shops are mentioned in the overall complex of the *haṭṭa*. Other records from the centre speak of *śaṅkhikas* or conch-shell workers, guild of artisans, guild of gardeners, guild of potters (mentioned separately)—all indicating the range of economic activities of the centre.[47] Similarly, the Arthuna (Banswara) record of 1080 lists, apart from the items sold at the *haṭṭa* in which shops were located, at least two categories of manufacturers: *kāṃsyakāras* or braziers and *kalyapālas* or distillers of liquor.[48] It can of course be assumed that each exchange centre may have been a manufacturing centre of some kind as well, but the actual dimensions of the centres are likely to have varied, depending on the range of economic and other activities taking place in the spatial contexts of such centres. No satisfactory finding in this regard is possible without detailed work in the historical geography of the period which also deals with such problems, but the question of hierarchy may, for the present, be approached from several angles. One approach would be to examine, as far as possible, the overall structure of a settlement to ascertain if it accommodates one or more points at which exchange transactions take place. Evidence of this kind is available from various regions of early medieval India,[49] and it may be worth-

[47] Ibid., vol. 24, pp. 329–36.

[48] H.V. Trivedi, *Inscriptions of the Paramāras* . . . .

[49] Siyadoni inscriptions, ranging in date from 903 to 968, list a number of such points of exchange, *EI*, vol. I, pp. 162–79; for other examples from early medieval India, see ibid., vol. 19, pp. 52–4; ibid., vol. 13, pp. 15–36, No. A.

while looking for such evidence in early medieval Rajasthan. The second approach would be to try and locate clusters of exchange centres; a series or succession of such centres in a given area is likely to yield, if not a hierarchical ordering of such centres, at least an idea of the areas of concentration. Thirdly, a dependable index for the purpose would be provided by an analysis of the range of goods which were regular items of exchange at a centre and the variety and number of social groups and institutions which were drawn into the network of exchange. This exercise may be considered relevant for a study of local commerce since no region as a whole represents equal potential for identical economic activities at any period of history, and a reconstruction of hierarchy may indicates the directions along which the flow of commercial traffic was important.

Although it would be impossible to work out the details of this pattern in this essay, particularly in view of the uneven exploration of the historical sites of Rajasthan, attempts may nevertheless be made in relation to a few areas. Clusters of exchange centres seem to have been located along a line from the Jodhpur area down to Banswara in the south. Around Jodhpur, exchange centres at Ghatiyala, Mandor and Ratanpur suggest some kind of cluster. References in twelfth century records suggest more than one exchange point at Ratnapura[50] or Ratanpur. Another cluster can be located about half way between Jodhpur and Udaipur in an area under the control of Cāhamāna lineages; here, the exchange centres at Nadol, Nāḍūlaḍāgikā or Narlai, Dhalopa, Sevadi and Badarī are located close to one another. Arthuna, Talabad and Panahera, all in Banswara, together seem to constitute another cluster in south Rajasthan. Towards the east, the exchange centre of Kāmyakīya-*koṭṭa*, taken along with the *maṇḍapikās* at Śrīpathā and Vūsavāṭa, may be taken to form another cluster. It is perhaps superfluous to add that considering the vastness of Rajasthan as a region, other such clusters may well have existed in this period, but even the kind of limited exercise done above may suggest a pattern of unequal intensity of commercial exchange (see map on page 101).

Insofar as the hierarchical order of exchange centres is concerned, two centres appear to stand out as exceedingly important, at least from

[50] P.C. Nahar, pp. 248–9.

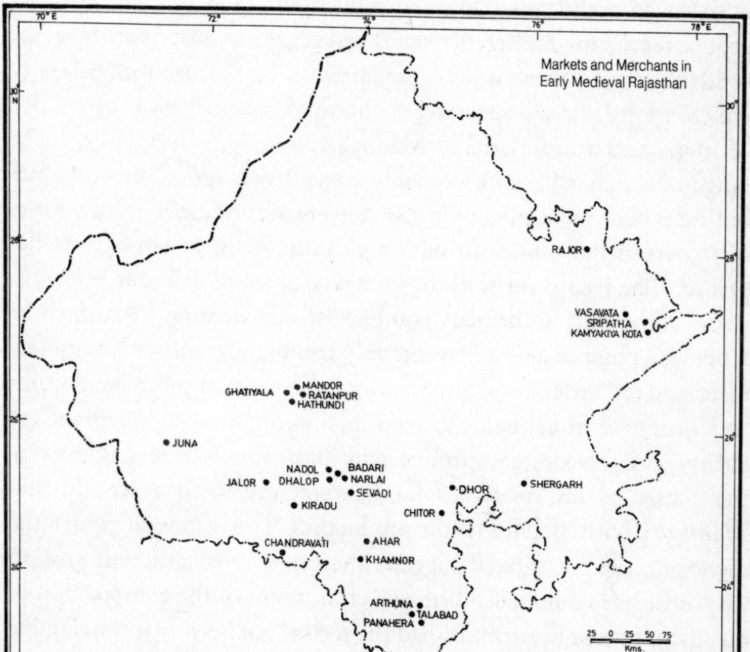
Markets and Merchants in
Early Medieval Rajasthan
70° E
72°
74°
76°
78° E
30° N
28°
26°
24°
RAJOR
VASAVATA
SRIPATHA
KAMYAKIYA KOTA
MANDOR
GHATIYALA
RATANPUR
HATHUNDI
JUNA
NADOL
BADARI
JALOR
DHALOP
NARLAI
SEVADI
DHOR
SHERGARH
KIRADU
CHITOR
CHANDRAVATI
AHAR
KHAMNOR
ARTHUNA
TALABAD
PANAHERA
25 0 25 50 75
Kms.

the manner in which they have been presented in the records. One is Āghāṭapura or Ahar, a part of Udaipur; the other is Arthuna near Banswara. Ahar seems to stand out alone but if the Arthuna evidence is any indication, it would seem that in both the cases there were minor exchange centres located around them. The importance of both lay in the fact that they were points at which varieties of resources converged; this impression is derived from the items which were listed for the purpose of religious levies and from the groups which were drawn into such transactions. At Āghāṭapura or Ahar, the merchant groups represented different origins and organizations. Apart from the resident *Vaṇiks*, there was an organization of the *deśīs*, members of which are mentioned separately. The third category was constituted of merchants from Karṇāṭa, Madhya-viṣaya, Lāṭa and Ṭakka. The range of the merchandize probably started with agricultural produce but extended, in keeping with the convergence of different categories of traders at the centre, to such high-value items as horses and elephants. The record suggests the existence of more than one exchange point within the settlement complex of Āghāṭapura.[51] Arthuna, to reiterate a point made earlier, certainly combined trade with manufacture; here too agricultural produce, including several commercial crops and products from them, formed an important component of exchange. Apart from items produced by local manufacturers, there were those used as raw materials for manufacture, such as cotton and *Mañjiṣṭhā*, both used for textile production. The manner in which the merchants are mentioned suggests the presence of different groups. Of course, we could have formed a clearer idea of the composition of merchant groups at Arthuna, had the record not been so unintelligible in most parts.[52]

III

The significant trend which can be seen in the increase in specific references to exchange centres coincides with references to items which were available at the centres. It is of course impossible to reconstruct

[51] *The Indian Antiquary*, vol. 58, pp. 161ff.
[52] H.V. Trivedi.

TABLE 3

LIST OF GOODS EXCHANGED

Date	*Centre*	*Agricultural Items Including Items of Commercial Agriculture, Processed Items and Dairy Products*	*Manufactured Items or Items used for Manufacturing*	*Other Items*	*High Value Items*
916, 939, 997	Hastikuṇḍikā, Godwar,[53] Pali district	1. wheat	1. cotton	1. salt	—
		2. barley	2. *mañjiṣṭhā*	2. *collika* of leaves	
		3. pulses	3. products of braziers	3. *kuṃkuma* (saffron)	
		4. product of oil-press	4. *rālaka* (stuff made from animal hair?)[54]	4. gum-resin (*guggula*)	
		5. *dhānya* (rice?)			

[53] Ibid., vol. 10, pp. 17–24.

[54] Angali Bagai, on the strength of the seventh century account of Hiuen Tsang and other sources, suggests that *rālaka* probably denoted some variety of stuff made from animal hair, 'Merchandise and Mercantile community in post-Gupta times in northern India', Ph. D. Dissertation submitted at the University of Delhi, 1985, p. 111, fn. 1. Dasarath Sharma, on the strength of the Jaina Prākṛta text, *Kuvalayamālā*, takes *rallaka* to mean winter cover prepared from goats' hair, Presidential Address, Ancient India Section, Indian History Congress, 29 session (Patiala, 1967).

Date	*Centre*	*Agricultural Items Including Items of Commercial Agriculture, Processed Items and Dairy Products*	*Manufactured Items or Items used for Manufacturing*	*Other Items*	*High Value Items*
953	Ahar, Udaipur[55]	i) unspecified agricultural produce for which two measures, *tulā* and *āḍhaka*, are mentioned ii) produce of *ghāṇaka* or oil mill iii) produce of confectioners			1. elephants 2. horses 3. horned animals (*śṛṅgī*)
960	Rajor, Alwar[56]	i) reference to sacks of agricultural produce? (*goṇi*) ii) butter and oil		*collikā* of leaves (*parṇa*)	
1080	Arthuna, Banswara[57]	i) barley (*yava*) ii) reference to *bhāṇḍa-dhānya*, possibly meaning 'loads of grain' iii) *Ikṣu* (sugar-cane); separate reference to *khaṇḍa-guḍa*, i.e. candy-sugar and jaggery	i) *tumbaka* of liquor ii) products of braziers (*kāṃsyakāra*) iii) *mañjiṣṭhā* or madder	i) salt ii) *parṇa* or leaves iii) cattle-fodder?	

[55] *The Indian Antiquary*, vol. 58, pp. 161ff.
[56] *EI*, vol. 3, pp. 263–67.
[57] Ibid., vol. 14, pp. 295–310; H.V. Trivedi, *Inscriptions of the Paramāras* . . . .

Date	Centre	Agricultural Items Including Items of Commercial Agriculture, Processed Items and Dairy Products	Manufactured Items or Items used for Manufacturing	Other Items	High Value Items
		iv) cotton (*kārpāsa*)			
		v) thread (*sūtra*)			
		vi) clothing fabric (*karppaṭa-koṭika*)			
		vii) sesame oil (*ajyataila*)			
		viii) oil (*taila*)			
		ix) areca-nut			
		x) coconut			
		xi) citron			
1143 and 1145	Nadlai,[58], Pali district	i) *dhāna*?	i) iron implements?	i) salt	i) jewels
		ii) *kirāḍauā*, covering such items as gum, black pepper, dry ginger and so on	ii) *mañjiṣṭhā*		
		iii) oil			
		iv) ghee			
		v) cotton			
		vi) *puga-haritakī* (myrobalan)			

[58] P.C. Nahar, pp. 213ff; *EI*, vol. 11, pp. 42–3.

the total range of goods since the levies or prestations imposed upon them were often specified in terms of total dues and not as dues from separate items: this would be suggested by such expressions as *mārgādāya*[59] (collection from *mārga*) or *maṇḍapikādāya*[60] (collection from *maṇḍapikā*) out of which a part would be set aside for the purpose of donation. It is only in cases where the levies are specified as collected from separate items that it is possible to form an idea of the range of goods which were exchanged. Comparisons between exchange centres in this respect would thus be imperfect, but for an understanding of the general trend it needs to be reiterated that clusters of exchange centres seem to occur in areas which were essentially agrarian settlements and that agricultural items entered the centres perhaps with as much regularity as did other items. Few records offer any details but those that do may be used to prepare a table which will provide, for generally fixed points of time represented by the available records, lists of items constituting the nexus of exchange at the exchange centres (see Table 3).

Even though the material collated in Table 3 is decidedly inadequate for generalizations, it is nevertheless an indicator, at least in two respects, of the nature of commerce in all major exchange centres: (i) the first point concerns the structure of contemporary demand which generated exchange as a major economic activity. In understanding this structure the crucial fact is the juxtaposition of agricultural goods with high-value items and manufactured items at several points where exchange took place; (ii) secondly, exchange took place at points where various social groups interacted—not periodically but on a regular basis, and in this sense the major exchange centres were different from periodical markets or fairs, references to which are available in early medieval records from different parts of India.[61] Movements of specific

[59] *EI*, vol. 23, pp. 137–41. Some inscriptions also have such expressions as *Svīyādāna-madhyāt mārge* (i.e. 'from our collections from the road'); see Nadlai record of Rāyapāladeva of 1138, *EI*, vol. 11, pp. 36–7.

[60] See for example, Shergarh inscription of 1018, *EI*, vol. 23, pp. 137–41. In fact both the terms—*mārgādāya* and *maṇḍapikādāya*—occur in this record.

[61] One piece of rather well-known evidence regarding the horse fair in north India is provided by the Pehoa (Karnal district, Haryana) record of the time of the Pratīhāras, *EI*, vol. I, pp. 184–90; the Bali record of 1143 from Rajasthan, referring

goods into the exchange centres could be periodical, but major exchange centres had resident populations, including resident *vaṇiks* and manufacturers, and one could thus suppose that exchange relations between these two groups and other sections of the population were not determined by periodical cycles in the movement of goods, even if such movements are taken as an essential component of the mobilization process. Both points, however, require further empirical substantiation. Two records of early medieval Rajasthan may be cited to reveal, at least partially, the pattern of contemporary requirements which would correlate with activities at the exchange centres. The Harsha record of AD 973 from the Shikar area speaks of Vigraharāja of the Cāhamāna lineage in the following terms:

> He has been served with many presents—with strings of pearls, gay steeds, fine garments and weapons; with camphor, quantities of betel, first rate sandal wood, and endless quantities of gold and with spirited rutting elephants, huge like mountains, together with their mates.[62]

The description of 'presents' is, in one sense, a conventional one, similar descriptions being found in other records of the period; in another sense, however, it represents the range of requirements among the ruling elites, which can be used for the purpose of correlation with contemporary commerce. Although the record chooses to list the items as 'presents', one is entitled to read beyond this label and, on the basis of other records of the period, broadly consider them as items which entered into the exchange activities of various of merchant groups. Indeed, the same Harsha record mentions that a levy of one *dramma* on every horse was imposed by the rulers on the Heḍāvika group of horse-dealers who visited the Shikar area from Uttarāpatha.[63]

---

to the sale of horses, may be another such piece of evidence, ibid., vol. 11, pp. 32–3. For references to fairs held in different parts of Karnataka and Andhra, see G.S. Dikshit, *Local Self-Government in Medieval Karnataka* (Dharwar, 1964), ch. 8; T. Venkateswara Rao, 'Local Bodies in Pre-Vijayanagara Andhra (AD 1000 to AD 1336)', Ph.D. thesis (Dharwar University, 1975), ch. 5.

[62] *EI*, vol. 2, p. 127. The term *puga* in the record (verse 24) seems to refer to betelnut and not betel.

[63] Ibid. The Heḍāvika horse-merchants are mentioned not only in the Harsha record of 973. The Heḍāvikas, the different variants of the name being Heṭāvuka and Heḍāvuka, are known from other epigraphic and literary sources as well.

The second record, of 1249, from Bhinmal[64] mentions an amount of several *drammas* deposited at the *bhāṇḍāgāra* of the Jagatsvāmī temple at Bhinmal, the deposit being intended to procure certain resources for the performance of a ritual at the temple. The items required for the ritual were: wheat, rice, pulses, ghee, betel-leaves and nuts, *aguru* and *kuṃkuma*.

Despite their distance in space and chronology, the juxtaposition of the two records cited above would surely reveal the complex pattern of early medieval trade involving a wide range of goods and of exchange relations, necessitating the use of coined money combined with other means of exchange. This will, in turn, reflect on the structure of the centres of exchange as points of convergence of movements of goods and acts of exchange. It may be worthwhile to attempt to examine, from a study, over a wide span of time, of movements of goods and of operations of trading groups, whether any particular form of operation can be seen to emerge as more significant than others. The movements of goods suggest differential distances covered. While the term *skandhaka*[65] (literally, imposts on items carried on shoulders) may refer to movement over a very short distance, intercentre movements, by the *vanajāraka* community of traders, for example, were undertaken by loading pack animals and carts.[66] Long-distance move-

---

Balambhaṭṭa, commentator of *Mitākṣarā*, associates them with Gurjjara-deśa, and it would appear that they constituted a sub-caste of the brāhmaṇas. See Chitrarekha Gupta, 'Horse Trade in North India: Some Reflections on Socio-Economic Life', *Journal of Ancient Indian History*, vol. 14, pts. 1–2 (1983–84), pp. 186–206.

The other point to note is that the horse, as an item of trade, was in demand throughout the country, and was a prized item among the royalty, which would explain its extensive itinerary. Apart from the Harsha record, see the evidence of the Kiradu inscription (1161) of Caulukya Kumārapala and his feudatory Paramāra Someśvara. Someśvara claims to have exacted 1700 horses, including one 'five-nailed' and eight 'peacock-breasted' from one prince Jajjāka, *The Indian Antiquary*, vol. 61, pp. 135–6.

64 Ibid., vol. 11, pp. 55–7.

65 Rajorgarh inscription of 961, *EI*, vol. 3, pp. 263–7. For a brief discussion of the term, see U.N. Ghosal, *Contributions to the History of the Hindu Revenue System*, 2nd edition (Calcutta, 1972), pp. 317–18, 420. The term resembles in its import *aṃsa-bhāra* (shoulder-load) occurring in the *Arthaśāstra*, 2.21.24, which specifies one *māṣaka* as the impost on a shoulder-load of goods.

66 For example, the expression *märgge gacchatānāmāgatānāṃ vṛṣabhānāṃ sekeṣu* (Nadlai record of 1138. *EI*, vol. 11, pp. 36–7) refers to incoming and outgoing

ments of exchangeable items were organized in the form of *sārthas.*[67] It can be assumed that traders from outside Rajasthan, to whom the Ahar record of 953 refers,[68] moved from one centre to another in periodic cycles in well-organized caravans.

The nature of the organization which cut across trading groups coming in over long distances as well as certain, though not necessarily all, groups which may be considered to have operated locally is mostly reflected in the use of the term *deśī. Deśī* can only loosely be taken in the sense of a guild of traders, and in the records of Rajasthan the term has been used in such expressions as *Bhammaha deśī*[69] and also in relation to the *Vanajārakas.*[70] The reference to the Heḍāvikas, the horse-dealers, in the plural perhaps suggests an organization similar to that of the *deśī.*[71] In the Ahar record of 953, seven members of a *deśī* are mentioned by name. It may be significant that the list of *deśī* names is juxtaposed with the name of an individual who is designated as a *vaṇik,*[72] perhaps indicating conscious differentiation between them by the community which was the immediate context of exchange.

The groups participating in commerce in early medieval Rajasthan may thus be considered to have ranged from non-resident merchants from other—sometimes distant—regions, locally mobile groups originating in different centres and coming together for the mobilization

---

loads on bullocks which passed through the road at Nadlai. The load of merchandise transported by the trading organization (*deśī*) of the *Vanajārakas* on bullocks (*vṛṣabha-bharita*) are mentioned in another Nadlai record of 1145, ibid., pp. 42–3. A fascinatingly visual idea of how goods were transported comes from the Mangarol inscription of 1144 from the Kathiawar area under the Caulukyas. Referring to the varieties of merchandise arriving at *Śrīmān Maṅgalapura-śulkamaṇḍapikā,* the record includes items transported by *balīvardda* (oxen), *rāsabha* (donkey) and *uṭa* (camel). For the text of the record, see G.V. Acharya, *Historical Inscriptions of Gujarat* (in Gujarati), Sri Forbes Gujarati Sabha Series, No. 15, pt. 2 (Bombay, 1935), No. 145.

[67] For occurrence of the term *sārtha,* consisting of oxen and camels, see the Juna record of 1295 from Mallani district, *EI,* vol. 11, pp. 59–60.

[68] *The Indian Antiquary,* vol. 58, pp. 161ff.

[69] *EI,* vol. 2, p. 124, line 38.

[70] Reference to the *deśī* of the Vanajārakas is available in the Narlai inscription of 1145 of Rāyapala, ibid., vol. 11, pp. 42–3.

[71] Ibid., vol. 2, p. 124, line 38.

[72] *The Indian Antiquary,* vol. 58, pp. 161ff.

of goods, to resident merchant-families. In trying to understand the overall pattern of commerce which the activities of these disparate groups reflected, it is necessary to reiterate two points already made: (i) such activities converged at sedentary points[73] where exchange took place; and (ii) such points were centres of ruling lineages of varying importance. Although the epigraphs do not directly relate to the mechanisms of commerce, the nature of transactions with which they are concerned throws up two impressions from which the commercial trend of the period may be sought to be reconstructed.

IV

The first impression is that of the ascendancy of several local merchant lineages and of the expansion of their network. Mention has previously been made of the Dhūsara and Dharkaṭa families of the ninth century from the Sekhavati area of the old Jaipur state.[74] Although reference to the Dhūsara *vaṃśa* of merchants does not seem to continue, the continuity of the Dharkaṭa lineage is attested by later records. A Rajorgarh record of 922 and another record of the tenth century, preserved in the Mandor museum, contain references to the Dharkaṭas.[75] A *vaṇigvara* of the Dharkaṭa family is mentioned in 986 in the Mandkila Tal record from Nagar.[76] The Dharkaṭa *Jati* further appears in the records of the eleventh century[77] and early thirteenth century.[78] It is believed that the Dharkaṭas or the Dhākaḍas repre-

[73] The use of the term 'sedentary' should however relate more to the organization of trade than to nodes of exchange; the point which emerges from this essay is that by the close of the period under review 'sedentary' merchants perhaps tended to become more important than itinerant and other categories of merchants in the region concerned. For conceptual clarification, see J. Bernard, 'Trade and Finance in the Middle Ages: 900–1500', in C.M. Cipolla, ed., *The Fontana Economic History of Europe: The Middle Ages* (London-Glasgow, 1973), pp. 308–09.

[74] See note 7.

[75] R.V. Somani, *Jain Inscriptions of Rajasthan* (Jaipur, 1982), p. 209.

[76] *EI*, vol. 34, pp. 77ff.

[77] A stone inscription, reported to have been discovered in Jodhpur district and dated V. S. 1165 (AD 1198), records the death of a merchant of Dharkaṭa lineage and of Khandasa *gotra*. This information is derived from the descriptive label of the record preserved in the Mandor Museum.

[78] P.C. Nahar, p. 220. See also *JPASB*, vol. 12 (1916), pp. 104–06.

sented a section of the later day Oswals.[79] The Sonis, taken to be another subdivision of the Oswals and deriving their name from Suvarṇagiri or Jalor,[80] are mentioned in a record of 1296 from Jalor.[81] In fact, the emergence of the Oswals as a major merchant group before the middle of the thirteenth century can be considered a certainty. A Mt. Abu record of 1230, while providing details of the composition of various *goṣṭhikas*, refers, at one place, to the merchants of Uesavāla-*jñātīya* from Kāsahradagrāma[82] and, at another, to merchants of Oisavāla-*jñātīya*, probably a more correct form of the name, of Sāhila-vāḍā.[83]

Another merchant lineage, that of the Śrīmālas, was also on the ascent from around this period. A Mt. Abu (Sirohi) record of 1144 mentions it as Śrīmāla-*kula*[84] and a Jalor record of 1183[85] has a eulogistic reference to an individual merchant of the lineage, who is described as *Śrī Śrī Mālavavaṃśavibhūṣaṇa Śreṣṭhī* Yaśodeva. The ascendancy of the merchant families of the period, some of whom, like the Sonis or the Śrīmālas, derived their caste or lineage names (the epigraphs use such terms as *kula*, *vaṃśa*, *jāti*, *jñāti*, etc.) from the centres of their origin and of the consolidation of their intraregional as well as interregional network, is perhaps best illustrated by the case of the Prāgvaṭas. The Prāgvaṭas are known from inscriptions at Sirohi (1031),[86] Kiradu (1132),[87] Nadol (1161)[88] and other places such as

[79] According to D.R. Bhandarkar, the name Dharkaṭa survives as Dhākaḍa, which he takes to represent a sub-section of the Oswals, *EI*, vol. 27, p. 29. The Dharkaṭas figure very prominently in the inscriptions at Osian, the temple site located 66 kms to the north-northwest of Jodhpur; the site is considered 'a cradle of the Oswals'. See Devendra Handa, *Osian: History, Archaeology, Art and Architecture* (Delhi, 1984), chs 1 and 6.

[80] *EI*, vol. 11, pp. 60–2.

[81] Ibid.

[82] G.V. Acharyya, Inscription No. 168.

[83] Ibid.

[84] *EI*, vol. 9, p. 151. Curiously, the person mentioned in the record is spoken of as belonging to *Śrīmālakula* and as being an ornament of the Prāgvaṭa *vaṃśa*.

[85] *EI*, vol. 11, pp. 52–4.

[86] Ibid., vol. 9, p. 149. The association of the Prāgvaṭas with Arbudagiri in Sirohi continued for centuries, ibid. Also G.V. Acharyya.

[87] Ibid., vol. 11, pp. 43–6.

[88] *EI*, vol. 9, pp. 62–3. For reference to *Śrī Nadrala* (Nadol)—*pura vāsī-Prāgvaṭa-vaṃśa*, see also G.V. Acharyya, Inscription No. 148.

Candrāvatī[89] but their network extended to Gujarat, and in fact the merchants of the Prāgvaṭa family developed a close association with the Caulukya court of Gujarat.[90] According to early medieval Jaina texts, Ninnaya of the Prāgvaṭa family, originally belonging to Śrīmāla or Bhinmal was invited to settle in Aṇahilavāḍa.[91] Individual members of the family were endowed with such official designations as *mahāmātyavara* and *daṇḍapati* or *daṇḍādhipati*, *mantrī* and *saciva*,[92] and if the evidence of literary texts is to be believed, Vimala of Prāgvaṭa descent was elevated to the rank of *nṛpati*[93] with proper insignias. The movement towards the ranks of the contemporary political elites is reflected further in the saying attributed to Vastupāla who won a military victory over a Muslim merchant, supported by the ruler of Lāṭa, from Cambay: 'It is delusion to think that kṣatriyas alone can fight and not a *vaṇik* . . . I am a *vaṇik* in the shop of battlefield'.[94]

Major merchant lineages such as those of the Prāgvaṭas had understandable links with important centres like Aṇahilapura or Candrāvatī and with royalty, but what is more significant for understanding the growth of their intraregional and interregional network is that they are found associated with various other, possibly rural, bases as well. The details of this phenomenon for different parts of Gujarat and Rajasthan are not available, but an idea of the network of the merchant lineages is nevertheless provided by the Mt. Abu record of 1230 which enumerates some of their bases. The Prāgvaṭas are thus found, apart from Aṇahilapura and Candrāvatī, at Uṃbaraṇīkīsaraulagrāma, Brahmaṇā, Ghauligrāma and Dāhaḍagrāma.[95] The merchants of the Śrīmāla lineage can be located, on the strength of the same record, at Phīliṇigrāma, Haṃḍāudrāgrāma and Dāvāṇīgrāma.[96] The Oswals are found to be associated with Kāsahradagrāma and Sāhilavāḍā.[97]

89 *EI*, vol. 9, pp. 149–50; also G.V. Acharyya, Inscription No. 168.

90 G.V. Acharyya, Inscriptions 167, 168.

91 V.K. Jain, *Trade and Traders in Western India (AD 1000–1300)* (Delhi, 1990), chs 9, 10. The epigraphic records of the Aṇahilapura family, however, trace the genealogy of the family from the time of Chaṇḍapa, *EI*, vol. 8, pp. 200ff.

92 See ibid., pp. 208–13; ibid., vol. 9, pp. 62–6; V.K. Jain.

93 V.K. Jain.

94 Ibid.

95 G.V. Acharyya, Inscription No. 168. See also *EI*, vol. 8, pp. 219–22.

96 Acharyya.

97 Acharyya.

The expansion of the network of lineages of local merchants, the history of some of which may be traced back at least to the ninth century, appears to have been the mechanism through which resource bases, arteries for the flow of resources and the centres of exchange came to be gradually integrated. The stages of this integration are still far from having been worked out; one may perhaps envisage a change from a situation in which itinerant merchants and the *vanajārakas* were an important component in commercial operations to a situation which was dominated by groups that were being crystallized into trading castes. Certainly by the close of the early medieval period the ascendancy of such merchant lineages as Dharkaṭa, Oisavāla, Śrīmāla and Prāgvaṭa was a phenomenon which patterned commercial as well as non-commercial activities at various centres in Rajasthan. To this may perhaps be added another dimension. The major merchant lineages had by now been considerably stratified. The segment of the Prāgvaṭas, resident at Aṇahilapura (*Aṇahilapuravāstavya* or *Śrīpattanavāstavya*)[98] and high up even in political hierarchy,[99] would be a case in point. It is likely that such merchant families were involved in trans-regional trades during the period through their agents[100] and mediated between them and local resource bases because of their expansive network.

[98] Ibid.

[99] Stratification was not necessarily confined within individual merchant lineages, although one could suppose that the difference between the Aṇahilapura Prāgvaṭas and those located in rural bases extended to other merchant lineages as well. Stratification related to different categories of merchants, of which there must have been a wide range. V.K. Jain cites contemporary literary references to Śūdra pedlars, to needy traders and farmers receiving liquid capital from merchants on interest and to the appointment of different types of traders by big individual merchants. The complementarity between big merchants and petty traders in the fifteenth and sixteenth centuries in which the terms *sāhu* and *banjārā* or *bāpāri* were used is brought out by Irfan Habib; in this relationship the great *sāhu* is spoken of as God 'served by his millions of *banjārās*, and one whose confidence it is not easy for new *bāpāris* to gain', 'Usury in Medieval India', *Comparative Studies in Society and History*, vol. 6, No. 4 (1964), p. 400.

[100] See A.K. Majumdar, *Chalukyas of Gujarat—A Survey of the History and Culture of Gujarat from the Middle of the Tenth to the End of the Thirteenth Century* (Bombay, 1956), pp. 266ff and V.K. Jain, ch. 9. It should, however, be made clear that no clear relationship between the major merchant lineages or individual merchants mentioned in this essay and the agents occasionally referred to in other types of

The second impression to which only a perfunctory reference will be made in this essay (since a fuller statement would require far more sustained and detailed work) relates to the manner in which money has been mentioned in the records. References to varieties of coins start appearing in the epigraphs of Rajasthan from about the tenth century. This phenomenon corresponds closely to the proliferation of epigraphic references to centres and items of exchange. Two points regarding the use of coins in contemporary economic relations may be noted at this stage. First, religious levies at centres of exchange were expressed both in terms of cash and kind;[101] thus monetization, even in the spatial context of exchange centres, was partial. In fact the contributions by ruling elites to the religious institutions were often made in the form of shares which they drew in kind from agricultural and related products—a practice suggested by such expressions as *ātmapāilāmadhyāt,*[102] *ātmaghāṇaka-madhyāt,*[103] etc. By contrast, religious levies are found to have been imposed in cash on communities in areas not necessarily commercial.[104]

Secondly, the situation of partial monetization may be assumed to have emerged because of certain needs for the circulation of money—needs which may be explained in terms of the range of relations from the primary producers to the itinerant merchants and of the varieties of demands, including preparations for the endemic wars of the period,[105] of the ruling elites. At other levels, in situations

sources can be established as yet. All that can be suggested is that it is not beyond the range of possibility.

[101] On this numerous examples can be cited from different parts of India; for early medieval Rajasthan, reference may be made to a select number of records already discussed above in some detail: Ahar record of 953 (*Indian Antiquary*, vol. 58, pp. 161ff); Arthuna record of 1080 (H.V. Trivedi); The Rajorgarh record of 961 (*EI*, vol. 3, pp. 263–7).

[102] Nadlai stone inscription of Rāyapāla of 1143, *EI*, vol. 11, pp. 41–2.

[103] Ibid.

[104] For example, 2 *drammas* were imposed as annual levy on each village attached to Naḍḍūlai, to be paid on a specified date to Śrī Mahāvīra Jina, *EI*, vol. 9, pp. 66–70.

[105] The support expected by the royalty from the merchants in this regard is a common feature of royalty–big merchant collaboration. V.K. Jain refers to the Caulukya king Siddharāja calculating the amount of cash he could expect a merchant to pay for raising an army against Malwa.

of direct appropriation of agrarian surplus, for example, the need for cash may not have been great, and with a few and rather unspectacular exceptions,[106] the evidence of local production of coins in this period is decidedly inadequate. And yet, varieties of coins such as *dramma*, *rūpaka* and *viṃśopaka*, along with such extensively used media of exchange as cowries, are found to have been in simultaneous circulation at single exchange centres.[107] As underlined earlier, this coexisted with the system of imposition of religious levies in kind as well, but its general implications for the mechanism of commerce at the exchange centres and more generally in the network of commerce cannot be overlooked.[108]

As a hypothesis, the situation of partial monetization in which the local supply of money was uncertain—an uncertainty perhaps confirmed by the emergence of myths concerning the minting of money[109]—would suggest that the supply of money itself was an important component of contemporary commercial enterprise. For the moment, attention may be drawn to certain contemporary practices which, located in the context of what has been outlined regarding the monetary situation, may be examined to generate further discus-

[106] Although no inventory of coin hoards relating to the early medieval period is available, references to finds of coins from this region would add up to a substantial quantity. However, coin series which can be definitely attributed to local ruling lineages are not many. Those that can be attributed with any certainty were based on the Indo-Sassanian and 'Bull and Horseman' types. See D. Sharma, *Rajasthan Through the Ages*, pp. 499–507. For a recent, detailed investigation, see John S. Deyell, *Living without Silver*: *The Monetary History of Early Medieval North India* (New Delhi, 1990), part 2.

[107] See, for example, the Shergarh inscription of 1018, *EI*, vol. 23, pp. 137–41; and the Arthuna inscription of 1080, Trivedi. For varieties of coin names in early medieval epigraphic and literary sources from Rajasthan and western India in general, see D. Sharma, *Rajasthan Through the Ages*, pp. 497–505.

[108] Maurice Aymard suggests that the role of money could be 'infinitely greater than the actual circulation of coins might suggest; even when physically absent, money dominated the core of economic activity and social relations'. See 'Money and Peasant Economy', *Studies in History*, vol. 2, No. 2 (1980), p. 15.

[109] This impression is derived from the way minting of coins by the Cāhamāna king Ajayarāja (twelfth century) and his queen Somalladevī is eulogized by Jayānaka in *Pṛthvīrāja-vijaya* and by his commentator Jonarāja. See D. Handa, 'Coins of Somalladevi', *Numismatic Digest*, vol. 2, pt. 2 (1978), pp. 42–57; also D. Sharma, *Early Cha̢uhan Dynasties*, p. 41, fn. 55.

sion on the relationship between money and commerce in general. The hypothesis presented here cannot be developed further without bringing in comparable and contemporary material from other regions. One can, however, underline the possibility of interconnections in areas of basically commercial import, which may be assumed to be related to the mechanism of money accumulation and circulation, and to provide an explanation of stratification within the community of merchants and perhaps also among manufacturers.

It would appear from the social composition of those who regulated *mārgādāya* and *maṇḍapikādāya* that some form of commercial revenue farming was gradually coming into existence.[110] This was true not only of early medieval Rajasthan but of other regions as well. The autonomous character of such bodies is suggested by the phenomenon that local merchant associations or other corporate bodies could impose levies on local communities and on the items of exchange.[111] To an extent this may have been so, but the phenomenon surely needs a more satisfactory explanation, and in a political situation where 'bureaucracy' lacked a distinctly identifiable character, one way of looking at it would be to consider it a mechanism of control over the acquisition of cash and kind and over their redistribution, assuring at the same time the concerned political powers of a regular return in the form of a share. Of course, this would not apply to ad hoc levies intended as contributions to religious institutions, but then terms such as *mārgādāya* or *maṇḍapikādāya* cannot be conceived in terms of ad hoc levies alone.

In early medieval Rajasthan, as in some other regions, a trend was

[110] This, we understand, is a statement likely to be vehemently challenged, but if followed up, it may lead to a new line of inquiry and explain why the ruling elites themselves are not directly involved in the collection of commercial revenue. For Rajasthan, one relevant record to analyse would be the Shergarh inscription of 1018 which refers to contributions made to Bhaṭṭāraka Śrī Nagnaka from *maṇḍapikādāya* by a body consisting mostly of *Śreṣṭhīs*, *EI*, vol. 23, pp. 137–41.

[111] For evidence of this kind, see G.S. Dikshit, ch. 7; T. Venkateswara Rao, pp. 134ff. For Tamilnadu, the functions in this regard of the merchant groups constituting the *nagaram* have been discussed in detail by K.R. Hall, *Trade and Statecraft in the Age of the Colas* (Delhi, 1980), chs 3 and 5. The details given by Hall in ch. 3 seem strongly to suggest that the *nagaram* could well have served as an agency for the collection and redistribution of royal revenues at one level.

developing towards the acquisition, among other things, of immovable assets such as *āvāsanikās* or residential buildings, *āvāris* and *vīthis* or shops.[112] The acquired assets are consistently found to have yielded a rent return in cash. This practice is of course found in our records of religious grants but perhaps a comparison may be made between the functions of cash deposits made with religious establishments in the early historical period[113] with at least one facet of the pattern emerging in the early medieval period. As the Bhinmal record of 1249 cited above shows, cash deposits could bring in resources[114] for keeping the ritual cycle of a temple in operation, but in trying to understand the relationship between cash and the mechanism of trade outside the ritual sphere of temples, the particular dimension of cash rent accruing from investments in immovable assets even for temple establishments cannot be lost sight of. Unlike immovable assets, money was more a part of a system of circulation, but its uncertain flow, in a situation of demand created for it by the existence of stages in the exchange process, may have assured it a high return in the form of non-cash resources which could then be put in the exchange-circuit[115] or could further be used to augment capital for the purpose of ensuring high

[112] For Rajasthan, the practice of assigning or acquiring such assets for religious purposes, sometimes made by the merchants or manufacturers themselves, is to be found in the Kaman inscriptions (*EI*, vol. 24, pp. 329–36) and the Shergarh inscription (Ibid., vol. 23, pp. 137–41). Outside Rajasthan the details from the Ahar record of the Gurjara-Pratīhāra period are quite revealing, ibid., vol. 19, pp. 52–4. For relevant analysis of the record, see R.S. Sharma, *Perspectives in Social and Economic History of Early India* (Delhi, 1983), pp. 212–13; also the essay, 'Trade and Urban Centres in Early Medieval North India' in this volume.

[113] For early historical evidence, see *EI*, vol. 8, pp. 82–3.

[114] *EI*, vol. 11, pp. 55–7.

[115] This point can be substantiated by citing once again the evidence of the Bhinmal record of 1249 (*EI*, vol. 11, pp. 56–8) which lists the items which two separate cash deposits were expected to yield. These items were a part of the total range of goods which entered the centres of exchange.

1. Annual interest on 40 *drammas*:

Wheat	2 *seis*
Ghee	8½ *kalasas* or jars
Muṅga pulse	1 *mana*
Chokhā (rice)	2 *pāilis*
Various articles for worship	7 *drammas* in value

rent in cash. The premium put on the acquisition of cash by the merchants of western India may be illustrated by citing two cases. D. Sharma cites the *Kharataragacchapaṭṭāvalī* to show that Sādhāraṇa, 'perhaps the richest of the merchants of Chitor fixed 1,00,000 *drammas* as the limit of the property that he would amass'.[116] A document in the *Lekhapaddhati* records that in 1230[117] a resident of a village issued a receipt to his father, in the presence of witnesses, for a sum of 500 *drammas* of his share which he had borrowed for the purpose of operating business transactions on his own. The document has interesting implications pointing to the existence and use of common capital which could be drawn upon before partition, but what is relevant in the *Kharataragacchapaṭṭāvalī* evidence as well as in the *Lekhapaddhati* is the control which could be exercised through access to such substantial amounts of cash over the exchange network.

This brings us finally to the question of the rate of return. The return in the form of resources in kind could, as suggested before, be considered high, but data for calculating actual rates of interest are rather meagre. Even so, barring a few curious exceptions, the rate of interest per annum may be put between 25 per cent and 30 per cent.[118] Despite the absence of evidence on how interest rates related to the general processes of commerce, it is certain that outside their known religious contexts they were also interwoven in the different tiers of secular exchange transactions. The three final sections of this essay relating to the accumulation and circulation of money can therefore be taken as pointers to go beyond the constraints implicit in the evidence and examine more thoroughly a process which evidence emanating from religious establishments partly reflects.

---

2. Interest on a deposit of 15 *drammas*:

Wheat	25 *pāilis*
Muṅga	4 *pāilis*
Chokhā	2 *pāilis*
Other articles of worship	2 *drammas* in value

See also D. Sharma, *Rajasthan Through the Ages*, p. 506.

[116] D. Sharma, ibid., p. 498.

[117] Cited in G.D. Sontheimer, *The Joint Hindu Family—Its Evolution as a Legal Institution* (Delhi, 1977), xix.

[118] This estimate is based on D. Sharma, *Rajasthan Through the Ages*, pp. 505–07.

To sum up, the broad survey of the commerce of early medieval Rajasthan offered in this essay seems to establish distinct stages in its history, with overlapping between them in certain respects. The first phase is essentially characterized by the proliferation of local centres of exchange which were situated within the domains of emergent Rajput lineages and the spatial contexts of which were agrarian. Despite being local centres of exchange, they were nevertheless points of intersection for traffic of varying origins, and it is perhaps the nature of the interaction with traffic from the outside that gave rise to a certain measure of hierarchy among exchange centres The second phase, dating roughly from the eleventh and twelfth centuries, witnessed the resurgence of local merchant lineages already in operation and the emergence of hitherto unfamiliar lineages which established wide intraregional and interregional networks. What this essay cannot claim to offer at this stage is a satisfactory exposition of the structure of commerce which these merchant lineages represented or what changes the structure underwent beyond the thirteenth century.

5

*Early Memorial Stones of Rajasthan: A Preliminary Analysis of their Inscriptions**

The memorial stones of Rajasthan cover a span of more than a thousand years. It was in this region that memorial stones developed in the medieval period into a form of architecture, the *catris* or memorial pavilions, which were put up to commemorate Rājput royal and associated families.[1] Seen in the light of the immense potentiality for a detailed study of the Rājasthānī memorial relics, the scope of the present note is rather limited; it covers the period roughly down to the close of the thirteenth century; furthermore, it is neither intended as a comprehensive survey, nor is it based on any extensive field work. Its main focus is on the social origins of the stones as they were fashioned in the early medieval period, and on how such origins were linked with the pattern of the Rajput polity, which was gradually consolidating itself in that period. Needless to say, the suggestions made here are purely tentative.

This essay is based on information from publications such as the *Epigraphia Indica; Progress Report of the Archaeological Survey of India, Western Circle; Annual Report on Indian Epigraphy; Indian Archaeology—A Review; Annual Report on the Working of the Rajaputana Museum, Ajmer*, and so on. The point that emerges from a study of these publications and which crucially relates to any meaningful future investigations of the memorial stones of Rajasthan is that, so far, a systematic presentation of the data has been largely neglected; this neglect, which probably stems from the fact that the stones were not considered a serious theme of study, has affected two aspects most

* Reprinted from S. Settar and G.D. Sontheimer, eds, *Memorial Stones: A Study of their Origin, Significance and Variety* (Dharwad, 1982).

[1] For some interesting remarks on *Chatris*, see Goetz H., *The Art and Architecture of Bikaner State* (Oxford, 1960), pp. 61ff.

vitally: (i) references in the publications are mostly to nondescript 'memorial stones' which, as the more satisfactorily published ones show, have significant typological variations; (ii) in the majority of cases, the complete texts of inscriptions on the stones are not available. Thus, the circumstances leading to a death which was commemorated remain largely unknown, as also the details of the person or persons commemorated. Such details are necessary for analysing the pattern of the incidence of memorial stones in relation to particular social groups in a region, and the diversity and intensity of their involvement in situations which caused the memorials to be erected. This kind of information is vital also in the case of *satī* stones, as the practice of *satī* is unlikely to have been current in all strata of society. After all, memorial stones are valuable documents of social history, and it is difficult to subject them to a social analysis if there are large gaps in our information.

The preliminary work, however, is to make a typological study of the stones and to study their distribution in space and time. From the available relics, there appear to have been two types of stones in the early medieval period: (i) memorial pillars with sculptured tops, the main variations within the type deriving from variations in the sculpture. The pillars are locally known as *govardhanas* and possibly also as *tīrthambas.*[2] The term *govardhana*[3] or *govardhanadhvaja*[4] is as early as the memorials themselves; (ii) the vertical slabs, with sculptures in relief, are known as *pāliyas* or *devalīs.* The term *devalī* is also old and occurs in the epigraphs[5] on the stones along with its variants, *deulī,*[6] *devakulikā,*[7] etc. The sculptural variations in this type are many, and seem to correspond, at least in some cases, to the type of occasion for which they were erected. Thus, in ordinary *satī* stones there would be a couple facing the front;[8] if the occasion was the death of an individual

[2] *PRASWC,* 1911–12, p. 51.
[3] *JPASB,* 1916, pp. 104–06.
[4] *ARIE,* 1964–5, p. 102.
[5] Ibid.
[6] *Rajasthan Bhāratī,* V, pts. III-IV, p. 12.
[7] *PRASWC,* 1911–12, p. 53.
[8] Agrawal, R.C., 'Paśchimī Rājasthān Ke Kuchh Prārambhik Smṛtistambha', *Varadā* (Hindi) (April, 1963), p. 70.

in battle, the battle scene would be depicted, as also the horse-man;[9] cattle raids would occasion the depiction of a man driving cattle.[10] Such close correspondence between the theme and the form of the memorial stone may not, however, have been universal, and, for a further analysis of the stones from a chronological perspective, it would be interesting to see if there was a trend towards a gradual standardization of their forms.

As a continuation of what has been said above, a few other points regarding the typology of the stones need further investigation: (i) the first concerns the relative chronology of the two types mentioned above. Goetz has made the point that by about the twelfth century *govardhanas* were generally replaced by *pāliyas.*[11] This statement needs further substantiation and, if found to be valid, some explanation should be thought of as to why pillars henceforth assumed a different commemorative function;[12] (ii) how did the memorials originate in this known form? Goetz's derivation of *govardhanas* from tribal memorial pillars of central India, Rajasthan and Gujarat[13] appears to be valid, and in fact, as a recent article has shown, the association of pillars with the cult of the dead is of extremely early origin.[14] But, if the social context of the transformation of pillars into impressive monoliths in the early historical period is provided by early Buddhism,[15] then the social process which transformed the humble wooden pillars of the tribals into stone memorials with sculptured tops is something which remains to be investigated. This would apply to the study of the *pāliyas* as well. They are believed to be of Central Asian origin, but the prototypes from western India to which they are related by Goetz[16] are far too early for the Rājasthānī specimens. If,

[9] See Agrawal, p. 70 for description of a hero on horseback with two *satīs.*

[10] *PRASWC,* 1908–9, p. 49.

[11] Goetz, p. 88.

[12] According to Goetz (Ibid.), the function of a *govardhana* was gradually reduced to that of a *kīrtistambha.*

[13] Goetz, p. 87.

[14] John Irwin, 'Asokan Pillars: A Reassessment of the Evidence', *The Burlington Magazine* (November, 1973), pp. 706–20.

[15] Ibid.

[16] Goetz, p. 88. For other stone memorials of an early date, see H. Sarkar, 'Chhayastambhas from Nagarjunakonda', *Seminar on Hero-stones,* R. Nagaswamy,

however, the connection between the Central Asian memorials and the *pāliyas* of Rajasthan is found to be irrefutable, it should still be examined as to why or from which particular period this type of memorial tended to proliferate.

Apart from the typology of the stones the typology of the contents of inscriptions that occur on the memorials needs detailed study and analysis. A primary classification may be made of what the memorials commemorate. Many of the memorials merely speak of the death of an individual. In some cases an individual's wife or wives performed *satī*. Under this category may be included some inscriptions issued in AD 686, AD 688, AD, 692 and AD 770 from Chhoti Khatu in the Nagaur Dt., where the death of four wives of four persons are commemorated separately.[17] Similarly, a Pushkar memorial stone inscription of 1130 records the death of one *Ṭhā* (*kurāṇī*) Hiravadevī, wife of *Ṭhā* (*kura*) Kolhava.[18] Others commemorate both the male member of the family and his wife or wives. Thus, the Lohari inscription of 1179[19] mentions Jalasala and his nine wives in whose names the memorial was erected. An identical specimen would be the one which was set up in honour of the Cāhamāna king, Ajayapāla, and his three wives, Somaladevī, Oṣṭhaladā and Śrīdevī, at Bassi, Nagaur Dt., in 1132.[20]

The region-wise spread as well as the spread in terms of social groups which such memorials covered appear to have been extensive. Two further instances, both from the Jaisalmer area, may be cited. An inscription of the Bhāṭika *saṃvat* 534 (1158 AD) (it is not clear whether the inscription is engraved on the usual type of memorial stone or not), from the temple of Cāmuṇḍā, four miles from Jaisalmer,[21] records the demise of Ādi Varāha of the Atri family, supposedly a great poet. Another inscription, engraved on a *govardhana*, about ten miles from Jaisalmer, records that during the reign of Vijayarāja, queen Rājaladevī built a tank and erected a *govardhana* in memory of her

ed. (Madras, 1974), pp. 93–7.

[17] Agrawal, R.C., pp. 68–9.

[18] *ARRM*, 1919–20, p. 3.

[19] Ibid., 1922–3, pp. 2–3.

[20] *EI*, XXXVII, pp. 163–4.

[21] *ARRM*, 1919–20, p. 3.

daughter's son, Sohāgapāla.[22] References may be cited in plenty to show that persons belonging to different castes, Brahmins, Jains and others, were commemorated through memorial stones; and, although such references may not necessarily be taken to suggest any universality of practice, they may nevertheless show that in all such cases it was not a hero whose death was being commemorated, but that commemoration of the dead had become a social practice, irrespective of the cause of death. We shall return to an elaboration of this point later on.

There are, at the same time, memorials to violent death, and an analysis of the circumstances which led to such deaths may bring out the significance society attached to them. One series among such memorials relates to the victims of cattleraids. A very well-known example of this type of memorial is a stone from about the eighth century from Bayana in Bharatpur. The rectangular slab 'sculptured along the top with a row of four animals being driven by a man' bears an inscription[23] which mentions that in the reign of Śrī-Nanna, in a place called Pimpala-Gaundala, a certain Durgāditya was killed by some robbers in a [cattleraid]. The term *go-graha* is mentioned also in a stone of possibly 1013 from a different region of Pokran in the Jodhpur area, where a *govardhana* was erected in the memory of a member of the Guhila family who had been killed in a cattleraid.[24] The Jaisalmer area also provides interesting information on memorial inscriptions, found in the form of a group, occasioned by such raids. One record (of Bhāṭika year 685 = 1309) from Gogaki-talai, five miles from Jaisalmer,[25] mentions Dhulā, the son of Īsara and belonging to the Cāhamāna family and Vatsa *gotra*, as having been killed while rescuing cows. The victim of another such raid was Palāniā, the son of Velāka and of the same descent.[26] The last record of this group commemorates Muñjaladeva, the son of Hemā, descended from the same Cāhamāna family and Vatsa *gotra*, who was killed by robbers

22 Ibid.
23 *PRASWC*, 1908–9, p. 49.
24 Agrawal, p. 70.
25 *ARRM*, 1936, p. 3.
26 Ibid.

while serving his master in the act of rescuing women, cows, horses and camels belonging to the Brāhmaṇas.[27]

The other series of such memorials relates to those who fell in battle. An interesting representative of this series would be the twelfth century group of Charlu inscriptions from the Bikaner area, which supply the names of several Mohila chiefs and record the death of Āhara and Ambāraka 'in the battle of Nāgapura', i.e. Nagaur.[28] The memorials (mentioned in the records as *devalī*) from Anakhisara in Bikaner—all dated 1283—possibly refer to such an event.[29] A similar group, known from three memorial records, is known to have been found in the Sekhawati area of the former Jaipur state. All the three records, referring to the reign of Pṛthvīrāja Cāhamāna, are from the village of Revasa in the Sikar Dt., and are of the same date, i.e. 1186.[30] The victims, Chandelā Nānnava, Chandelā Dulabhadeva and Chandelā Singhara, were killed apparently in the same encounter at the village of Khaluvānā. There is another *devalī* of 1104 from Berasar, Bikaner, wherein occurs the inscription '*suhāgu raṣasanā*', or 'protection of Suhāgu (?)'.[31]

These memorials, then, appear to have been erected to those who were victims of raids, and elsewhere in the country also, such memorials were erected.

While no detailed study can be made of the contents of the inscriptions in this preliminary essay, what may be underlined is that a classification of the contents is useful for analysing the social composition of the people who were commemorated. Secondly, an attempt may be made to correlate particular situations resulting in commemorations, to particular social groups. Any deviations from the pattern of correlation that may emerge will have to be explained, not in terms of the caste or clan of the person commemorated, but in terms of how much he may be supposed to have deviated from the position warranted by his caste or clan. Thus, while ordinary memorials could be erected for a Brahmin, a Jaina or a Rajput, a memorial for violent

27 Ibid.
28 *JPASB*, 1920, pp. 256ff.
29 Ibid.
30 *ARRM*, 1935, pp. 3–5.
31 Agrawal, p. 71.

death in the case of a Brahmin will be explained by how he was involved in such a situation. Again, an analysis of the cases of violent death would show which social groups were generally involved in situations leading to such death. In short, future investigations, relying on the evidence of number, will be able to establish a more effective correlation between inscriptional types and social types.[32]

But first, in continuation of what has been said at the beginning, it may be pertinent to ask: How universal was the practice of commemoration? Broadly speaking, the practice seems to have been fairly widespread in space and time. For example, apart from the Brahmins[33] and Jainas,[34] mentioned earlier, there was a broad spectrum of other groups which were also represented. Memorials to *śreṣṭhis*, or merchants, of the early twelfth century have been found.[35] A member of a Naigama Kāyastha family, Talhā, the son of Bilhaṇa and grandson of *Ṭhā* (*kura*) Candra, was commemorated by *Ṭhākura* Somadeva in

[32] The memorial stones, in cases where they are available in clusters, also provide some clue for a study of the single clan or multi-clan composition of a region; and where the memorials were the result of raids, an analysis of such composition may give some idea of the pattern of inter-clan conflict as also of inter-clan alignment in a particular period. For example, a memorial cluster in the Sekhawati area of the former Jaipur state relates to a Cāndela *pratigaṇaka* (an area held by the Cāndelas) and to Cāndelas who apparently fought for the Cāhamānas in the period of Pṛthvīrāja III (*ARRM*, 1935, pp. 3–5). Similarly, it has been remarked in the light of the evidence of memorial stones, that the 'whole of the Medta province was only held by Guhilots' (*PRASWC*, 1909–10, p. 61). On the other hand, a cluster of 12 *govardhanas*, found at Pāla near Jodhpur and ranging in date between AD 1161 and 1187, refer to at least four castes, Bhici, Gaṃghala, Dharkaṭa and Pratīhāra, *JPASB*, 1916, pp. 104–06.

[33] The memorial records occasionally refer to different sections among the Brahmins. For example, a record speaks of a memorial to Pallival Brahmins, *IA*, XL, p. 183.

[34] There are a few interesting specimens of Jaina memorials, termed *niṣedhikā* in the records, from the Kishengarh area. One such *niṣedhikā*, from a record from Rūpnagar, was erected in AD 961, in memory of Meghasenācārya by his pupil Vimalasenapaṇḍita (*PRASWC*, 1910–11, p. 43). Another, from the same place, was erected in AD 1019, in memory of Padmasenācārya, by Citranandin (ibid.). A third, from a site three miles to the south of Rūpnagar, refers to the memorial of Vāliya Ṣaḍḍika erected by Chāhchideva and does not seem to be Jaina in origin (ibid.).

[35] Inscriptions of Jhalrapatan of AD 1109 and AD 1113, *ARRM*, 1912–13, Appendix B.

AD 1158, as is evident from a stone at Pilani.[36] There is, also, perhaps quite an early memorial (AD 764?) erected to the daughter of a *veśyā* (courtesan) at Osian in the Jodhpur area.[37] Another, a *satī* slab, from Kalyanpur in the Udaipur area, records the death of a member of the *Kamhāra*, i.e. potters' caste.[38]

While these cases do relate to a wide cross-section of society, what may be highlighted, again from a rough calculation of the number of records available, is that the memorials—to both normal and violent deaths—were predominantly to the following castes and clans: Pratīhāra (*jāti*[39] and *gotra*[40]); Varāha[41] and Mahāvarāha;[42] Rāṭhoda;[43] Guhila,[44] and Māṅgalīya,[45] a subdivision of the Guhila; Cāhamāna,[46] and Bodānā[47] and Mohili,[48] subdivisions of the Cāhamāna;[49] Debrā;[50] Doḍā;[51] Solāṅki;[52] Dahiyā;[53] Paramāra;[54] Pavāra;[55] Doharā;[56] Bhichi;[57] Ghaṃgala;[58] Dharkaṭa;[59] and so on. Further, in a number of cases,

[36] Ibid., 1933, p. 2.

[37] *ARIE*, 1961–62, p. 114.

[38] Agrawal, p. 78.

[39] One of two memorials dated AD 936 from Cherai, Jodhpur, mentions Arjuna, the son of Durlabharaja of Pratihāra *jāti* (*Indian Archaeology*—1959–60 *A Review*, p. 60).

[40] A record of AD 1015, from Cherai, Jodhpur, speaks of a memorial to one of Pratīhāra *gotra* (*Indian Archaeology*—1959–60 *A Review*).

[41] *PRASWC*, 1911–12, p. 53.

[42] Ibid.

[43] *IA*, XL, pp. 181–83.

[44] *PRASWC*, 1909–10, p. 61; *PRASWC*, 1911–12, p. 52.

[45] Ibid., 1911–12, p. 53.

[46] *Indian Archaeology*—1962–63 *A Review*, p. 54.

[47] *PRASWC*, 1911–12, p. 53.

[48] Ibid.

[49] *ARRM*, 1935, pp. 3–5.

[50] Ibid., 1909–10, Appendix D.

[51] Ibid., 1922–23, p. 2.

[52] *IA*, XL, p. 183.

[53] Ibid., XLII, pp. 267–69.

[54] *PRASWC*, 1916–17, p. 70.

[55] Ibid., 1911–12, p. 53; also *ARIE*, 1964–65, p. 102.

[56] *ARIE*, 1959–60, p. 113.

[57] *JPASB*, 1916, pp. 104–06.

[58] Ibid.

[59] Ibid.

official titles or titles indicative of social status, occur on the same records, such titles being *rā(uta)*,[60] *rājā*,[61] *mahāsāmanta*,[62] *rājaputra*,[63] *rāṇā*,[64] etc. In short, where it is possible to relate the memorial stones to any clans or castes, it is mostly the Rajputs that we come across. Chronologically, too, the early memorials of Rajasthan correspond to the formative period of the Rajput polity. It is true that the memorials were not erected to the Rajputs alone, but such diffusion as penetrated different sections of society may suggest that the formalization of death through stones by the members of the deceased's family had come to be accepted as a symbol of status in society. The stones also gave sanction to the practice of *satī*, which was becoming increasingly common and the incidence of which was quite frequent among the ruling elite of this period. One should further take into consideration the expenses involved in getting the stone sculpted and incised with the inscription by, as one record mentions, a professional craftsman (*rūpakāra*).[65]

The process of the transformation of tribal wooden pillars into memorial stones may also be viewed in this light. The Rajput polity evolved, at least to an extent, as a result of confrontation with original settlers, and inscriptional references, though veiled, bear testimony to Rajput expansion at the expense of the Bhīls, Āhirs[66] and others. This interaction may have resulted in the Rajputs (and it may be underlined here that all Rajputs were not colonizers, as might be suggested from

[60] *ARIE*, 1954–55, p. 69.

[61] *PRASWC*, 1909–10, p. 51.

[62] *ARIE*, 1961–62, p. 115.

[63] Ibid.

[64] A record of 1191 from Unstra, four miles west of Barlu in Jodhpur area, speaks of *rāṇā* Motīśvara, a Guhilautra, as having been followed in *satī* by his chief queen, Rāji, a Mohili (*PRASWC* 1911–12, p. 53).

[65] *ARIE* 1952–53, p. 67.

[66] Such ideas about colonization emerge from several records of early medieval Rajasthan. Thus, the Ghatiyala inscription of Kakkuka, of AD 861, from the Jodhpur area, credits Kakkuka with taking away herds of cattle (implying that *go-graha* was not always a defensive measure) and with the destruction by fire of a village on the hill in the inaccessible Vaṭanānaka, *JRASGBI*, 1895, pp. 513–21. See also *EI*, IX, p. 80 for another record of AD 996 of the same family for the settlement of an area called *Ābhirajanadāruṇaḥ*, 'terrible because of being inhabited by the Ābhīras'.

the gradual proliferation of Rajput castes)[67] taking over a simple form of memorial and transforming it into something vastly more elaborate, in keeping with the art tradition of the time, which also found its source of patronage among the emergent Rajput political elites as well as among other categories of elites in the early medieval society of Rajasthan.

[67] For the process of the Rajputization of local tribes, see B.N.S. Yadava, *Society and Culture in Northern India in the Twelfth Century* (Allahabad, 1973), p. 34.

6

Trade and Urban Centres in Early Medieval North India[*]

Recent studies have attempted to show that a major socio-economic change took place in early India from roughly the close of the Gupta period.[1] This change is elucidated in terms of the gradual crystallization of 'Indian feudalism',[2] the origins of which can be traced to the land grants of the pre-Gupta period; 'and the two centuries preceding the Turkish conquest marked both the climax and the decline of feudal economy of India'.[3] As a new system,

[*] Reprinted from *The Indian Historical Review*, vol. I, No. 2 (1974).

[An earlier draft of this paper was read at a seminar on 'Cities and Towns in Ancient India' organized in March 1974 by the Centre of Advanced Study in Ancient Indian History and Culture, University of Calcutta. My attention was later drawn by Dr Sanjay Chandra of the Centre for the Study of Regional Development, Jawaharlal Nehru University, to E.M. Medvedev's 'The Towns of Northern India during the 6th–7th Centuries (according to Hiuen Tsang)' in *India—Land and People*, Book 3 (vol. 14 of Countries and Peoples of the East), compiled and edited by I.V. Sakharov (Moscow, 1972), pp. 168–83. I am extremely grateful to Dr Chandra for this reference and also for translating the entire paper from the original Russian into English. Medvedev makes a thorough study of Hiuen Tsang, but my use of his account is limited to the passages cited in the original draft of the present paper.]

[1] For a statement of different facets of this change, see R.S. Sharma, 'Problem of Transition from Ancient to Medieval in Indian History', *The Indian Historical Review*, i, No. 1 (1974), pp. 1–9; also his *Social Changes in Early Medieval India (c. AD 500–1200)* (Delhi, 1969).

[2] For the first important empirical study of early Indian feudalism, see D.D. Kosambi, *An Introduction to the Study of Indian History* (Bombay, 1956), ch. IX in particular; the most comprehensive work on it is by R.S. Sharma, *Indian Feudalism, c. 300–1200* (University of Calcutta, 1965). For a bibliography on early Indian feudalism, see R.S. Sharma and D.N. Jha, 'The Economic History of India upto AD 1200: Trends and Prospects', *Journal of the Economic and Social History of the Orient*, vol. 17, No. I (1974), pp. 48–80. For a rather inadequate analysis of the literature, see V.K. Thakur, *Historiography of Indian Feudalism* (Patna, 1989).

[3] R.S. Sharma, *Indian Feudalism*, p. 262. However, the chronology of 'Indian feudalism' is not as yet precisely ascertained. While early indications of feudal

it is naturally assumed to have marked a departure from the early historical pattern. The economic implications of the suggested change are believed to be represented by a situation of increasing ruralization in which the self-sufficient villages became the foci of production.[4]

This hypothesis has gained considerable strength from the substantive arguments put forward from time to time in the process of its elaboration. Two deductions, following from the idea of self-sufficient village economy, have been made: (i) decline of trade, including long-distance trade; and (ii) decline of urban centres. The paucity of indigenous dynastic coinage, which suggests rarity of exchange at commercial levels, has been taken to substantiate the first point.[5] It has derived support from an analysis of some literary material as well.[6] For the second point considerable support comes from a recent survey of the early north Indian urban centres, many of which reached a state of decay in Gupta and post-Gupta times.[7]

Even if, as suggested by the hypothesis thus outlined, trade and urban centres suffered a setback in early India,[8] resulting in the growth of a closed village economy over a considerable stretch of time, one cannot still view this validly in terms of 'production for use' as opposed to 'production for exchange'.[9] While, therefore, it is necessary to

---

development are traced to inscriptions of the late Sātavāhana period, i.e. second century AD (Kosambi, p. 276), the historians of medieval India apply the same term, albeit with reservations, to the Mughal economy, S. Nurul Hasan, *Thoughts on Agrarian Relations in Mughal India* (New Delhi, 1973), pp. 1–2.

[4] R.S. Sharma, *Indian Feudalism*, pp. 127–34.

[5] For a list of coin-types in circulation in the early medieval period, see L. Gopal, *Early Medieval Coin-types of Northern India, Numismatic Notes and Monographs*, No. 12 (Varanasi, 1966). A recent detailed study is by John S. Deyell, *Living without-Silver: The Monetary History of Early Medieval North India* (Delhi, 1990).

[6] L. Gopal, *The Economic Life of Northern India, c. AD 700–1200* (Delhi, 1965), pp. 102–4.

[7] R.S. Sharma, 'Decay of Gangetic Towns in Gupta and post-Gupta Times', *Proceedings of the Indian History Congress*, 33rd session (Muzaffarpur, 1972), pp. 92–104. A more recent and detailed publication by R.S. Sharma on the same theme is: *Urban Decay in India, c. 300–c. 1000* (Delhi, 1987).

[8] This may have been so, but if the history of Indian feudalism extends from the second to the seventeenth–eighteenth centuries, then it has to be reconsidered whether a relative decline of trade or urban centres really constitutes an essential variable in the study of this system.

[9] For the difficulty involved in thinking in terms of such a distinction, see

examine closely as to what extent and in what precise form trade and urbanism survived[10] in the post-Gupta period, the scope of the present paper is rather limited. Here only a few known documents have been chosen for a detailed analysis—documents which bear upon the close link between trade and urbanization. These pertain to several distinct geographical regions, and it can at least partly be tested whether what emerges from them will have uniform applicability for different parts of north India. In the final part of the paper an attempt has been made to review the entire problem of the decline of trade and urban centres in the light of the documents selected as well as some other material.

I

The geographical areas to which the documents relate are: (i) the Indo-Gangetic divide; (ii) the upper Ganga basin; and (iii) the Malwa plateau.[11] This location pattern is crucial since it is known that in at least two of them, the upper Ganga basin and the Malwa plateau, important urban centres had developed in the early historical period.[12]

We may start with a site in the Indo-Gangetic divide which, if at

---

H.K. Takahashi in *The Transition from Feudalism to Capitalism* (London, 1954), pp. 35ff; also the important remarks of Marx, 'The extent to which products enter trade and go through the merchants' hands depends on the mode of production . . . on the basis of every mode of production, trade facilitates the production of surplus products destined for exchange, in order to increase the enjoyments, or the wealth, of the producers (here the owners of products are meant)', who are specified as the 'slave-owner, the feudal lord, the tribute-collecting state', etc., *Capital* (Foreign Languages Publishing House, Moscow, 1962), iii, pp. 320–1.

10 This need is also suggested in the important writings on Indian feudalism. Although Kosambi speaks of the 'ominous spread of closed village economy' in the context of feudalism (p. 288), he underlines the process of the 'development of new trade centres' in his criticism of Marx's concept of the Asiatic mode (p. 11). R.S. Sharma has made a study of trade and urban centres in the context of early medieval feudalism, *Indian Feudalism*, pp. 238ff.

11 See O.H.K. Spate and A.T.A. Learmonth, *India and Pakistan: A General and Regional Geography*, 3rd edn. (London, 1967), pp. 534ff, 546, 625–7.

12 For a distribution of the important early historical urban sites of north India, see A. Ghosh, *The City in Early Historical India* (Simla, 1973), map facing p. 90; also, G. Erdosy, 'Early Historic Cities of Northern India', *South Asian Studies*, vol. 3 (1987), pp. 1–23.

all it has to be given the label 'urban', may at best be called an incipient urban centre. This site is Pṛthūdaka, modern Pehoa in the Karnal district of Haryana. Pṛthūdaka is called an *adhiṣṭhāna* in an inscription (AD 882–3)[13] of the Gurjara-Pratihāra period which also provides some details of a fair at this place in which different animals—the most important of which was the horse—were sold and bought. Several points emerging from this record are of relevance here. First, the horse dealers headed by a foreman (which suggests that the horse dealers were organized into a guild) were not local; they hailed from nine different localities: Cūṭavārṣika, Utpalika, Cikkariselavaṇapura, Baladevapura, Śāraṅkadika, Sīharudukkaka, Traighāṭaka, Ghaṃghaka and Aśvalauhavoka; one of these is tentatively identified with a locality near Lahore. Secondly, the dealers do not seem to have been non-Indian traders of the period, although horse trade is not usually associated with Indians in the contemporary sources.[14] According to the editor of the record the names appear to be Hindu[15] and it is likely that some of them were brāhmaṇas (for example, Vāmuka or Bhaṭṭa Vīraka's sons, Vanda and Rājyabala). The evidence of the Pehoa record may thus suggest that in the ninth century Indians of the north-west at least acted as intermediary dealers in horse trade and, if the guess regarding the participation by brāhmaṇas in it is correct, the restrictions in the brāhmaṇical texts[16] weighed lightly on them. Thirdly, the donations which the horse dealers agreed to make went not only to a religious shrine at Pṛthūdaka, but also to Kānyakubja, Gotīrtha and Bhojapura—all widely distant from Pṛthūdaka. Fourthly, among the buyers of horses figure the king, *ṭhakkuras* and provincials who were, however, not necessarily physically present at Pṛthūdaka. It would appear from all this that Pṛthūdaka was a focal point in the network

[13] G. Bühler, 'The Peheva Inscription from the Temple of Garibnath, *Epigraphia Indica*, vol. I, pp. 184–90.

[14] For countries from which the horse was imported, see L. Gopal, *The Economic Life of Northern India*, p. 113. The information that horse trade extended up to Bengal in the early thirteenth century and that Turkish invaders of Bengal posed as horse traders is given by *Tabaqāt-i-Nāsirī*, tr., H.G. Raverty (reprinted in New Delhi, 1970), i, p. 557.

[15] G. Bühler.

[16] See *Manusmṛti*, x, pp. 86, 89, and also Kullūkabhaṭṭa's commentary, which prohibit brāhmaṇas from participating in animal trade.

of north-western horse dealers and although the record does not positively show it to be an urban centre, it may be labelled at least as a *nigama*—a market centre occupying a somewhat intermediary position between a village and a developed township.[17] This supposition seems to be confirmed by its characterization in the record as an *adhiṣṭhāna* which, in Gupta and post-Gupta terminology, would signify an urban centre as well.[18]

Tattānandapura, identified with Ahar near Bulandshahar and situated on the western bank of the Ganga, was on the other hand a fully developed township of the upper Ganga basin. It has yielded a set of ten inscriptions dated between AD 867 and 904,[19] which show it to have been included in the Gurjara-Pratihāra empire. The urban character of the settlement emerges from a number of indications in the record. First, the suffix *pura* in its name and the fact that it was called *pattana*[20] distinguish it from *grāma, pallī* or *agrahāra* by which village settlements of the period were known.[21] Secondly, whatever meagre information is available regarding its lay-out confirms this. It was intersected by a number of roads, *kurathyā* (small or narrow roads, lanes?), *bṛhadrathyā* (big roads) and *haṭṭamārga* (roads leading to the market area).[22] Since such expressions have been used in relation to

[17] A. Ghosh, pp. 38, 46–7.

[18] Vaiśālī (modern Basarh in Vaisali district of north Bihar) which was an urban centre in the Gupta period was called an *adhiṣṭhāna* in that period, cf. the expression *vaiśālyadhiṣṭhānādhikaraṇasya*, seal No. 25 in T. Bloch, 'Excavations at Basarh', *Archaeological Survey of India, Annual Report, 1903–4*, p. 109. Gopagiri (Gwalior), an urban centre of the tenth century, is mentioned in its records as an *adhiṣṭhāna.* It may be noted that by the time of Rājaśekhara, Pṛthūdaka was considered to be so important as to be mentioned as the point beyond which the northern region began, *pṛthūdakāt parata uttarāpathaḥ, Kāvyamīmāṃsā*, G.S. Rai, ed. (Varanasi, 1964), ch. XII, p. 264.

[19] D.R. Sahni, 'Ahar Stone Inscription', *Epigraphia Indica*, xix, pp. 52–4; also C.D. Chatterjee, 'The Ahar Stone Inscription', *The Journal of the United Provinces Historical Society*, iii, pt. iii (1926), pp. 83–119. (I owe the second reference to Mr M.C. Joshi).

[20] Ahar Inscription, Nos. 1, 2, etc. (The numbers cited here refer to D.R. Sahni's edition).

[21] A.K. Choudhary, *Early Medieval Village in North-eastern India (AD 600–1200)* (Calcutta, 1971), pp. 42–9.

[22] Ahar Inscription, Nos. 4, 5, 6, etc.

townships in early medieval literature,[23] some functional differences between them in the context of urban settlements may be inferred. The impression one gets from the records is that the eastern market area (*pūrvahaṭṭapradeśa*) was one of the nerve-centres of the town,[24] dotted as it was with shops and residential buildings. The reference to the eastern market implies that there were several other such centres which, as is clear from the eastern market cluster, were not necessarily located in one part of the town, but were dispersed among different residential areas. The inscriptions mention six temples (those of Kāñcanaśrīdevī or Kanakadevī, Nandābhagavatīdevī, Vāmanasvāmī, Gandhadevī, Daśāvatāra and Sarvamaṅgalā) which formed a distinct part of the urban set-up. At least two of them, enshrining Nandābhagavatīdevī and Kāñcanaśrīdevī, seem to have been located a little away from the town (*ihaiva pattanādvahi dakṣiṇasyāṃ diśi*), but both owned property in the eastern market area.[25] Thirdly, the constructional details and dimensions of some of the buildings are given in the records in clear terms. Two types of buildings are generally mentioned: *āvāris* (shops and enclosures) and *gṛhas* (residential buildings). The *āvāris* seem in some cases to have combined the functions of a shop and a residential building. In one case an *āvāri* with its elevations is said to have consisted of three rooms of burnt bricks; in another it had a few inner apartments.[26] The *gṛhas* were also constructed with burnt bricks. The inscriptions abound in references to house sites (*gṛhabhūmi*) contiguously situated and belonging to persons of different castes.[27]

That Tattānandapura was an important urban settlement of the early medieval period is confirmed by archaeologists as well,[28] although no attempt at correlation between epigraphic and archaeological material is possible at present. The mounds at Ahar cover a total area of 3800 acres and five trial trenches laid at the site are scattered over a

[23] L. Gopal, *The Economic Life of Northern India*, p. 96.
[24] Ahar Inscription, Nos. 4, 6, 7, 9, etc.
[25] Ibid., No. 2.
[26] Ibid., Nos. 2, 10.
[27] Ibid., Nos. 4, 5, 9, etc.
[28] *Archaeological Survey of India, Annual Report, 1925–6*, pp. 56–8; plates X–XII (I owe this reference to Mr B.M. Pande).

stretch of nearly one and a half miles. At site B, which dates back to about ninth century AD were discovered, apart from burnt brick structures of residential character, excellent specimens of pottery, hand-grinding mills, a mortar, household articles of copper, an iron scythe and early medieval coins of at least three varieties.

All the urban characteristics of Tattānandapura or Ahar revealed by epigraphy were present at Sīyaḍoni near Lalitpur in Jhansi district. The dates of its records ranging from between AD 907 and 968[29] relate, as in the case of the other inscriptions cited, to the Gurjara-Pratihāra period. It was also a *pattana* intersected by a variety of roads, *rathyā*, *haṭṭarathyā*, etc.[30] The functional differences between different varieties of roads may be assumed here again; besides, there is clear mention in one case of a road belonging to the merchants (*vaṇijonijarathyā*).[31] The residential sites included *aparasaraka* (houses with a porch or vestibule), *āvāsanikā* (dwellings) and *gṛhabhitti* (a house site) owned by different communities.[32] The spatial dimensions of the town may be assumed to have been larger than those of Ahar, considering the number of market centres it had. Five of them figure in the records: Dosihaṭṭa, Prasannahaṭṭa, Caturhaṭṭa (possibly identical with Catuṣkahaṭṭa of no. 25), Kallapālānāmsatkahaṭṭa (*haṭṭa* belonging to the Kallapālas) and Vasantamahattakahaṭṭa (possibly named after the chief of a guild).[33] *Vīthis* or shops owned by merchants and manufacturers of different categories constituted the nucleus of a *haṭṭa*, though not the entire *haṭṭa* complex. Although, as in the case of the Kallapālānāmsatkahaṭṭa,[34] the entire *haṭṭa* appears to have been owned by and to have specialized in the merchandise of the Kallapālas, this was not the general pattern. At Caturhaṭṭa, for example, the *vīthi* owned by *grahapatika tāmbulika* Keśava is mentioned along with that of the *kaṃsāraka*.[35] Nor was there any clear distinction between commercial and residential areas and in this regard too the lay-out was similar to

[29] F. Kielhorn, 'Siyadoni Stone Inscription', *Epigraphia Indica*, i, pp. 162–79.
[30] Ibid., Nos. 6, 7, 9, 10, etc.
[31] Ibid., No. 27.
[32] Ibid., Nos. 3, 6, 7, 14, etc.
[33] Ibid., Nos. 6, 7, 8, 27.
[34] Ibid., No. 11.
[35] Ibid., No. 8.

that at Ahar. The residence of a brāhmaṇa or a religious shrine could be a part of the total *haṭṭa* complex.[36] As at Ahar, temples formed a part of the urban set-up; there were several of them at Sīyaḍoni, dedicated to Nārāyaṇabhaṭṭāraka, Śivabhaṭṭāraka, Bhaillasvāmī, Sīgākīyadeva, etc.[37] Sīyaḍoni was, however, primarily a commercial centre, as is suggested not only by the number of its *haṭṭas*, but also by a customs house attached to it (*Sīyaḍonisatkamaṇḍapikā*).[38] A mint also seems to have been located there.[39] Sīyaḍoni served as a political centre as well, but this point will be elaborated later on.

Though not very close to Sīyaḍoni, yet in the same geographical region, was Gopagiri (Gwalior) which, as the analysis of its two inscriptions dated AD 875 and 876[40] shows, appears to have been a fort town. The settlement was administered by a chief of the boundaries (*maryādādhūrya*), appointed by a Gurjara-Pratihāra king. The second record refers to the presence at the fort town of a *koṭṭapāla*, also appointed by the Gurjara-Pratihāra ruler, and a *balādhikṛta* (commander of the army).[41] The settlement seems to have covered both the hills and the plains, as suggested by an incidental reference to the dwellers of the plateau of Gopagiri (*gopagiritalopari*). Gopagiri was a commercial centre as well, as *śreṣṭhīs* and *sārthavāhas* were counted among its residents and as members of a local council. Two *haṭṭikās*, Cacchikā and Nimbāditya, are mentioned as those parts of Gopagiri where oil-millers (*tailikas*) lived, and on the strength of this indication it may be inferred that Śrīsarveśvarapura and Śrīvatsasvāmīpura, residential areas of several other oil-millers mentioned in the records, were also parts of the Gopagiri urban complex.

On the basis of the discussion so far, some typological differences that seem to have existed between the four urban centres may be briefly

[36] Ibid., No. 7.

[37] Ibid., Nos. 1, 10, 14, 15, 20, 25, etc.

[38] Ibid., Nos. 2, 11, 27, etc.

[39] Ibid., No. 2.

[40] E. Hultzsch, 'The Two Inscriptions of Vaillabhattasvamin Temple at Gwalior', *Epigraphia Indica*, i, pp. 154–62.

[41] It is significant that while in connection with either Tattānandapura or Sīyaḍoni no *rājamārga* (royal road) is mentioned (for *narapatipatha* at Ujjayinī, see *Meghadūtam*, *Pūrvamegha*, 37), Gopagiri Inscription, No. 2, refers to *śrībhojadevapratolyavatāre*, 'the descent of the road of Bhojadeva', the Gurjara-Pratihāra ruler.

reiterated. While Pṛthūdaka was perhaps not a fully developed urban centre (although the holding of a fair would imply a commercial status already achieved), Tattānandapura and Sīyaḍoni were certainly so. Some typological distinction seems, however, to have existed between the two. Despite some incidental references to a *uttarasabhā*, the meaning of which is not clear, and a *daṇḍapāśika* and a *dūtaka* at Tattānandapura,[42] the records do not mention any ruler or other important officials in connection with the town or its activities. At Sīyaḍoni, on the other hand, four rulers—all feudatories of the Gurjara-Pratihāras—are mentioned within a span of about sixty years.[43] The *pañcakulas*, appointed by the rulers in each case,[44] represented the administrative body of the township; there are, besides, references to such officials as *karaṇikas* and *kauptikas*.[45] Sīyaḍoni was thus on all counts an important political centre of the Gurjara-Pratihāra empire. The point of contrast between Sīyaḍoni and Gopagiri would be that the latter's political importance was more military than administrative.[46] The character of the rule, suggested by the presence of a *koṭṭapāla* and a *balādhikṛta*, would be a sufficient indication of this. Another significant piece of information is also available in the Gopagiri records, if the suggested interpretation of the relevant passages is correct. They record that a piece of land belonging to the village of Cūḍāpallikā and the entire village of Jayapuraka were the properties of the city (*svabhujyamāna*). This may suggest the measure of the fort town's control over the countryside, evidence regarding which is absent in other records.

II

To what extent the suggested typological differences had a bearing on the nature and organization of the commerce and certain other related aspects at these urban centres cannot be satisfactorily ascertained from

[42] Ahar Inscription, Nos. 1, 3.
[43] Sīyaḍoni Inscription, Nos. 1, 2, 11, 20.
[44] Ibid.
[45] Ibid., Nos. 1, 22, 26.
[46] Gopagiri may thus well compare with the fortified settlements under the Pālas and the Candellas listed by R.S. Sharma, *Indian Feudalism*, Appendix II.

the records which are not primarily concerned with such matters. Only a few guesses can be made. What strikes as a possibility in the cases of Tattānandapura, Sīyaḍoni and Gopagiri is that they were not planned townships—a point suggested by the disparate location pattern of the *haṭṭas* which, as mentioned earlier, included shops, temples and residential buildings. There is no evidence that caste distinctions were made in the selection of residential sites.[47] At Tattānandapura the house site of a brāhmaṇa is mentioned as lying next to that of a *vaṇik* in the eastern market area.[48] Similar evidence is available from Sīyaḍoni. At Gopagiri the headmen of the oil-millers are mentioned in connection with two *haṭṭas* and Śrīsarveśvarapura and Śrīvatsasvāmīpura, and this may again endorse the supposition that the latter two were *haṭṭa*-cum-residential areas integrated within the township. At Sīyaḍoni two types of shops are mentioned: (i) *pitṛpitāmahopārjita*; and (ii) *svopārjita.*[49] While the latter category suggests an expansion of activities by the town's merchants, the former testifies to the antiquity of commerce at the *haṭṭas* carried down family lines.

This type of evidence may be taken to suggest that before emerging as fully developed urban centres all these sites were central points in local commerce, an assumption which may explain the concentration of a number of *haṭṭas* in one area. It was the process of the conglomeration of such *haṭṭas* and residential areas which led to the initial urbanization of these settlements.[50] Such a developmental process of

[47] All the four inscriptions discussed here offer an interesting insight into the working of the caste system at the urban centres: brāhmaṇas participated in the horse trade at Pehoa; at Tattānandapura a kṣatriya *vaṇik* was engaged in commerce (Ahar Inscription, No. 6); Sīyaḍoni and Gopagiri records mention respectively a brāhmaṇa *tambolika* (No. 17) and a kṣatriya cultivator.

[48] Ahar Inscription, No. 4.

[49] Sīyaḍoni Inscription, Nos. 13, 15, etc.

[50] This seems to be more forcefully suggested by the evidence relating to Aṇahilapāṭaka, an early medieval urban centre in Gujarat, which consisted of 84 marts; cf. *Kumārapālacarita* cited by P. Niyogi, *Contributions to the Economic History of Northern India (from the tenth to the twelfth century* AD) (Calcutta, 1962), p. 120. One wonders how V.K. Thakur who chose to reuse the same records as have been analyzed in this paper came to the rather astounding conclusion that 'early medieval urban centres of different regions clearly bring out to the fore their non-commercial nature' and that 'they betray distinct non-commercial ethos', 'Towns in Early Medieval India', in K.V. Raman *et al* (eds), *Śrīnidhiḥ* (*Perspectives in Indian Ar-*

urban centres would not, however, preclude the possibility of long-distance contacts; that such contacts did exist is borne out by all the records discussed here. At Tattānandapura lived (and got involved in local property transactions) the Varkkaṭavaṇik community from Bhillamāla (Bhinmal in south-west Rajasthan),[51] the Gandhikavaṇik community from Mathura and also merchants from Apāpura, a place not yet identified. At Sīyaḍoni the presence of a *maṇḍapikā* would imply outside trade contacts. The merchant community of Gopagiri included *sārthavāhas* who may be assumed to have headed long-distance commercial ventures. Considered along with other evidence relating to early medieval India,[52] which includes the Pehoa record, such examples would testify to the existence of a network of trade routes cutting across boundaries of local commerce.

The three urban centres, Tattānandapura, Sīyaḍoni and Gopagiri, seem to have been different in certain respects from townships founded by rulers, to which reference will be made later. Apart from their process of growth, the Sīyaḍoni evidence may bring out the difference further. Although it was a political centre, its importance in that respect lay essentially in the fact that it was assigned to the feudatories (the town is referred to as *paribhujyamāna* a number of times)[53] of the Gurjara-Pratihāras. The assignment was perhaps not permanent, an

---

chaeology, Art and Culture: K.R. Srinivasan Festschrift) (Madras, 1983), pp. 389–97. Unlike temples elsewhere receiving donations in the form of extensive landgrants, the major sources of income of temples located in urban centres were in the form of contributions by merchant groups or cesses on their incomes. The urban process was therefore exactly the opposite of what V.K. Thakur considers it to have been; the resource bases of the urban centres—and of temples located in them—were created by the activities and convergence of merchant groups and artisans; it was not the temples which created such resource bases.

51 C.D. Chatterjee (p. 102) suggests that Varkkaṭa and Lambakañcuka, mentioned in the Ahar records, 'refer to the different sections of the Gurjara stock'.

52 A relatively early evidence would be the account of I-tsing who refers in the second half of the seventh century to many hundreds of merchants coming to central India from Tāmralipti, *A Record of the Buddhist Religion as Practised in India and the Malay Archipelago*, tr., J. Takakusu (Oxford, 1896), p. xxxi; for other examples, see L. Gopal, *The Economic Life of Northern India*, pp. 90–1; it is significant that the vaiśyas who are believed to have become hardly distinguishable from the śūdras in the early medieval period were, as traders, urged by Medhātithi to get themselves familiarized with the products, customs and languages of different countries (ibid.).

53 Sīyaḍoni Inscription, Nos. 11, 20, etc.

assumption suggested by the mention of four feudatories within a span of sixty years and the absence in all cases of any reference to their predecessors. There is nothing surprising in an urban centre being assigned to feudatories. Document number 27 of the Sīyaḍoni group of inscriptions clearly refers to a township, Rāyakka, made over to some brāhmaṇas by a prince of Mahodaya. Similarly, in the eleventh century, one-half of a town along with a number of villages was assigned by Paramāra Bhoja to a feudatory in the Nasik area (*Śrī Bhojadevaprasādāvāpta nagarasellakārddha-sārddhasahasragrāmā-nāṃ bhoktā Śrī Yaśovarmā*).[54]

The fact that Sīyaḍoni was an assigned area (and as a political centre it has to be viewed from this perspective) would not by itself have made much difference in the nature of its commerce. As commercial centres, the real points of difference among the townships—which would perhaps also explain the necessity and forms of communication among them—would emerge from the composition of their artisan and merchant groups. It may be assumed that the records leave out a number of social groups from their purview, but the most dominant groups do nevertheless seem to have been different at different urban centres. At Tattānandapura, apart from the Cāturvaidya brāhmaṇas, various *vaṇikjātis* are mentioned: Vaṇik Varkkaṭajāti, Lambakañcukvaṇikjāti, Sauvarṇikavaṇikmahājana, Māthurajātīya, Gandhikavaṇik and Kṣatriyavaṇik. If any conjecture can be made from their recorded activities, the Sauvarṇikamahājanas appear to have been the most dominant group. At Gopagiri, apart from the *śreṣṭhīs* and *sārthavāhas*, the nature of whose trade is not specified, are mentioned heads of oil-millers (*tailika-mahattaka*) who alone numbered more than twenty and heads of gardeners (*mālika-maharas*) who numbered more than fourteen. Social groups other than merchants and artisans were represented at Sīyaḍoni by different types of *rāja-puruṣas* (*karaṇikas*, *kauptikas*, etc.), brāhmaṇas and *mātangas* (i.e. Caṇḍālas), but the records are concerned more with merchants and artisans: ***nemakavaṇik*** (salt-merchants), ***kumbhakāra*** (potters), ***kallapāla*** (distillers of liquor), ***kanduka*** (?), ***tāmbulika*** (betel-leaf traders),

[54] See R.D. Banerji, 'The Kalvan Plates of Yaśovarman', *Epigraphia Indica*, xix, pp. 69–75; ll, pp. 7–8.

tailika (oil-millers), *śilākūṭa* (stone-cutters) and *lohavana* (blacksmiths ?). Here again, if any guess is hazarded, the *nemakavaṇiks* would stand out as the most important group.

A guild was the organization which integrated the activities, secular as well as religious, of the merchants and artisans. As in the early period, the term is *śreṇī*, which occurs in the Gopagiri inscriptions. The chief of each guild was a *mahattama*, as in the case of the *tailikas* of Gopagiri or *mahara*, as in the case of the gardeners of the same place or the *tāmbulikas* of Sīyaḍoni.[55] Perhaps the term *grahapatika* referring to a *tāmbulika* at Sīyaḍoni[56] carried the same sense. The use of the term *jāti* in respect of some merchant communities at Tattānandapura raises certain problems regarding the organization of guilds in the early medieval period. It may be taken to suggest that guilds invariably corresponded to specific castes.[57] However, if this was so, one would expect that not more than one guild, representing a group of merchants or that of manufacturers, would exist at an urban centre. The *tailikas* and gardeners at Gopagiri had, however, a number of chiefs, and this fact, along with references to a series of mostly religious activities undertaken by individuals and their family members, may imply that guilds were organized more on family lines than in terms of all the members of the same caste or even of practitioners of the same trade. That they were united at certain levels is evident from such expressions as *samastakallapālānām, samastamahājanena, samasta . . . śilākūṭānām*, etc.[58] In any case one may perhaps think in terms of variations in guild organizations from a number of contemporary sources. That guilds cut across the frontiers of caste and narrow regions is suggested not only by the Pehoa record, but also and more forcefully by contemporary south Indian evidence.[59]

[55] Sīyaḍoni Inscription, No. 18.

[56] Ibid., No. 8.

[57] See L. Gopal, *The Economic Life of Northern India*, p. 82.

[58] Sīyaḍoni Inscription, Nos. 4, 11, 20, 21.

[59] For example, a record of *c.* AD 800 from Mulgund speaks of four heads of a guild belonging to 360 towns, see A.S. Altekar, *The Rashtrakutas and Their Times* (Poona, 1934), pp. 368ff for this and other cases. Vijñāneśvara in the *Mitākṣarā* (ii, p. 30) defined a *śreṇī* as a guild of persons earning its livelihood by the same kind of labour, though belonging to different castes or the same caste, cited by R. Narasimha Rao, *Corporate Life in Medieval Āndhradeśa* (Secunderabad, 1967), p. 5.

What is most difficult to reconstruct is the relationship between the merchants, artisans and officials, because what brings them together in the records are religious donations and levies and not any economic transactions. Two separate pieces of information may, however, have some bearing on this point. At Sīyaḍoni the authority for levying contributions from the *maṇḍapikā* was the local ruler or the *pañcakula* appointed by him. While the composition of the *pañcakulas* is not known (only the names of individuals are known), both at Sīyaḍoni and Gopagiri the actual *sthānādhikṛta* or *sthānādhiṣṭhita* was the *vāra* which, as the Gopagiri evidence shows, was constituted by the *śreṣṭhīs* and *sārthavāhas.* Secondly, the temples which received donations in different forms either through official intervention or by arrangements initiated by their patrons were mostly built by merchants. Of the six deities at Tattānandapura two were clearly caste deities—Kanakadevī or Kāñcanaśrīdevī of the Sauvarṇikamahājanas and Gandhaśrīdevī of the Gandhikavaṇikjāti. At Sīyaḍoni too the shrines for Viṣṇubhaṭṭāraka, Bhaillasvāmī, etc., were all constructed by merchants.[60]

Paradoxical though it may sound, it is the pattern of donations and more generally the activities centring round these temples that suggest the commercial ethos of these urban centres. While certain fields and villages belonging to the township were made over to the temples at Gopagiri (and here one temple was built by the local rulers), the contributions from the itinerant merchants at Pṛthūdaka were in the form of *dharma,* certainly a corruption of *dramma,* the most common coin-name in early medieval records.[61] At Sīyaḍoni such contributions were in the form of a daily levy of one quarter of *pañcīyakadramma* at the *maṇḍapikā* made over, under the *akṣaya-nīvi* tenure, to Viṣṇubhaṭṭāraka enshrined by a salt-merchant.[62] But

[60] Sīyaḍoni Inscription, Nos. 1, 20.

[61] G. Bühler seems wrong in taking it in the sense of a tithe set apart for religious purposes; for a general survey of *dramma* in early medieval literature and epigraphs, see R.C. Agrawala, 'Dramma in Ancient Indian Epigraphs and Literature', *The Journal of the Numismatic Society of India,* xvii, pp. 64–82; also L. Gopal, 'Coins in the Epigraphic and Literary Records of Northern India in the Early Medieval Period', ibid., xxv, pp. 1–16.

[62] Sīyaḍoni Inscription, No. 2.

another type of arrangement, of which the temple would be a beneficiary, was the investment of a substantial amount of cash with a group of manufacturers (for example, record no. 11 at Sīyaḍoni shows that 1350 *ādivarāhadrammas* were deposited with the distillers of liquor who were to pay every month *tuṅgīyadramma* on every cask of liquor). This type of investment, perhaps implied by the expression *aparimitamūlyena kṛtvā* (i.e. having bought with excessive price), involved other groups of artisans and manufacturing communities at Sīyaḍoni,[63] and in all cases except a few (where it was not necessary to convert kind into cash) the purpose of such investments was a return in the form of a regular interest in cash.[64]

It was the prospect of this form of regular return on investments which governed the most typical transactions, made on behalf of the deities, both at Tattānandapura and Sīyaḍoni. Most of the Tattānandapura documents deal with the purchase, with cash belonging to Kāñcanaśrīdevī, of houses and house sites owned sometimes for generations by different communities (Cāturvaidya brāhmaṇa, Kṣatriyānvaya vaṇik, etc.). The deed of ninety-nine years (*navanavatipatra*) through which such transactions were formalized assured the investor

[63] Ibid., Nos. 4, 5, 11, etc.

[64] The transactions were all in cash except where contributions in kind could be used by temples (for example, oil levied on the *tailikas* and garlands on the gardeners at Gopagiri); see also Sīyaḍoni record No. 22. Elsewhere contributions or interests on deposits realized even from the local manufacturers were in the form of cash, as is clear from the arrangements made with the distillers of liquor at Sīyaḍoni (Nos. 4, 5, 11, etc.). The Pehoa record mentions one type of coin: *dramma*, and the Ahar inscriptions two: *dramma* and *viṃśopaka*. Sīyaḍoni records on the other hand give a much more comprehensive idea of the types of coins that circulated in the Gurjara-Pratihāra kingdom, not all of them necessarily representing indigenous or dynastic coinage, or even metallic currency: *pañcīyakadramma*, *yuga*, *vigrahapāladramma*, *varāhakayaviṃśopaka*, *ādivarāhadramma*, *kapardaka*, *vigrahapālīyadramma* and *dramma*. What these names represented is at least partly known from the Ahar finds of three types of silver coins: (i) Indo-Sassanid; (ii) with legend *śrī śrī vi* or *vigra* (definitely identical with *vigrahapāladramma*); and (iii) uncertain, possibly with a Bull device (*Archaeological Survey of India, Annual Report, 1925–6*, pp. 56–8). A hoard of *ādivarāha* and *vigraha* type of coins was found at Ahicchatra (*Ancient India*, i, pp. 39–40), whereas at Kashipur (Nainital district) early medieval currency is represented by the 'Bull/Horseman' type (*Indian Archaeology, 1970–71, A Review*, pp. 41ff).

of varying types of sureties.[65] In some cases, where initially the surety was of a limited kind, fresh arrangements were later made to transfer the entire property and thus the entire rent to the deity.[66] At Sīyaḍoni although no clear references to such purchase[67] are available (unless the expression *aparimitamūlyena kṛtvā* refers to buying up of some kind of property), houses and shops were assigned in large numbers to various deities of the town.[68] The purpose of such assignments was obviously to secure a regular rent, and the patterns at Tattānandapura and Sīyaḍoni were identical, because in substance the rent accruing from the assigned houses and shops was the same as the return on the money with which the houses were purchased.[69] As mentioned earlier, all these transactions revolved round the temple establishments at these two places, but one may not be entirely wrong in supposing that the trend was not substantially different in secular commerce.

III

Pṛthūdaka, Tattānandapura, Sīyaḍoni and Gopagiri are useful examples—and more so because of their chronology—of the continuity of inland trade and of urbanization associated with it in the early medieval period, but by themselves they can hardly answer whether or not the early medieval pattern was completely different from the early historical. For such an answer one may think of two sets of comparisons between the two periods in the following terms: (i) a comparison, region-wise, of the number of different categories of urban centres and of the social composition of population in them; (ii) a comparison of the pattern of trade and of petty commodity production. No such detailed comparisons, particularly in quantitative

[65] For a relevant analysis of the Ahar documents, see R.S. Sharma, 'Usury in Early Medieval India (*c*. AD 400–1200)' in *Light on Early Indian Society and Economy* (Bombay, 1966), pp. 138–9.

[66] Ahar Inscription, compare 4 and 8 and 2 and 9.

[67] See, however, Sīyaḍoni document No. 17, which refers to the purchase of a *uvaṭaka* which was assigned to the deity *Śrī Umāmaheśvara.*

[68] Sīyaḍoni Inscription, Nos. 6, 7, 8, 9, 10, 13, 15, 16, 17, etc.

[69] The term used in the two records is *bhāṭaka*. For the significance of the term, see C.D. Chatterjee, p. 92. See also Sīyaḍoni Inscription, No. 24.

terms, are available,[70] and, given the nature of the data, are hardly likely to be undertaken. But then one can legitimately raise a question: if early historical economy had reached a certain level of urbanization and petty commodity production, what were the reasons for the apparent swing back to the state of 'natural economy' in the post-Gupta period?

One possible explanation suggests itself in the form of the decline of trade relations with the West,[71] indicated archaeologically by the gradual disappearance of the flow of Roman coins into India after the first three centuries of the Christian era. It should be noted, however, that the majority of the hoards of Roman coins relate to the first century AD and not later.[72] Secondly, although the relative prosperity of the Śaka-Kuṣāṇa-Sātavāhana urban phases[73] may to some extent be linked with Roman trade, it has to be remembered that 'India had . . . lost its principal source of the precious metal (i.e. gold) just before the beginning of the Christian era'—a phenomenon which has been taken to explain convincingly the genesis of Indian contacts with South-East Asia.[74] This may further show that the spate of gold currency throughout the Gupta period, despite its debasement in the later period of the empire,[75] cannot be entirely attributed to trade with the West, because, if the chronology of the hoards of Roman coins is any indication, relations with that area had already declined by that period. In the post-Gupta period India was no doubt not a serious contender in the contemporary international trade,[76] but so was the

[70] For a rather incomplete list of the urban centres of north India, see P. Niyogi, pp. 117–22; for several other references where such lists are available, see R.S. Sharma, *Indian Feudalism*, p. 245ff; also Appendix II.

[71] R.S. Sharma, *Social Changes in Early Medieval India*, p. 2; Idem, 'Decay of Gangetic Towns in Gupta and post-Gupta Times', pp. 101–2.

[72] E.H. Warmington, *The Commerce between the Roman Empire and India* (Cambridge, 1928), pp. 272ff; P.L. Gupta, *Roman Coins from Andhra Pradesh* (Hyderabad, 1965), pp. 47–53.

[73] R.S. Sharma, 'Decay of Gangetic Towns in Gupta and post-Gupta Times'.

[74] G. Coedes, *The Indianized States of South East Asia* (East-West Center Press, Hawaii, 1968), p. 20.

[75] S.K. Maity, *Economic Life in Northern India in the Gupta Period (c.* AD *300–550)*. 2nd edn. (Delhi, 1970), Appendix III.

[76] This is the impression one gets from L. Gopal, *The Economic Life of Northern India*, chs VI and VII.

case even during the period of Roman trade.[77] However, the continued participation by Indians in this trade and the presence of non-Indian merchants, particularly the Tājikas and the Turuṣkas in different parts of India, are attested by a variety of sources.[78] The Arab conquest of Sind[79] and the occasional raids in the western and central parts of India are initial indications of commercial motivations turned political.

Foreign trade, however, is not central to the argument here, as even a decline in foreign trade may not necessarily imply a decline in internal trade or petty commodity production. The same applies to urban centres as well. It emerges from a number of recent discussions that the economic basis of the early urban centres of the Ganga basin was an agricultural surplus generated by new methods as well as expansion of cultivation[80] and by the gradual crystallization of a power structure which ensured the production of surplus.[81] A certain amount of commercialization of this surplus was necessitated by the presence of specialized labour and of surplus appropriated by social groups which were not necessarily confined to the monarch, his kin and his

[77] In northern India, on which the focus of the present paper is, the pattern of trade seems to have been different from that in the south and local Indians were one among the many middlemen in the Indo-Roman trade; see G.L. Adhya, *Early Indian Economics (Studies in the Economic Life of Northern and Western India, c. 200 BC–300 AD)* (Asia Publishing House, Bombay, 1966), pp. 46–94.

[78] L. Gopal, *The Economic Life of Northern India*, pp. 113–15. *Turuṣkadaṇḍa*, occurring commonly in the Gāhaḍavāla records of the Ganga basin, has been taken by a number of writers as a tax on Turkish settlers, see R.S. Avasthy and A. Ghosh, 'References to Muhammadans in Sanskrit Inscriptions in Northern India—AD 730 to 1320', *Journal of Indian History*, xv, p. 171; also L. Gopal, *Economic Life*, pp. 116–18. It is well-known from the Arab geographers' accounts that the Tājikas or the Arabs were patronized by Rāṣṭrakūṭa rulers, for which corroboration is available in the epigraphic records of the western Deccan. The Chinchani Charter of AD 926 mentions that the entire *maṇḍala* of Saṃyāna (Sanjan) was made over by Kṛṣṇa II to Madhumatī (Muhammad) of the Tājika community who conquered the chiefs of all the harbours of the neighbourhood on behalf of his master and placed his own officials in them, D.C. Sircar, 'Rāshṭrakūṭa Charters from Chinchani', *Epigraphia Indica*, xxxii, pp. 45ff.

[79] This point has been made by M. Mujeeb, *Islamic Influence on Indian Society* (Meerut-Delhi-Kanpur, 1972), pp. v-vi.

[80] R.S. Sharma, *Light on Early Indian Society and Economy*, pp. 57–9.

[81] A. Ghosh, p. 20.

officials. Viewed from such a perspective, it stands to reason that trade (and not necessarily foreign trade) and a power structure which needs it and hence may promote it, are essential factors in urban growth. If foreign trade did not play a crucial role in the birth of early urban centres, a reduced volume of such trade may hardly be held responsible for their decay in the post-Kuṣāṇa or post-Gupta period.

Secondly, and this is more important, the alleged decay of urban settlements coincides with, and in a number of cases even precedes, the period when land grants actually start proliferating.[82] This may preclude any possible connection between them, as the full impact of land grant economy, if any such impact is highlighted to explain the decay of urban centres,[83] ought to have taken some more time to assert itself. This point needs to be stressed, as decline of trade and of urban centres may not have logically followed from the types of assignments that were made in early and medieval India. For the present this has to remain at the level of a theoretical discussion, but it may be pointed out that some trends to the contrary have already been discovered. Of south-east Bengal, which initially as a peripheral area offers a good example of the working of land grant economy, Morrison writes:[84]

> Such an extensive series of occupation sites . . . indicates a concentration of population whose food needs would have been met by the surplus production of the local agriculturists. There may well have been a commodity market with a currency to facilitate exchange[85] as well as the transfer of extensive lands to temples and monasteries to secure to them productive land from which their own food needs might be supplied.

An increase in the number of assignees with their bases at already existing urban centres perhaps served as an impetus to further urban

[82] So far as the urban centres along the Himalayan foothills are concerned, Medvedev points out that the account of Fa-hien tallies with that of Hiuen Tsang.

[83] R.S. Sharma, *Social Changes in Early Medieval India*, pp. 3–6.

[84] B.M. Morrison, *Political Centers and Cultural Regions in Early Bengal* (The University of Arizona Press, 1970), p. 153.

[85] For currency in early medieval south-east Bengal see my paper, 'Currency in Early Bengal', *Journal of Indian History*, vol. 55, pt. 3 (1977), pp. 41ff; for relevant bibliographical references to the extensive writings of B.N. Mukherjee on the coinage of southeast Bengal, see B.N. Mukherjee, *Post-Gupta Coinages of Bengal* (Coin Study Circle, Calcutta, 1989).

growth and trade, as it seems to have done in Mughal India,[86] while their presence in rural areas could have created conditions for what Medvedev calls 'commodity-money relations'.[87] Thus rural market centres named after kings, like the Devapāladevahaṭṭa mentioned in a Nalanda inscription,[88] or created by feudatories, like the market centre founded by Kakkuka in the Jodhpur area of Rajasthan,[89] could and did emerge in the context of a land grant economy. A conglomeration of such *haṭṭas* could evolve, as shown by Tattānandapura and Sīyaḍoni evidence, into an urban centre where urban property along with marketed goods would become objects of commercial transactions. It may be mentioned that a good amount of *Śilpaśāstra* material[90] on towns and town-planning, despite its being highly stereotyped, relates to the early medieval period and the ranking of houses prescribed by early medieval texts for princes and different categories of *sāmantas*[91] may be accommodated within the framework of what they say about towns and town-planning.

One has at the same time to contend with the unassailable archaeological evidence, which shows that many of the important—and not so important—urban centres decayed in north India in the Gupta and post-Gupta times. An alternative way of looking at this process of decay would be to start with a study of the geographical distribution of the centres, for which, apart from archaeology, the travel account

[86] I. Habib, 'Potentialities of Capitalistiç Development in the Economy of Mughal India', *Enquiry*, new series, iii, No. 3 (1971), p. 10; also A.I. Chicherov, *India: Economic Development in the 16th–18th Centuries* (Moscow, 1971), ch. III. It may be argued, of course, that conditions in Mughal India were completely different from those of early medieval times as Mughal India was characterized by 'the separation of the crafts from agriculture and the town from the countryside' (Chicherov, p. 95), but then we are only thinking in terms of a theoretical possibility here.

[87] Medvedev.

[88] *Epigraphia Indica*, xxv, p. 335.

[89] Ibid., ix, pp. 277–80. The inscription refers not only to the establishment of a *haṭṭa* but also to the settling of merchants in it, *haṭṭo mahājanaśca sthāpita*(-).

[90] For example, *Samarāṅganasūtradhāra* of Bhoja, T. Ganapati Sastri and V.S. Agrawala, eds (Baroda, 1966), chs 10, 15, 18, 30, etc.; for a list of *Śilpaśāstra* texts, see D.N. Sukla, *Vāstuśāstra*, i, *Hindu Science of Architecture* (Chandigarh, no date), p. 83. See also B.B. Dutta, *Townplanning in Ancient India* (Calcutta, 1925), *passim.*

[91] R.S. Sharma, *Social Changes in Early Medieval India*, pp. 6–7.

of Hiuen Tsang, which is regarded as a standard source for the first half of the seventh century,[92] may be useful.[93] Hiuen Tsang too refers to a number of decayed urban centres and in the Indus valley one such typical site was Śākala.[94] Such sites were, however, much more numerous in the Ganga basin proper and the adjoining areas where a selected list would include Kauśāmbī,[95] Śrāvastī,[96] Kapilavāstu,[97] Rāmagrāma,[98] Kuśīnagara,[99] and Vaiśālī[100], the capital of the Vajjis.[101] The point to be noted in this account is that in many of the regions where these centres lay it was not only the townships which had gone into decay, but the 'peopled villages' too were 'few and waste'.[102] Hiuen Tsang seems also to have made a conscious distinction between a city and a town. With reference to the capital of the Vajjis, he remarked that '. . . the capital is ruined' and that 'it may be called a village or town'.[103] His statement about Magadha has similar implications: 'The walled cities have but few inhabitants but the towns are thickly populated'.[104] It would appear from his descriptions that this distinction would also apply to the urban centres which he found surviving and some of them would come under his category of cities. Thus Kānyakubja and Varanasi may be definitely labelled as cities of his period. Both of them were 'thickly populated' and 'valuable merchandise was collected' at them 'in great quantities'.[105] Urban characteristics were present also at a number of sites listed by Hiuen Tsang in the Indo-Gangetic divide, the Ganga valley and its extension, covering a recog-

[92] Medvedev gives convincing reasons for treating it as a standard source.

[93] From the tenth century onward the accounts of Arab geographers and others contain much useful material, but they have not been used in this paper.

[94] S. Beal, *Si-yu-ki: Buddhist Records of the Western World* (Indian reprint, Delhi, 1969), i, pp. 166–7.

[95] Ibid., pp. 235–9.

[96] Ibid., ii, p. 1.

[97] Ibid., p. 14.

[98] Ibid., p. 26.

[99] Ibid., pp. 31–2.

[100] Ibid., p. 66.

[101] Ibid., p. 78.

[102] Ibid., p. 32.

[103] Ibid., p. 78.

[104] Ibid., p. 82.

[105] Ibid., i, p. 206; ii, p. 44.

nizable stretch along the Himalayan foothills. At Thaneswar 'rare and valuable' merchandise was brought from elsewhere;[106] the chief town of P'o-lo-hih-mo-pu-lo was densely populated and most of its people were 'engaged in commerce';[107] at Kiu-pi-shwang-na too the population was numerous.[108]

The survival of old urban centres or the emergence of new ones in these areas is attested by archaeology as well, although, owing to the insignificant progress made in historical archaeology so far, our information is scanty here. The most important representative of the old urban centres is Ahicchatrā in Bareilly district, which reveals an unbroken sequence in the early medieval context.[109] At Purana Qila in Delhi the Gupta, post-Gupta and Rajput phases show that here also the sequence was uninterrupted between the Kuṣāṇa and the Turkish periods, though the quality of the structures at these phases appears to have been poor.[110] Atranjikhera in Etah district has remains of Gupta and post-Gupta times.[111] At Rajghat near Varanasi, period IV lasted from AD 300 to 700 and period V from AD 700 to 1200.[112] At Chirand in Saran district, representing the middle Ganga basin, a new occupational stratum was discovered in 1968–9 and the coins of Gāṅgeyadeva and other metal objects marked it out to be the early medieval phase of the site.[113] Among the sites that appear to have emerged in the post-Gupta period, apart from Ahar, Sankara in Aligarh district may be mentioned. Structures at this site have been dated from between the ninth and twelfth centuries.[114]

To return to Hiuen Tsang, the deserted and deurbanized areas of

[106] Ibid., i, p. 183.

[107] Ibid., p. 198.

[108] Ibid., p. 199. Excavations at Kashipur (Nainital district), generally identified with Hiuen Tsang's Kui-pi-shwang-na, have revealed imposing religious structures of the early medieval period; see *Indian Archaeology 1970–1 A Review*, pp. 41ff.

[109] A. Ghosh and K.C. Panigrahi, 'The Pottery of Ahichchhatra, District Bareilly, U.P.', *Ancient India*, i, pp. 38–40.

[110] *Indian Archaeology 1969–70 A Review*, pp. 4–5.

[111] Ibid., 1960–1, pp. 32–3.

[112] Ibid., p. 39. See also ibid., 1957–8, pp. 50–1, where period IV was dated between the fifth and eighth centuries and period V between the ninth and fourteenth centuries.

[113] Ibid., 1968–9, p. 6.

[114] Ibid., 1960–1, pp. 32–3.

his account, so far as the Ganga basin and the adjoining areas along the Himalayan foothills are concerned, correspond to a stretch which was in early times intersected by a number of important trade routes. They connected Gaya, Pāṭaliputra, Vaiśālī, Kuśīnagara, Nepalese *tarai*, Śrāvastī and Kauśāmbī,[115] covering precisely an area in which were located the most important urban centres which had decayed by Hiuen Tsang's time. No detailed history of these trade routes is as yet available, but the impression that they had decayed fairly early may still be tested by analysing the chronology of the sources in which some of them are mentioned. Mithila in north Bihar is believed to have been touched by eight trade routes: (i) Mithila-Rājagṛha; (ii) Mithila-Śrāvastī; (iii) Mithila-Kapilavāstu; (iv) Videha-Puṣkalāvatī; (v) Mithila-Pratiṣṭhāna; (vi) Mithila-Sindhu; (vii) Mithila-Campā; and (viii) Mithila-Tāmralipti.[116] From the direction of these routes their actual number may be reduced to three or four, but even so it is significant that not a single reference to them is of the early medieval period, perhaps suggesting that they had become defunct by that time. This apparently provides us with an explanation as to why the urban centres in this area decayed, but it does not answer why the trade routes themselves had dried up.

There is another dimension to the problem already briefly touched upon, and it bears upon the relationship between trade, urban centres and a stable political structure. The role of the political organism in the formation of early historical urban centres has often been stressed to the extent that according to one writer '. . . if any priority is to be established, the ruler should get the credit because he happens to symbolize a power structure very necessary for the maintenance of any economic system represented by the merchants'.[117] The problem of the decay of urban centres has also to be viewed in this light. It is common knowledge that the *mahājanapadas*, within the framework of which emerged the urban centres of the Buddha's time, were not

[115] D.D. Kosambi, op. cit., p. 132.

[116] Md. Aquique, *Economic History of Mithila (c. 600 BC–1097 AD)* (New Delhi, 1974), pp. 141–4.

[117] Dilip K. Chakrabarti, Review of *The City in Early Historical India* by A. Ghosh, *Journal of Ancient Indian History*, vi, pts. 1–2 (1972–3), pp. 314–9.

merely territorial structures but political structures as well.[118] With regard to the urban sites along the Himalayan foothills, Medvedev's formulation that 'with the dissolution of Kṣatriya oligarchical state-clan formations (*gaṇas*) the Himalayan area lost its past political significance and came to occupy the position of an unimportant outlying province of economically advanced north Indian states',[119] may be only partly true.[120] But it is significant that even in the Ganga basin and the Indo-Gangetic divide there is in the post-Gupta period no substantial evidence of any well-knit kingdoms, apart from the ephemeral empire of the Vardhanas. Even in this short-lived empire two urban centres, Thaneswar and Kanauj, stand out in the account of Hiuen Tsang and in Harṣa's time they were important political centres as well. Instances of early medieval rulers establishing new townships abound in literature and in epigraphs and they cover such widely distant regions as Kashmir,[121] Rajasthan[122] and Bengal.[123] Tattānandapura, Sīyaḍoni and Gopagiri, although not founded by any ruler, are all examples of townships which emerged along with the rise of the Gurjara-Pratihāra empire.

This, however, does not guarantee that the rise of a kingdom or an empire would necessarily bring in trade and urbanism. We have as yet no substantial evidence of either, for example, in the long-lasting kingdom of the Eastern Cālukyas of Andhra. And despite political vicissitudes a number of traditional urban centres survived; such survivals were the measure not of the stability of a kingdom but of (i) some important trade routes; and (ii) the location of a traditional seat of manufacture at the centre. A single but representative example would be Varanasi, which was not only located on a traditional artery

[118] See H.C. Raychaudhuri, *Political History of Ancient India*, 6th edn. (University of Calcutta, 1953), part i, ch. III; also A. Ghosh, p. 13.

[119] Medvedev.

[120] The oligarchical states disappeared as a result of Magadhan expansion, but archaeologically the region, including the Nepalese *tarai*, is well-documented down to the Kuṣāṇa period, if not later, Debala Mitra, *Excavations at Tilaura-kot and Explorations in the Nepalese Tarai* (The Department of Archaeology, Nepal, 1972), p. 15; also R.S. Sharma, 'Decay of Gangetic Towns in Gupta and post-Gupta Times', p. 97.

[121] See *Rājataraṅgiṇī*, iv. 10; v. 156, etc.

[122] *Epigraphia Indica*, xviii, pp. 87–99.

[123] See *Rāmacarita* of Sandhyākaranandī, v. 32.

of trade, the Ganga, but was also an important centre of textile and ivory products in the early historical period.[124] As a centre of textile manufacture, its importance continued till early medieval times.[125] When new centres emerged in different regional contexts—and studies on early medieval India have to think in terms of such possibilities—the pattern of petty production was not substantially different from that of earlier times. Of the most important guilds of early historical times[126] at least seven existed at Tattānandapura, Sīyaḍoni and Gopagiri, those of the goldsmiths, stone-masons, braziers, oil-pressers, garland-makers, potters and caravan traders.[127]

[124] See B. Srivastava, *Trade and Commerce in Ancient India (from the earliest times to c. AD 300)*, Appendix A, pp. 278–9.

[125] L. Gopal, 'The Textile Industry in Early Medieval India', *Journal of the Asiatic Society of Bombay*, 1964–5, p. 103.

[126] See R.C. Majumdar, *Corporate Life in Ancient India*, 3rd edn. (Calcutta, 1969), ch. I, pp. 15–17.

[127] For a list of 18 guilds mentioned in *Jambudvīpaprajñapti*, see A.K. Majumdar, *Chaulukyas of Gujarat* (Bombay, 1956), pp. 263–4; also L. Gopal, *The Economic Life of Northern India*, ch. IV.

7

Urban Centres in Early Medieval India: An Overview*

Urbanization in early medieval India is as yet a little understood phenomenon. Compared to the quantum of writing on urbanization in other phases of early India the research available on this phase is decidedly inadequate.[1] This inadequacy is apparent at two levels. First, in the absence of any substantial empirical work, the intensity or otherwise of urbanization and the distribution of urban centres in the period can only be impressionistically gauged. Second, general works on the period which touch on the problem of urbanization lack an appropriate analytical framework. The existence of urban centres is taken for granted in such works and no reference is usually made to the historical context in which they may have emerged. Such studies are therefore in the nature of compilations of urban place names from epigraphs and literature,[2] or they state what, according

* Reprinted from S. Bhattacharyya and Romila Thapar, eds., *Situating Indian History* (Oxford University Press, 1986).

[1] General works on early medieval India hardly touch upon the problem of urbanization; even a work which purports to trace the history of urban development in India in a broad sweep rests content with Al Beruni's evidence so far as the early medieval period is concerned. See B. Bhattacharya, *Urban Development in India (Since Prehistoric Times)* (Delhi, 1979), ch. III. The position is no better in standard works on economic history in which a synthesis of voluminous empirical material has been attempted. See Tapan Ray Chaudhuri and Irfan Habib (eds), *The Cambridge Economic History of India, c. 1200–c. 1750* (Cambridge University Press, 1982). The section on 'Economic Conditions before 1200' (pp. 45–7) presents a rather dismal picture of the decline the economy suffered in the post-Gupta period. In the context of south India, however, Burton Stein recognizes the development of urban places, but generally from the thirteenth century. Ibid., pp. 36–42.

[2] Only a few examples need to be cited. P. Niyogi's *Contributions to the Economic History of Northern India (from the tenth to the twelfth century AD)* (Calcutta, 1962), has a chapter (ch. V) on 'Towns and Town-planning'. The chapter compiles, from indigenous and non-indigenous sources, a list of place names which are regarded as urban centres of the period with which the work deals. The information on town-

to prescriptive *Śilpaśāstra* texts, the various forms of urban settlements were in terms of their plan or layout.[3] Whereas such compilations do not lay down specific criteria by which a settlement area may be defined as urban, the prescriptive texts, in the absence of any attempted correlation with other types of evidence and in view of their uncertain chronology, are, in the final analysis, hardly of any use in understanding the nature and process of urbanization in the early medieval period.

Although some beginnings have now been made in understanding urban processes in various regional contexts,[4] in the absence of an

---

planning is based on some literary evidence which cannot be further tested; material which is datable to a much earlier period is also used. K.C. Jain's *Ancient Cities and Towns of Rajasthan (A Study of Culture and Civilization)* (Delhi-Varanasi-Patna, 1972) has a rather confused chapter on 'Principles of Selection' (ch. V) and takes the 'criteria on the basis of which the selection of cities and towns has been made' as self-evident. This work is really in the nature of a compilation of brief sketches of settlements in Rajasthan and does not distinguish between the early historical and the early medieval period. P.K. Bhattacharya's compilation of a list of rural and urban centres in Madhya Pradesh in *Historical Geography of Madhya Pradesh from Early Records* (Delhi-Varanasi-Patna, 1977), pp. 198–225, is similarly of little use for distinguishing between rural and urban and between early historical and early medieval. In fact all the works cited above take the existence of urban centres so much for granted that they do not regard the problem of urbanization as a theme requiring serious analysis.

[3] See B.B. Dutt, *Town Planning in Ancient India* (Calcutta, 1925; reprinted, New Asian Publishers, Delhi, 1977). Dutt's work is based largely on such texts as *Vāstuvidyā, Mānasāra, Mayāmatam, Manuṣālaya-Candrikā, Viśvakarmaprakāśa* and so on. Apart from the fact that the dates of most texts cannot be ascertained with certainty, the material contained in such works is of doubtful relevance for the study of urbanization. This is not to imply that literary texts have no historical value; much of our understanding of early historical urban centres is in fact derived from literary evidence. I merely suggest that the use of literary material requires a different kind of critical apparatus, which is generally absent in works which depend on it. That literary evidence can have exciting and suggestive details is revealed by the text *Kumārapālacarita*, which describes the urban centre of Aṇahilapura in Gujarat; the text has been cited by P. Niyogi, p. 125, and B.N.S. Yadava, *Society and Culture in Northern India in the Twelfth Century* (Allahabad, 1973), p. 241.

[4] Regional studies in the form of monographs on urbanization in early medieval India are rather rare. O.P. Prasad's Ph.D. dissertation, 'Towns in Karnataka', submitted at Patna University, has only recently been published under the title *Decay and Revival of Urban Centres in Medieval South India (c. AD 600–1200)* (Patna-Delhi, 1989). A few articles by him on this theme are also available: (i) 'A Study of Towns

overall perspective there is a tendency to isolate factors and elements relevant to a local situation rather than view local developments as expressions of a broader general process. Notwithstanding the possibility that urban centres represented varied typologies or that they were generated by different 'immediate' factors, there is a need to transcend locality-centred perspectives and view urbanization as corresponding to a process, which alone can satisfactorily explain its emergence and structure. Even the range of issues involved in the study of early medieval urbanization remains to be properly defined and empirically worked out, and I shall only underline some of the issues and present a viewpoint. In so doing, it may be found necessary to introduce some empirical material in various regional contexts, but the main purpose of this would be not to highlight regional trends but to identify factors which cut across what may have been taking place at a purely regional level. If urbanization was a phenomenon which was geographically widely distributed in the early medieval period, then one is entitled to speculate as to what the commonality of elements was between the urban centres of the period. This will be a valid exercise.

---

in Karnataka on the Basis of Epigraphic Sources: *c.* AD 600–1200', *Indian History Congress, Proceedings of the 38th Session* (1977), pp. 151–60; (ii) 'Two Ancient Port Towns of Karnataka—Goa and Mangalore', ibid., 39th Session (1978), pp. 55–61. Also unpublished is T. Venkateswara Rao's Ph.D. dissertation, 'Local Bodies in Pre-Vijayanagara Andhra', submitted at Karnataka University in 1975; it contains much material on urban centres in the Andhra region.

The picture of early medieval urbanism is thus only slowly emerging and is still mostly to be got from articles. For urban centres in the areas under Gurjara-Pratīhāra rule, see B.D. Chattopadhyaya, 'Trade and Urban Centres in Early Medieval North India' in this collection. For the growth of urban centres in the Coḷa area of Tamilnadu, see R. Champakalakshmi, 'Growth of Urban Centres in South India: Kuḍamūkku-Palaiyārai, the Twin-city of the Coḷas', *Studies in History*, vol. I, No. I (1979), pp. 1–29; also Idem., 'Urban Process in Early Medieval Tamilnadu', Occasional Papers Series, No. 3, Urban History Association of India (1982). See also, K.R. Hall, 'Peasant State and Society in Chola Times: A View from the Tiruvidaimarudur Urban Complex', *The Indian Economic and Social History Review*, vol. 18, Nos. 3–4 (1981), pp. 393–410. See also R. Champakalakshmi, 'Urbanization in Medieval Tamilnadu', in S. Bhattacharyya and Romila Thapar, eds, *Situating Indian History*, pp. 34–105; Idem., 'Urbanisation in South India: The Role of Ideology and Polity', Presidential Address, Ancient India Section, Indian History Congress, 47 session, 1986 (Srinagar).

In defining the issues, the first point to be made is that urbanization in the early medieval period is here taken as the beginning of the third phase of the phenomenon in India. Two distinct phases of urbanization in early India have already been demarcated. The first and perhaps the more readily recognized phase is represented by the planned cities of the Harappan culture, and in several ways this phase stands apart from the historical context which gave rise to India's second urbanization. Covering a long time span between about the middle of the third and the middle of the second millennium BC, the Harappan cities were mainly distributed over the Indus drainage system, extending to what Spate calls 'one of the major structure-lines of Indian history', namely 'the Delhi-Aravalli axis and the Cambay node'.[5] The Indus civilization sites did spill over into other geographical regions and did interact with other cultures, but beyond the 'structure line' there was no gradual territorial extension of the Indus urban sites. In other words, the major part of the Indian subcontinent remained unaffected by Indus urbanism. Secondly, the Indus cities, with their accent on rigid and unfailingly uniform layouts,[6] reflect a kind of spatial and social organization which would be unfamiliar on such a scale in any other phase of Indian history. The Indus valley urbanism thus did not continue as a legacy beyond the middle of the second millennium BC.[7]

The second phase of urbanization, the beginnings of which have been dated around the sixth century BC, coincided with a gradual maturation of the iron age. As a causative factor of the second phase

[5] O.H.K. Spate and A.T.A. Learmonth, *India and Pakistan: A General and Regional Geography* (Methuen & Co., 3rd edition, 1967), pp. 175–9.

[6] The literature on Harappan urbanism is extensive and to form satisfactory impressions of Harappan urban centres the best guides are the excavation reports. For a useful though by now dated bibliography, see B.M. Pande and K.S. Ramachandran, *Bibliography of the Harappan Culture* (Florida, 1971). For recent perspectives and bibliographical references, see G.L. Possehl, ed., *Harappan Civilisation: A Contemporary Perspective* (New Delhi, 1982).

[7] Despite oft-repeated suggestions to the effect that Harappan cultural traditions continue into later Indian history, this point has been made with considerable emphasis in A. Ghosh, *The City in Early Historical India* (Simla, 1973) and S. Ratnagar, *Encounters: The Westerly Trade of the Harappa Civilization* (New Delhi, Oxford University Press, 1981), p. xiii.

of urbanization iron has been a subject of some debate.[8] The second phase of urbanization reveals stages of internal growth and of horizontal expansion. The distribution of two new and crucial cultural elements, namely a multifunctional syllabic script and coinage, which are associated with this phase, serves as an effective indicator of the geographical spread of urbanism.[9] The factor adding substantially to the internal growth process was an enormous expansion of trade networks in the period when India's early contact with Central Asia and the Roman world reached its peak,[10] and despite physical variations between the urban centres, between Ujjayinī[11] and Nagarjunakonda[12] for example, this network is evident in the unprecedented mobility of men and goods in the period. It is probably not coincidental that a shrinkage in this network coincides with the decline of urban centres from the post-Kuṣāṇa period through the Gupta period.[13] The decline was geographically widely distributed, and since this observation is based on a study of archaeological sequences at a number of

[8] See for example R.S. Sharma, 'Material Background of the Origin of Buddhism', in M. Sen and M.B. Rao, eds, *Das Kapital Centenary Volume—A Symposium* (Delhi-Ahmedabad-Bombay, 1968), p. 61; A. Ghosh, ch. IV; R.S. Sharma, 'Iron and Urbanization in the Ganga Basin', *The Indian Historical Review*, vol. I, No. 1 (1974), pp. 98–103; Dilip Chakrabarti, 'Beginning of Iron and Social Change in India', *Indian Studies: Past and Present*, vol. 14, No. 4, pp. 329–38.

[9] Although the Brāhmī and Kharoṣṭhī scripts emerged together, for the major part of India it was Brāhmī which was in use.

[10] For a general survey of the trade networks of this period, the following works may be consulted: G.L. Adhya, *Early Indian Economics* (Bombay, 1966); E.H. Warmington, *The Commerce Between the Roman Empire and India* (Cambridge, 1928); R.E.M. Wheeler, *Rome Beyond the Imperial Frontiers* (London, 1954); P.H.L. Eggermont, 'The Murundas and the ancient trade route from Taxila to Ujjain', *Journal of the Economic and Social History of the Orient*, vol. 9 (1966), pp. 257–96.

[11] No detailed report of Ujjayinī excavations is available yet. Brief notices were published in *Indian Archaeology—A Review (1956–7)*, pp. 20–8; and ibid. (1957–8), pp. 32–6.

[12] See H. Sarkar and B.N. Misra, *Nagarjunakonda* (New Delhi, Archaeological Survey of India, 1980).

[13] R.S. Sharma, in an attempt to add to the empirical base of his hypothesis that decline of trade and urbanism is associated with Indian feudalism (see his *Indian Feudalism*, University of Calcutta, 1965, pp. 65ff), provided the first archaeological documentation of this decline. 'Decay of Gangetic towns in Gupta and post-Gupta times', *Proceedings of the Indian History Congress, 33rd session* (Muzaffarpur, 1972), pp. 92–104; Idem., *Urban Decay in India (c. 300–c. 1000)* (New Delhi, 1987).

early historical sites, both of northern and southern India, the chronology of the decline of this urban phase is not a matter of speculation.[14] Thus if the phenomenon of urbanism is noticeable again from the early medieval period, one may not be off the mark in calling it the third phase of urbanization in India.[15] At the same time to characterize this as a distinct phase in early Indian urban history leaves one with two vital questions: (i) what contributed to the fresh emergence of urbanization after a recognizable, although perhaps not total, lapse? and (ii) in what way did early medieval urbanism differ from early historical urbanism? Once it is categorically asserted that early medieval urbanism represented a distinct phase, there is no way in which one can avoid confronting these two questions. These questions are particularly relevant because the comparison intended in this essay is between the early historical and the early medieval; the proto-historic Indus valley does not come within its purview.

[14] That the decline of the early historical urban phase was a widespread geographical phenomenon is becoming increasingly evident with the progress of empirical research. See V.K. Thakur, *Urbanisation in Ancient India* (New Delhi, 1981), ch. 7: 'Decline of Urban Centres'; R. Champakalakshmi, 'Urban Processes in Early Medieval Tamilnadu'; R.N. Nandi, 'Client, Ritual and Conflict in Early Brahmanical Order', *The Indian Historical Review*, vol. 6, Nos. 1–2 (1979), pp. 74ff.

[15] The use of the term 'third urbanization' seems to have become necessary in view of the current historiography which points to a break in the early historical urbanization sequence but does not at the same time properly recognize early medieval urbanism as a phenomenon to be placed outside the context of the early historical urban phase. For example, V.K. Thakur, who has a lengthy chapter on the decline of early urban centres, starts with a categorical statement: 'Urbanisation in ancient India had two distinct phases' (p. 1). Where does one then place urban centres of the tenth or eleventh centuries? 'Third urbanization' may imply a partial rejection of my earlier views (in 'Trade and Urban Centres in Early Medieval North India'), but the point made in that essay was not so much to underline the continuity of early historical urbanism into the early medieval period as to structurally examine 'urban centres', so often projected as a crucial variable in the idea of 'Indian feudalism'. Cf. R.S. Sharma, *Indian Feudalism.* By talking about distinct phases of urbanization in early India, one may be drawn somewhat towards the two models of urbanization developed by R.M. Adams: the 'Rump' process and the 'Step' process. See *The Evolution of Urban Society (Early Mesopotamia and pre-Hispanic Mexico)* (Chicago, 1966), p. 170. The formulation of 'third urbanization' seems to establish a close parallel between the 'Step' process and the early Indian experience. Adams' model, however, does not provide for an examination of the historical contexts, which alone explain the emergence and collapse of distinct urban stages: the parallel therefore can at best be external.

The hazards of defining an urban centre are more acute in the early medieval context than in the context of the early historical phase. The problem derives largely from the nature of the source material. While there is a happy convergence of archaeological and literary material (and to these was added epigraphical material at a later stage) for the study of early historical urbanism, the only kind of material on which the historian has to depend for information on early medieval urban centres is epigraphic. Indeed the almost total absence of archaeological material on early medieval urban centres is perhaps the chief reason why our understanding of the chronology and character of early medieval urbanism remains imperfect, and will continue to remain so unless, at some time or the other, early medieval archaeology draws the attention of the practising archaeologists of the country. If Taxila or Kauśāmbī, to name only two among many, offer a visual idea of early historical urban centres, or Hampi[16] and Champaner[17] of that of the medieval period, there is not a single urban centre of the tenth or the eleventh century of which we can form a similar idea.[18] Further, early historical urban centres are known both from literature and archaeology; what was known for long from literary references came to be confirmed, though in a necessarily modified form, when literary references were geographically located and excavations exposed various stages of the history of the sites. Literary reference alone cannot provide the definition of an urban centre; archaeologists and historians can more meaningfully start talking about differentiation between an urban and a non-urban centre when the actual dimensions of a settlement are revealed by archaeology.[19] Since early

[16] For Hampi, see A.H. Longhurst, *Hampi Ruins Described and Illustrated* (Madras, 1917); D. Devakunjari, *Hampi* (New Delhi, Archaeological Survey of India, 1970); S. Settar, *Hampi* (Bangalore, 1990).

[17] R.N. Mehta, *Medieval Archaeology* (Delhi, 1979), ch. 18, 'Townplanning at Champaner', pp. 140ff, fig. 5.

[18] The early medieval phase is represented at a number of archaeological sites which have sequences dating to earlier periods, but owing to the absence of a horizontal clearing of this phase it is impossible to form any idea of settlement structure. The archaeological potential of early medieval urban centres is revealed by such sites as Ahar, *Archaeological Survey of India, Annual Report, 1925–1926*, pp. 56–8.

[19] An attempt was made by R.S. Sharma to lay down certain criteria in the context of the early historical sites in 'Decay of Gangetic Towns'; also, *Urban Decay.*

medieval archaeology is still an elusive proposition, historians of early medieval settlements depend entirely on epigraphic data to stipulate the recognizable characteristics of urban centres. The uncertainty of historians in regard to this problem can be illustrated. Writing in general terms on urbanization in Karnataka between AD 973 and 1336, G.R. Kuppuswamy states:

> It is futile to attempt a clear cut classification of medieval economy of Karnataka into different sectors, namely urban and rural. For in actual practice there were many things common to village and town life—industries, banking, fairs, corporations or guilds and religious beliefs. The distinction was only one of degree and not of kind. The villages exhibited more the features of a rural or agricultural economy while the towns or cities betrayed more of an urban or industrial and commercial economy.[20]

Viewed from this angle it is futile to attempt any distinction at all, since the 'distinction of degree' is impossible to measure; nevertheless the quotation does underscore the basic difficulty of isolating and defining a settlement as urban without being arbitrary.

The two major preliminary problems in the study of early medieval urban centres are thus of locating them among rather voluminous epigraphic references to place names of the period, and of explaining their growth. Both call for sifting the epigraphic material with caution.

II

If archaeology is more or less silent on the dimensions of early medieval settlements, how should one determine their nature? The initial method is to depend on contemporary perceptions regarding the differential characters and typologies of the settlements. These perceptions are conveyed by the use of terminologies which (as in the early historical period) relate to what must have been distinguishable categories, although the distinctions could not have been immutable. In fact we have evidence of attempts to transfer, under certain situations, settlements of one category into another.[21] The range of both

[20] *Economic Conditions in Karnataka, AD 973–AD 1336* (Dharwar, 1975), p. 95.
[21] For examples of this in early medieval Karnataka, see G.S. Dikshit, *Local Self-government in Medieval Karnataka* (Dharwar, 1964), pp. 140–2.

early historical and early medieval settlement terminology, if we are to use literary references as well, is extensive. The major categories for the early historical period are those of *grāma, nigama, pura, nagara* and *mahānagara*,[22] and although *nigama* seems to have been in infrequent use in the later period, there was really no break in the use of the terms *grāma* and *pura* or *nagara*. This indicates that the idea of two essentially different categories of settlements, representing two opposite points on a continuum pole, continued to survive, whatever the stages in the history of urbanism.[23]

Yet this polarity at the conceptual level is not enough, since *pura* or *nagara* seem at the same level to have represented some form of ranking as well, and the use of the *pura* or *nagara* suffix could easily have been a way of underlining the assumed or induced status of a particular settlement space. Admittedly then, among the multitude of settlement names mentioned and very infrequently described in any detail in epigraphs, it is hazardous, without applying further tests, to try and locate urban centres and comprehend their structure.

Clues to further tests are, fortunately, provided by the epigraphs themselves. In the majority of cases, villages appear in the epigraphs in the context of grants of land.[24] The reference may be to an individual village or to villages distributed around the village in which the grant was made. The object of the grant and the details associated with it almost invariably occur in the context of space which the records themselves specify as rural. So when one comes across cases where the object of grant and its associated details are sharply different, one can legitimately assume that the nature of the spatial context in which the grant was made was necessarily different. The objects of grant in this

[22] For discussions on units and terminologies of settlements, see N. Wagle, *Society at the Time of the Buddha* (Bombay, 1966), ch. 2; A. Ghosh, ch. 3.

[23] For a brief discussion of urban terminology, see B.D. Chattopadhyaya; also R.N. Nandi. Nandi cites O.P. Prasad's dissertation to show that such terms as *pura, durga, rājadhanī* and *skandhāvāra*, which occur in the epigraphs of the sixth-tenth centuries, are replaced by *pattana, nagara, mahāpattana, mahānagara* in the eleventh-thirteenth centuries.

[24] For the general features of such documents, see D.C. Sircar, *Indian Epigraphy* (Delhi, 1965), ch. V. Epigraphs also refer to the creation of rural habitats in areas previously not settled, and the distribution of land by specifying shares in such areas would indicate the stress put on bringing the land under cultivation.

different spatial context consist of levies on industrial items locally manufactured or brought from outside, on items brought for purposes of sale or exchange, on shops and residential quarters, and so on. Land is not entirely absent as an object of grant in such spatial contexts, but only rarely does one find it even as a subsidiary item.

The two types of grants thus relate to how spaces are differently occupied and used, and with this primary distinction in epigraphic references to early medieval settlements one can tentatively perceive the difference between rural and non-rural spaces. Thus, irrespective of whether rural space incorporated such activities as industry or commerce, land as the major item of grant would be the determinant of its nature as a human settlement; if the major object of grant, by contrast, relates to industrial and/or commercial items, then the spatial context within which such grants are made can justifiably be characterized as non-rural. It is perhaps necessary to add that a study of the different natures of the grants is essential since, despite its volume, the epigraphic material almost invariably records various types of grants.

There is one more general feature of the epigraphic evidence bearing on this distinction. Land, cultivated or uncultivated—and occasionally residential—being the major object of grant in rural space, there is hardly any need in epigraphs to furnish details of the rural settlement structure. The reference is specifically to land donated in relation to surrounding plots and villages. Although a typical village settlement is known to have consisted of three components, the *vāstu* (residential land), *kṣetra* (cultivable) and *gocara* (pasture),[25] the relationship between the three is generally absent in epigraphic material, except perhaps in south Indian records.[26] It can therefore be assumed that one is moving away from a purely rural landscape when one comes across references (although provided in fragments in the

[25] For discussions on various components of rural settlements, see A.K. Chaudhary, *Early Medieval Village in North-Eastern India (AD 600–1200)* (Calcutta, 1971), ch. 3; also, B.D. Chattopadhyaya, *Aspects of Rural Settlements and Rural Society in Early Medieval India* (Calcutta, 1990).

[26] For an introduction to the material bearing on rural settlements in early medieval Tamilnadu, see the interesting paper by N. Karashima, 'The Village Communities in Chola times: Myth or Reality', *Journal of the Epigraphical Society of India*, vol. 8 (1971), pp. 85–96, now included in his *South Indian History and Society: Studies from Inscriptions AD 850–1800* (Delhi, 1984), pp. 40–5.

same category of material) to centres of exchange, residential structures and their occupants, manufacturing quarters, functionally different streets, and so on.[27]

This should not suggest, however, that a rural settlement was essentially devoid of such features. It appears that urban centres can be identified from among a multitude of references in epigraphic records only by isolating what is stereotypical of the rural. This has nothing to do with the mention of a place as a *grāma* or a *nagara*; it is the relevance of how much is described in the context of what is being recorded that will finally count in assessing the character of each settlement. The method proposed here is admittedly inadequate and will appear more so whenever an attempt is made at detailed empirical study, and while preparing a distribution map of the urban centres of the period. For the present, however, the epigraphs do not appear to offer many more options.

III

Having suggested that urban centres of the early medieval period may be so considered because they are presented in epigraphic sources of the period as spatial units distinguishable from more readily recognizable rural ones, one is led to ask if this difference can be stretched, on the strength of the ideally exclusive categories of *grāma* and *nagara*, to the point of polarity. This question is to a large measure related to the problem of the genesis of urban spaces because acceptance of the idea of polarity—in spatial as well as social terms—would correspond to viewing urban settlements as growths from above. This, while not placing urban settlements totally outside the context of rural settlements, would nevertheless tend to suggest that the sphere of interaction between the two was largely induced.

As growths from above urban centres could be expected to exhibit characteristics of planned settlements, marked to a considerable degree by an absence of the components of rural settlements. There are numerous references in early medieval records to the creation of

[27] See B.D. Chattopadhyaya, 'Trade and Urban Centres in Early Medieval North India' in this collection.

townships by rulers and officials,[28] but not a single record seems to reveal how such settlements were planned. In fact an analysis of such references merely suggests an extension, through official initiative, of an already emergent process; the creation of townships in such cases consisted of laying the foundation of a core exchange centre[29] or a ceremonial centre or a combination of both in areas where there was need for them: such initiatives would hardly be equivalent to the urban process as a whole. Secondly, the very fact that urban centres of various dimensions become readily recognizable in records from a particular point of time immediately relates to the problem of social change, of which urbanization is only an aspect. Considering the nature of the social formation of the early medieval period, urban centres were likely to represent 'an extension of that of the countryside'.[30] However, if this perspective is adopted, it cannot then be added in the same breath that they have to be viewed 'as works of artifice . . . erected above the economic construction proper'.[31] Indeed they could not be, since it

[28] Ibid. Also, T. Venkateswara Rao, pp. 124ff.

[29] This is conveyed by an interesting passage in a Ghatiyala inscription of AD 861 from the Jodhpur area, which records the establishment of *haṭṭas* and *mahājanas* by a Pratīhāra king: *Epigraphia Indica*, vol. 9, p. 280. References to fairs or periodical markets are quite common in early medieval records, and while fairs cannot be considered necessarily equivalent to urban nuclei they do nevertheless suggest movement and concentrations, which are associated with the urban process. One may here recall the interesting observation of Fernand Braudel: 'town or market or fair, the result was the same—movements towards concentration, then dispersion, without which no economic life of any energy could have been created . . . ' *The Structures of Everyday Life* (London, 1981), p. 503.

[30] John Merrington, 'Town and Country in the Transition to Capitalism', in *The Transition from Feudalism to Capitalism*, introduced by Rodney Hilton (London, 1982), p. 178.

[31] Karl Marx, *Grundrisse* (Penguin edition, Harmondsworth, 1973), p. 479. Marx applies this statement to 'really large cities', which he would consider 'merely as royal camps'. Apart from the fact that the two constituents of the sentence sound somewhat contradictory—mere royal camps being in the nature of really large cities—Marx's characterization of 'Asiatic' cities leaves, by merely suggesting 'the indifferent unity of town and countryside', the issue of the emergence of towns as non-rural settlements unaccounted for. After all, 'ruralization of the city as in antiquity', to use his expression, is a general proposition and does not decrease the burden of finding out what is distinct between town and country. In fact Marx's formulation regarding the Asiatic city, if one goes by the statement in the *Grundrisse*, is a component of his Asiatic Mode of Production formulation. Parallel to its

was the nature of the economy which largely determined the spatial and social shape that the urban centres took.

To the issue of genesis must be added another dimension on which I have already focused, namely that the spurt of a new phase of urbanism became noticeable several centuries after the earlier phase had become moribund. There is no reason to suppose that the spurt in early medieval urbanism became possible only with a noticeable revival in India's external trade network,[32] or with the arrival of new cultural elements with the establishment of the Sultanate;[33] to stress this is to miss an important element in the significant changes taking place in the earlier period to which the establishment of the Sultanate added substantially. The existence of fully developed urban centres in some parts of the country can be traced to the close of the ninth century, if not earlier.[34] References to them increase numerically, suggesting the crystallization of a process, and unlike the early historical urban phase there is no suggestion as yet that this phase too reached a stage of decay. The early medieval thus seems to have advanced into the medieval, although this is a surmise which can only be validated by substantial empirical work.

A work which deals with corporate activities in the Andhra region from between AD 1000 and 1336 and dwells at some length on urban

---

dichotomy between the Absolute Despot and society is the dichotomy between the large city and the countryside.

[32] See L. Gopal, *The Economic Life in Northern India, c. AD 700–1200* (Delhi, 1965); A. Appadorai, *Economic Conditions in Southern India (AD 1000–1500)*, vol. I (Madras, 1936), ch. 5.

[33] Irfan Habib's suggestion that there was 'considerable expansion of the urban economy' during the Sultanate, is fully convincing (see his 'Economic History of the Delhi Sultanate—an Essay in Interpretation', *The Indian Historical Review*, vol. 4, No. 2, 1978, pp. 287–303), but the degree and nature of this expansion will have to be assessed in relation to the kind of change that surely was taking place in the pre-Sultanate period. The epigraphic data of the tenth to thirteenth centuries relating to the number and distribution of urban centres, whatever the inadequacies of the estimates available at present, make one hesitant about accepting Habib's tentative statement: 'It is possible that there was a modest revival of commerce and towns before the Ghorian conquests . . . ' 'The Peasant in the Indian History', Presidential Address, The Indian History Congress, 43rd session (Kurukshetra, 1982), p. 34, fn. 4.

[34] B.D. Chattopadhyaya, 'Trade and Urban Centres in Early Medieval North India'.

organizations[35] lists several factors which resulted in urban growth in the region: (i) the holding of fairs; (ii) the emergence of religious centres; (iii) commercial activities centred around ports; (iv) the bestowal of urban status on rural settlements; (v) initiatives taken by kings and ministers in the creation of urban centres, and so on. A basically similar approach to causality is present in a substantive recent study on the urbanization process in south India in which the growth of Kuḍamūkku-Palaiyārai, twin cities of the Colas in the Kaveri valley, is analysed.[36] The factors which seem to be highlighted in the context of the growth of this complex are: (i) the geographical location, making it 'a point of convergence of all major routes which passed through the core region of the Cola kingdom'; (ii) trade, which, however, to begin with, was 'incidental in the process of urbanization'; (iii) importance as a centre of political and administrative activities; and (iv) religious importance, indicated by the presence of a large number of temple shrines. In fact the study speaks of 'four major criteria' which 'emerge as determinant factors in urban development, leading to the evolution of four main categories of urban centres', although it is underlined 'that in most cases, while trade was a secondary factor, religious activity was a dominant and persistent, though not necessarily the sole, factor'.[37]

[35] T. Venkateswara Rao, pp. 124–5.

[36] R. Champakalakshmi, 'Growth of Urban Centres in South India . . . '

[37] Ibid., p. 26. The facts that temple shrines were the most dominant monuments of the urban landscape and that the available records mostly relate to them have considerably coloured the perspective regarding the growth of urban centres. This is evident, for example, from the juxtaposition of the statements which K.R. Hall makes regarding the urban complex of Tiruvidaimarudur. In trying to controvert Burton Stein's argument that the religious importance of such a centre comes first, Hall states, 'Tiruvidaimarudur, strategically located at an important intersection of the Kaveri communication network, had natural advantages which encouraged its development as a centre of exchange'; and further, 'Tiruvidaimarudur's *nagaram* fulfilled the area's commercial needs, specialising as the centre of a community of exchange . . . [It] was the locus for local economic interaction with higher order networks of exchange'. And yet the temple remains the final contributory factor: 'Tiruvidaimarudur provides an example of an urban centre which as a major religious hub was a participant in the pilgrimage networks of that era, but also, and possibly as a consequence of this influx of religious pilgrims, developed as a supra-local centre of consumption as well, requiring goods supplied not only by area residents but also goods acquired from distant places: e.g. condiments used in temple rituals as well

One could add a few more to the list of the multiplicity of factors behind each historical phenomenon; but while the factor complex approach may be of some use in understanding the separate personalities of contemporary settlement centres, the simultaneity with which factors became operative ultimately calls for a look at the process of which the factors were many facets. It is necessary to see what separates one phase from another and explain how one phase gradually changes over to another.

In a study of early medieval urban centres no detailed reconstruction is possible of the stages of their growth since archaeology alone can unravel these stages. Epigraphy, when it happens to refer to an urban centre, presents us with a *fait accompli*, and it is rare to find epigraphic material on an urban centre covering a long chronological span. How then is the process to be reconstructed?

The epigraphic references to urban centres—keeping in mind the criteria laid down above—present, among a variety of other details, two crucial items of information. The first relates to their linkage with the space outside. The second bears on the nucleus or nuclei within an urban area through which interaction, as a regular urban activity, takes place. These two features are present more or less uniformly in relevant epigraphs from different regions, and a digression will be in order to introduce some empirical material on the significance of these two interrelated features for a study of early medieval urban growth.

Two inscriptions, both dated to the tenth century and belonging to the region of the Kalacuris, refer to the existence of about seven urban centres in the Jabalpur area of Madhya Pradesh.[38] Of these, some details regarding two centres are available. The Karitalai record, coming from the watershed area between the upper Son and the Narmada,[39] of the time of Lakṣmaṇarāja II, mentions four major categories of grants to a newly constructed temple and the brāhmaṇas

---

as provisions for the consumption of visitors to the temple compound', K.R. Hall, 'Peasant State and Society in Chola times: A View From the Tiruvidaimarudur Urban Complex', *Indian Economic and Social History Review*, vol. 18, Nos. 3–4 (1981), pp. 397–8.

[38] V.V. Mirashi, 'Inscriptions of the Kalachuri-Chedi Era', *Corpus Inscriptionum Indicarum*, vol. 4, part I (Ootacamund, 1955), pp. 204–24.

[39] Ibid., pp. 186–95.

associated with it:[39a] (i) villages and fields, all located within a distance of about twenty miles (see map on facing page); (ii) *khalabhikṣā* or levies from threshing floors of the *maṇḍala*, probably a term denoting the geographical unit within which the urban centre was located; (iii) levies on agricultural produce—covering, it would seem, both food-grains and commercial items—as well as industrial items brought to the *purapattana* or the township for sale; and (iv) income from fairs held at the place. The second record, from Bilhari[40] in the same geographical region and datable to the close of the tenth century in the period of Yuvarāja II, provides a more detailed list of articles brought to the *pattanamaṇḍapikā* and of the levies imposed on them in the form of cash: salt (the quantity of which is specified and expressed in a term not understandable); products from oilmills; betelnuts; black pepper; dried ginger; varieties of vegetables, and so on. Items of considerable value on the sale of which levies were also imposed were horses and elephants.

To start with, let us assume that these two represent the typical urban centres of the early medieval period.[41] The epigraphs provide only partial glimpses of them; nevertheless several things are clear. First, there is the imposition of levies as a source of urban income, indicating the nature of activities predominant at the urban centres; second, the nucleus of urban space in which urban economic activities take place; third, the nature of the interaction with settlements outside; and, finally, the nature of urban hierarchy, which may be derived from an analysis of their respective networks.

Both Karitalai and Bilhari, as the epigraphs would have us view them, were centres of exchange of goods. The centre of this activity was the *maṇḍapikā*, a term which literally means 'a pavilion' but the

[39a] Another Kalacuri record, also of the time of Lakṣmaṇarāja II, calls this centre Somasvāmīpura, B.C. Jain, 'Kalachuri Inscription from Karitalai', *Epigraphia Indica*, vol. 33 (1959–60), pp. 186–8.

[40] Ibid., pp. 204–24.

[41] Both Karitalai and Bilhari appear to have been urban centres of modest dimensions with a limited range of functions, but they are nevertheless useful as samples of the kind of urban settlements which were coming up in the early medieval period. It is profitable to refer to Braudel again in this context: 'it would be a mistake only to count the sun-cities . . . Towns form hierarchies everywhere, but the tip of the pyramid does not tell us everything, important though it may be', pp. 482–3.

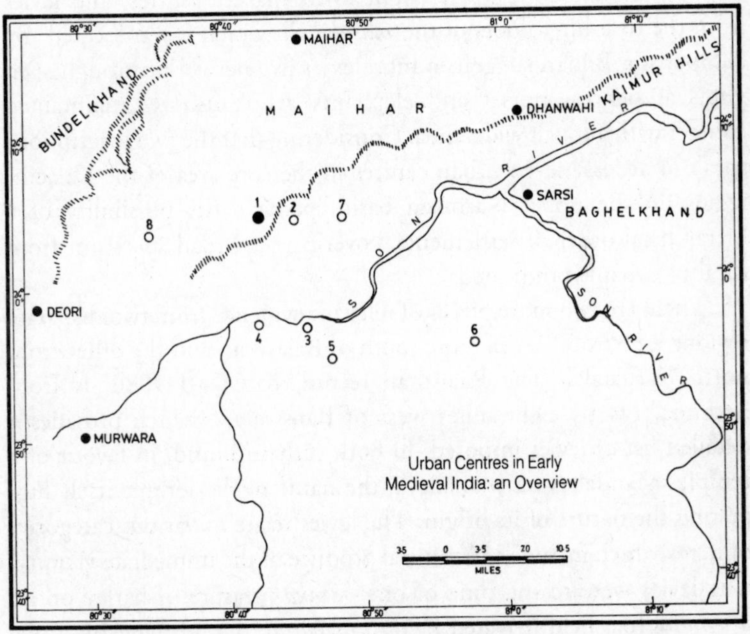

Karitalai and its neighbouring places.

1. Karitalai or Somasvâmīpura
2. Brahmapurī or settlement of brâhmaṇas; identified with Bamhori, 2 miles east of Karitalai.
3. Dīrghaśâkhika: Village donated by king; identified with Dighi, 6 miles southeast of karitalai.
4. Cakrahradī, village granted by queen with the permission of the King; identified with Chakadabi, 7 miles south of Karitalai.
5. Dhavala: *âhâra* or administrative unit in which the village of Challipataka was located; identified with Dhawaia, 4 miles south of Dighi.
6. Challipâṭaka: village given by the prince; identified with Chilhari, about 11 miles east of Dhavala.
7. Antarapâṭa: appears to have been another donated village; identified with Amaturra, 7 miles east of Karitalai.
8. Vaṭagartikâ: donated village; identified with Barhati, 10 miles west by south of Karitalai.

contextual meaning of which is suggested by its survival in the form of *mandi* in Hindi and *mandai* in Marathi. For Karitalai the range of spatial interaction seems to have remained limited to its immediate rural context, not only because the epigraph does not mention any item of exchange which could be of distant origin but also because the centre derived its resources, *inter alia*, from its immediate rural hinterland. These were villages and land assigned to its inhabitants, imposts on varied articles brought to its market centres, and levies from the threshing floors of the *maṇḍala* in which it was located. By comparison Bilhari suggests a more extensive network: through such items as pepper, horses and elephants, its *maṇḍapikā* maintained contact with a much wider area. Considering that the two inscriptions speak of at least seven urban centres in the core area of the Kalacuri region in the upper Narmada basin, perhaps the possibility of a hierarchical order of settlements, covering the broad spectrum from rural to urban, is indicated.

There are two more pieces of relevant evidence from two disparate regions, one from the extreme south of Rajasthan and the other from north Karnataka. The Rajasthan record, dated AD 1080, is from Arthuna, twenty-eight miles west of Banswara,[42] which provides a detailed list of levies imposed, in both cash and kind, in favour of a temple, Maṇḍaleśvara Mahādeva, the name of the temple itself suggesting the nature of its origin. The levies relate to various categories of items which include agricultural produce of the immediate vicinity. The levies were to the tune of one *hāraka* measure of barley on an *araghaṭṭa* (i.e. field irrigated by an *araghaṭṭa*), one *dramma* on a pile of sugarcane and a *bharaka* measure on twenty packs of loaded grain (*bhāṇḍadhānyānām*). The imposts on merchants and merchant organizations are mentioned separately from those on items sold at the market centre (*haṭṭa*). On each *bharaka* measure of candied sugar and jaggery (*khaṇḍagurayorbharakam*) belonging to the traders (*vaṇijām*) was imposed an amount which is not intelligible from the record; on each *bharaka* measure of *mañjiṣṭhā*, which obviously was to be used

[42] *Epigraphia Indica*, vol. 14, pp. 295–310. See also H.V. Trivedi, 'Inscriptions of the Paramāras, Chandellas, Kachchapaghātas and Two Minor Dynasties', *Corpus Inscriptionum Indicarum*, vol. 7.2 (Delhi, n.d.). pp. 286–96.

as a dye, and on thread and cotton, the amount was one *rūpaka.* In another part of the record is mentioned the *vaṇikmaṇḍala* or association of traders, which was required to pay one *dramma* each month.

The items which were sold at the market or were associated with it appear to have been subjected to meticulous assessment, although it is impossible to determine the basis on which the amount of impost was worked out. On every *bharaka* of coconuts was assigned one coconut; on each bullock load of salt one *mānaka* measure of salt; one nut on every thousand arecanuts; on every *ghaṭaka* of butter and sesame oil one *pālika* measure; and on each '*kotika* of clothing fabric' one and a half *rūpakas.* Owing to the obsolete terms used in the record, the nature of other items listed cannot be ascertained with any certainty; nevertheless it seems that the decision to impose contributions in cash or in kind was determined on the basis of whether the items were divisible into required shares or not. On each shop of the traders in the market area was fixed a contribution of one *dramma* during the *caitra* festival and the sacred thread festival. The braziers, located in the same area, paid a *dramma* a month, and each distillery, run by the *kalyapālas,* paid four *rūpakas.* Besides, each household was required to pay one *dramma,* whereas the contribution from a gambling house was fixed at two *rūpakas.* The record refers to other items which too were assessed and contributions from which were received either in kind or in some other variety of cash, such as *vṛṣaviṃśopaka,* but owing to the uncertainty of the meanings of the terms used in the record they are left out of the present discussion. In any case they would do no more than supplement the details already given.

The north Karnataka record of 1204 from Belgaum,[43] called Veṇugrāma in the record, is another detailed statement of several varieties of grants. They were made over to Śubhacandra Bhaṭṭāraka, *ācārya* of the Jaina shrine Raṭṭa Jinālaya of Belgaum. The record is of the period of Raṭṭa Kārttavīrya IV of Saundatti; the building of the temple too, as is evident from its name, was an act of patronage by this local ruler. Unlike the records analysed above, the Belgaum record provides a partial glimpse into the layout of urban space by mentioning land,

[43] *Epigraphia Indica,* vol. 13, pp. 15–36, No. A.

including arable land, as an item of grant within the territorial limits of Veṇugrāma. Thus an area, included in the twenty-fourth *haṭṭi* or division of Veṇugrāma, was given on a tenure of *sthalavṛtti*. The context and other details are even more telling:

In the aforesaid Veṇugrāma, in the western course of the great eastern street, on the north of the house of Duggiyara Ṭikāṇa, one house; in the western course of the western street, one house; in the western towngate, one house; in front of the white-plastered building of the god Kapileśvara, on the east of the Sāla-basadi, three houses; on the north of the road going to Āneyakeṛe (elephant's tank), a flower garden of two *mattars* and 276 *kammas* according to the rod of Veṇugrāma; on the west of the great tank of Āḷur of Kaṇamburige, twelve *mattar* of arable land; in the street on the south of the western market, one house, five cubits in width and twenty-one in length.[44]

To this may be added another significant detail, given toward the close of the record, that Raṭṭa Kārttavīrya donated to the Jaina sanctuary four bazaars 'on the east of the high road at the western end of the northern course of the north street'.[45]

The reference to the twenty-fourth *haṭṭi* or division is a sufficient indication not only of the vast dimension of the settlement space marked off as Veṇugrāma but of considerable intermingling of residential-cum-institutional and non-residential space as well. However, the focus of the record shifts immediately to the area of crucial economic activities of Veṇugrāma, which centred around the professionals of two major categories, the merchants and manufacturers. The decision to make a comprehensive coverage of items on which levies were imposed for the purpose of contribution to the sanctuary of Śāntinātha emanates from an assembly composed of the professionals of these two categories, headed by their leaders.

The category of merchants includes not only the *mummuridaṇḍas* of Veṇugrāma itself; it also comprises several groups of itinerant traders: the *pattanigas* of the total hereditary area of the Raṭṭas, namely Kundi, 3,000; the traders of Lāḷa or south Gujarat and those of Maleyāḷa or Kerala. Their representation in the assembly is understandable since they were all involved in the movement of a great bulk

[44] Ibid., lines 42–5.
[45] Ibid., line 59.

of goods that converged at Veṇugrāma. Since the terms used in the record for indicating quantity elude explanation, only a bare list of items which are specifically mentioned as coming from outside is all that can be provided.[46] They include various loads of paddy as well as husked rice, suggesting the importance of the cereal as an item of import (this supposition is further strengthened by references to separate levies on bazaars of paddy shops and shops of husked rice),[47] loads of black pepper, asafoetida, green ginger and turmeric, betel leaves and arecanuts, coconuts, palm leaves and grass, sugarcane and coarse sugar, plantains and myrobalans. The list further extends to include raw and consumer items such as cotton and finished cloth, parcels of perfumery and horses.[48] What is curious and defies explanation, however, is why the assembly decided to grant immunity on all imports 'in the case of sixty-five oxen and buffaloes, however they be laden'.[49] Since the loads are not specified, this clearly deprives us of further details of the goods that came to Veṇugrāma from outside.

Despite its monotony, it was necessary to consolidate the list given above on the basis of the record: its range, covering a wide variety from paddy to horses, can alone make the composition of merchants who participated in the economic and other activities at Veṇugrāma—as also the nature of transactions which obviously formed the core of its activities—understandable. There was a range of goods, starting from those which can be related to Veṇugrāma's immediate rural context to those which could be brought only through the organizations of professional itinerant merchants. The local participants in the assembly, besides the *mummuridaṇḍas*, were headed by goldsmiths, clothiers, oil merchants and others. The imposts on local manufactures were on clothiers' shops, a goldsmith's 'booth', a jeweller's shop and a perfumer's shop.[50] It is impossible to ascertain the point of time at which Veṇugrāma started developing as a centre of manufacture. All that the Belgaum record suggests is that a space, initially of a rural character and still retaining a measure of that character, came, over

[46] Ibid., lines 53–8.
[47] Ibid., lines 54–5.
[48] Ibid., lines 51–3.
[49] Ibid., lines 51–2.
[50] Ibid., lines 52–3.

time, to be a point of convergence of goods, obviously from varied distances, and of specialized items of manufacture for sale. If there were other crafts which did not come under the purview of imposts, the record has very naturally chosen to ignore them.

Starting from the significant fact that the urban settlement mentioned in the Belgaum record of 1204, which included cultivable land within a defined urban space, was known as Veṇugrāma, several inferences can be drawn from the early medieval evidence discussed so far. Although not invariably in a uniform manner, urban space represented a slow transformation of rural space, perhaps reflecting in most cases a non-nuclear organization of such space.[51] Epigraphy provides inadequate evidence on how a total urban space was defined, but considering what was relevant to this evidence *haṭṭa* or *maṇḍapikā* emerge as key terms for understanding the core of the urban space structure. They appear to have combined manufacture and exchange—two dominant activities of any settlement worth being considered a township. That their potential as sources of revenue is recognized by the ruling elite is the criterion by which such activities are assumed to be dominant. The details of items of exchange vary from one centre to another, but there is one common denominator: the mobilization of agricultural products, both in the form of foodgrains and commercial items, at certain points in space where the act of exchange is intermingled with other economic and non-economic activities. It is essential to remember that the process of mobilization has a history which precedes the imposition of levies—an event with which alone the epigraphs are concerned—as a form of religious patronage. In other words, the 'ceremonial' or 'ritual' centres which represented the important foci of many urban settlements were themselves part of a system of resource mobilization and redistribution.

[51] This has been suggested elsewhere as well with regard both to the urban centres of early historical and early medieval periods: B.D. Chattopadhyaya, 'Mathurā from the Śuṅga to the Kuṣāna Period: An Historical Outline' in Doris M. Srinivasan, ed., *Mathurā: The Cultural Heritage* (Delhi, 1989), pp. 19–30; Idem, 'Urban Centres in Early Bengal: Archaeological Perspectives' (forthcoming). This, however, should not be taken to mean that there was no nucleation of professional or caste groups within the urban space. Early medieval records, in fact, abound in references to such agglomerations.

The total complex of these will have to be underscored if one were to understand the specificity of the urbanization process in early medieval India.

The 'gross' surplus[52] which constituted the subsistence base of this urbanization covered a noticeably wide range of commercial and industrial items, including commercial crops. The production and variety of these appear, from the surveys available for this period, to have been on the increase.[53] The exchange 'nodes' pre-suppose a productive rural hinterland, and that this essential link has not gone entirely unnoticed is evident from the relationship which has sometimes been suggested between some urban centres and their local rural contexts. Of Kuḍamūkku-Palaiyārai in the Cola region the following comments bring out the relevance of this relationship:

> Numerous peasant settlements arose in this region from the Sangam period down to the thirteenth century, forming the main resource base of the Colas. The crucial stage in its development into an urban centre would be the period of the proliferation of *brahmadeyadevadānas,* the seventh to ninth centuries AD, henceforth a continuous phenomenon, showing the availability of sufficient resources for supporting a large population.[54]

Similarly Māmallapuram, which, in the reign of Rājarāja I, was administered by a *mānagaram*—signifying its status as an urban centre—'was said to have received the products of the fifty villages of Āmūr Koṭṭam (the regional unit of government) that were under the juris-

[52] For an elaboration of the concept of 'gross-surplus', see R.M. Adams, *The Evolution of Urban Society,* p. 46.

[53] While any estimate, in comparative terms, would be impossible to cite, this is an impression which general works on early medieval India seem to convey: (i) references to frequency and variety of such crops; (ii) regular movements of such crops for purposes of exchange. See A.K. Chaudhary, ch. 6; P. Niyogi, pp. 23–37; B.P. Mazumdar, *Socio-economic History of Northern India (1030–1194 AD)* (Calcutta, 1960), pp. 177–80; S. Gururajachar, *Some Aspects of Economic and Social Life in Karnataka (AD 1000–1300)* (Mysore, 1974), ch. 3. G.R. Kuppuswamy has attempted a distribution map of crops in Karnataka from between the close of the tenth and the middle of the fourteenth century; see Kuppuswamy, pp. 60–6, map facing p. 48.

[54] R. Champakalakshmi, 'Growth of Urban Centres in South India', p. 22.

diction of a Coḷa official'.[55] Veṇugrāma is similarly believed to have been the chief town of a small district of seventy villages.[56]

Despite their disparate geographical locations the point to be considered regarding urban centres is the kind of centripetality of surplus flow which alone could make urbanization a viable socio-economic process. The mobilization of surplus is invariably associated with an 'elaboration of complex institutional mechanisms'.[57] The mechanisms of production and mobilization of agricultural items—which have been underlined as the major economic activities that generated and sustained urban centres of the early medieval period—are ultimately tied up with the hierarchized structure of the polity in the period.[58] An elaboration of this linkage is not possible within the brief span of this essay. It suffices to say that this complex power structure not only skimmed the surface of what was brought to the market in the form of levies but that, in the final analysis, this structure was responsible for drawing the rural productive units—and groups with exchangeable commercial items—into the network of urban centres. It could do this because the various groups of élites were not only the ideal customers for circulating high value goods but because they were also, in a complex situation of land distribution (partly characterized by the system of assignments), the ultimate destination towards which the surplus was to move.

IV

If the urbanization process of the early medieval period with its continuity into the medieval period is taken as a case of the third phase of urbanization, in what ways did it differ from early historical urbanization? Only a tentative response to this question is attempted here. It has been remarked that early historical urban centres were all characterized by, first, being centres of political power, second, by

[55] K.R. Hall, *Trade and Statecraft in the Age of the Colas* (New Delhi, 1980), p. 166.

[56] *Epigraphia Indica*, vol. 13, p. 18.

[57] R.M. Adams, p. 46.

[58] For details, see R.S. Sharma, *Indian Feudalism*, chs 2 and 5; B.N.S. Yadava, ch. 3.

large agricultural hinterlands, and third, by their location along well developed trade routes.[59] The conjunction of these features may go well with the earliest phase of early historical urbanization, but it is doubtful if this conjunction continued with the horizontal expansion of the urbanization process. In the context of early historical urbanism it is legitimate to think in terms of an epicentre—really the region spread over the stretch of the upper Ganges and middle Ganges basin—and a subsequent expansion reaching out in stages to different parts of the subcontinent. There thus developed a wide network accentuated by new factors, which accounts for a certain uniformity in cultural items unearthed by archaeology at the early urban centres. They did each have an agrarian base, with the exception perhaps of those which, with their littoral locations, were more tied up with maritime trade than with an agricultural hinterland. But it is not adequate to try to understand early urban centres, particularly those of the early centuries of the Christian era, only in terms of their interaction and integration with an immediate hinterland. If Taxila was one point in the network which linked up early urban centres, the other points could well have been as distant as Pāṭaliputra in the east, Barygaza in the west and Ter or Paithan in the south.[60]

Early medieval urban centres did not have an epicentre, even though it may be empirically established that urban centres in different regional contexts represent different chronological stages. There is again no lack of interregional linkage, for we do often come across references to the presence of distant merchants in various urban centres.[61] But there is nothing in the records which could indicate the

[59] Dilip K. Chakrabarti, 'Concept of Urban Revolution and the Indian Context', *Puratattva* (Bulletin of the Archaeological Society of India), No. 6 (1972–3), pp. 30–1.

[60] See, as illustration of this, the evidence of *The Periplus of the Erythraean Sea*, translated and edited by W.H. Schoff (reprinted in Delhi, 1974), pp. 41–3.

[61] Evidence for the itinerary of *nānādeśis* or merchants of disparate regional origins is more readily available for the south than the north; B. Stein, 'Coromandel Trade in Medieval India', in John Parker, ed., *Merchants and Scholars* (University of Minnesota Press, 1965), pp. 47–62; K.R. Hall, *Trade and Statecraft in the Age of the Coḷas*, ch. 6; S. Gururajachar, *Some Aspects of Economic and Social Life in Karnataka (AD 1000–1300)*, ch. 5. However, in different parts of north and west India too, distant merchants can be seen to converge at points which serve as foci of commercial transactions. See, for example, *Epigraphia Indica*, vol. I, pp. 184–90;

regularity of such exchanges on a subcontinental level, notwithstanding the possibility that certain prized items of trade may have had a fairly extensive itinerary. Epigraphic evidence bearing on the range of interaction of early medieval urban centres *seems* to suggest that they were far more rooted in their regional contexts than their early historical predecessors. No early medieval centre seems to be comparable—and the absence of archaeological information alone may not be a sufficient explanation—with such early fortified settlements as Kauśāmbī or Ahicchatrā, but it may be significant that the estimates available regarding the numerical strength of early medieval urban centres suggest a high incidence. The estimates are imperfect, irregular and only incidentally done, and are cited only for their dubious worth.

According to one estimate the Malwa area in the Paramāra period had twenty towns.[62] The number is eight, obviously an extremely low figure, for the Caulukya period in Gujarat.[63] T. Venkateswara Rao estimates the number to have been more than seventy in Andhra between 1000 and 1336,[64] and Dasaratha Sharma has compiled a list of 131 places in the Cāhamāna dominions, 'most of which seem to have been towns'.[65] In a century-wise estimate for Karnataka, made on the basis of epigraphic sources, it has been shown that compared to seventeen in the seventh century and 'more than twenty-one' in the eighth century there was a 'sudden increase' from the tenth century onward, and 'more than seventy-eight towns are noticed in the inscriptions of the eleventh century'.[66] The numbers are clearly uneven, and this is largely due to the absence of any criteria for identifying urban centres.

But the estimates do make one positive point: the emergence of centres which could be considered distinct from rural settlement units was phenomenal in the early medieval period. This is not surprising

The Indian Antiquary, vol. 58, pp. 161ff.

[62] R.S. Sharma, *Indian Feudalism*, p. 245.

[63] P. Niyogi, pp. 120–1.

[64] T. Venketeswara Rao, pp. 124–9; map 3.

[65] D. Sharma, *Early Chauhan Dynasties (A Study of Chauhan Political History, Chauhan Political Institutions and Life in the Chauhan Dominions from c. 800 to 1316 AD)* (Delhi, 1959), pp. 311–16.

[66] O.P. Prasad, 'A Study of Towns in Karnataka', pp. 151–9.

if considered in the light of the profusion of place names in early medieval records. Since the majority of the urban centres of this period were primarily nodal points in local exchange networks, the numerical strength of settlements and the growth in the number of locality elites would tend to result in the proliferation of urban centres of relatively modest dimensions. They would thus reflect the character of the economy and polity of the period: unlike the early historical centres, which were directly linked with centres of authority with supra-regional loci, the majority of the early medieval centres would correspond to different tiers of regional power. Like land, urban settlements too came to be objects of assignment—a phenomenon which further reinforced the intimate linkage between them and their immediate locality.[67]

In the final analysis, however, was the basic nature of early medieval urban centres so very different from that of their predecessors of the early historical period? With our limited understanding it may be too early to say, but even so M.I. Finley's broad typologies of 'consumer' cities and 'commercial' cities, which correspond to cities of the classical and the medieval west respectively, do not seem to relate to the Indian urban phases.[68] If his major variable, the rentiers and revenue collectors, was what characterized the ancient city, this variable was characteristic of both the early historical and early medieval phases of Indian urbanization. At the same time the organizational and occupational specificities of Indian urban centres accommodated the commercial elite, organized into guilds, as a substantial component in their structure. It was this juxtaposition which may have prevented both the emergence of two distinct typologies as well as the Indian urban groups from approximating to the category of the 'burgher' in the medieval west.[69] Even the aspired mobility of the Indian social

[67] For examples of this from the early medieval period, see *Epigraphia Indica*, vol. I, pp. 162–79, document No. 27; ibid., vol. 19, pp. 69–75; the Gurgi record of the Kalacuris, urban centres in whose dominions have been discussed above, also mentions that the king donated a whole city crowded with citizens as a grant (*Puraṃ paurajanākīrṇaṃ samastakaml bhaktyā samarpayāmāsa śāsanatvena bhūpatiḥ*), Mirashi, p. 230, verse 41.

[68] M.I. Finley, 'The Ancient City: From Fustel de Coulanges to Max Weber and Beyond', *Comparative Studies in Society and History*, vol. 19 (1977), pp. 305–27.

[69] Cf. the perceptive comments of Carlo M. Cipolla, 'The Origins', in Carlo M.

groups did not extend beyond validation within the norms of a traditional social order, the broad contours of which remained identical in both early historical and early medieval phases.[70]

Cipolla, ed., *The Fontana Economic History of Europe*, vol. I: *The Middle Ages* (Collins/Fontana, 1973), pp. 12–23. The contrast is brought out also by John Merrington, pp. 178ff.

The separation of the town from the country, which set a pace of change in the medieval west, did not take place in India. It would thus be futile to try to see in the emergence of early medieval towns a possible dissolvent of 'Indian Feudalism'. For a critique of such attempts, see D.N. Jha, 'Early Indian Feudalism: A Historiographical Critique', Presidential Address, Section I, Ancient India, Indian History Congress, 40th session (Waltair, 1979).

[70] *Vaiśyapurāṇamu*, a medieval Telugu *Purāṇa* based apparently on earlier historical events, is an excellent example of this conformity to societal norms. The *Purāṇa* relates to the *Komatis*, also known in early medieval records as *Nakaramu*-102 or merchants of 102 *gotras*. The ascendancy of the merchants is evident from the way they styled themselves lords of the city of Penugoṇḍa and the way they were organized into a highly closed group. Their social organization sought validation not only through claiming the *vaiśya* status but also through rigid observance of the social customs of the community, called *menarikam* or *kulācāra-dharmamu*. For details, see T. Venkateswara Rao, pp. 240–5.

8

Political Processes and Structure of Polity in Early Medieval India[*]

Colleagues,

I am grateful to the Executive Committee of the Indian History Congress for the honour they have done me by inviting me to preside over the Ancient India section at the session this year. I confess that I am as surprised as I am overwhelmed at this honour, not only because my association with the Congress has so far been only minimal but also because my own assessment of my meagre research output, mainly of an exploratory nature, falls far short of the value the Committee have so kindly chosen to attach to it. I suppose being in the profession commits one to the responsibility of presenting one's credentials publicly to fellow-practitioners at some stage or the other; in me the responsibility has evoked a sense of awe, and all that I can do to get over this is to try and turn it to my advantage by bringing to you a problem which, for me, is beginning to take the shape of a major academic concern. Unable to present the results of a sustained empirical research, I am here instead with my uncertainties, but as I see it there can be no better forum for bringing one's problems to than this annual meet of historians, which accommodates various shades of thinking and encourages exchange of ideas beyond narrow barriers.

The problem I refer to concerns the study of polity in early medieval India. There is hardly any need to underline that this erstwhile 'dark period' of Indian history (a characterization deriving incidentally from the 'absence' of vast territorial empires in the period) is fast emerging as one in which significant changes were taking

[*] Presidential Address, Ancient India Section, Indian History Congress, 44th session (Burdwan, 1983).

[Due to constraints of space, I have tried to limit the references to recent writings and to use earlier publications mostly for the purpose of comparison. My thanks are due to Sri Asok V. Settar and especially to Sri P.K. Basant, research students at place[1]—a useful reminder that historical assessments never remain static and need to go through a process of constant revaluation. As one interested in the study of early medieval India, my feeling has been that the problem of the political formation of this period is in an urgent need of revaluation, and while it is presumptuous to think in terms of a single empirical work which will cover the problem at the level of the entire subcontinent, one can at least pose the problem, constant reminders regarding regional variations notwithstanding, at the subcontinental level, from the perspective of the possible processes in operation. My own interest in the study of the early medieval polity derives not so much from the recent spate of publications on the early state and the possibility of analysing early Indian political systems in the light of new ideas[2] but from more pragmatic considerations. The foremost among these is the resurrection, through the study of polity, of an interest in the study of the political history of the period. I apprehend that this sentiment is likely to raise a murmur of protest and I am also likely to be reminded that we have had enough of political history which may be sanctioned well-earned rest for some time to come. I wonder if this is really so, since I feel that historical

---

the Centre for Historical Studies, Jawaharlal Nehru University, for the help that I have received from them in the preparation of this Address].

[1] The stereotype of the 'dark period', however, seems to persist; see Simon Digby in T. Raychaudhuri and Irfan Habib, eds, *The Cambridge Economic History of India*, volume I: *c.* 1200–*c.* 1750 (Cambridge University Press, 1982), pp. 45–7.

[2] Evidence of recent interest in the study of the early state will be found in the range of contributions and bibliographies in two recent publications: H.J.M. Claessen and Peter Skalnik, eds, *The Early State* (Mouton Publishers, 1978); and *The Study of the State* (Mouton Publishers, 1981). The focus of most of the contributions in such publications is on the emergence of the early state which is often distinguished only from the modern industrial state and is therefore of little value in understanding processes of change. Relevant ideas on the emergence of the state have been used for the study of the pre-state and origin of the state society in India by Romila Thapar, 'State Formation in Early India', *International Social Science Journal*, 32.4 (1980), pp. 655–669 and *From Lineage to State:: Social Formation in the Mid-first Millennium* BC *in the Ganga Valley* (Bombay, 1984), and by R.S. Sharma, *Material Culture and Social Formations in Ancient India* (Delhi, 1983); 'Taxation and State Formation in Northern India in Pre-Maurya Times (*c.* 600–300 BC)', reprinted in R.S. Sharma, *Aspects of Political Ideas and Institutions in Ancient India*, third revised edition (Delhi, 1991), ch. 15; Idem, 'From Gopati to Bhupati (a review of the changing position of the king)', *Studies in History*, 2.2 (1980), pp. 1–10.

revaluation of the nature of change in a period implies revaluation of its sources in their entirety. As a teacher of ancient Indian history I notice a growing trend among students to be interested only in 'social and economic history' since political history with its endless dates, genealogical charts and catalogues of battles involves senseless cramming and serves no intellectual purpose at all.[3] Given the nature of ancient Indian political historiography,[4] the distaste is understandable, but if in sheer frustration we turn away from a serious study of political history, we shall, perhaps unwittingly, be leaving out a substantial chunk of Indian history. After all, the study of polity essentially involves an analysis of the nature, organization and distribution of power, and in a state society in which the contours of inequality are sharp, relations of power encompass relations at other levels in some form or the other.[5] Even the seemingly bewildering variety of details of the political history of early medieval India—the absurdly long genealogies, the inflated records of achievements of microscopic king-

[3] It is necessary to keep it in mind that a study of social and economic history by itself is not a sufficient guarantee of the quality of history. Most available monographs on social and economic history of the period, including my own, are no more interesting readings than dynastic accounts.

[4] The dominant trend in the writing of the political history of early medieval India is towards the reconstruction of dynastic accounts, and the trend carried to an extreme has yielded more than one monograph for a single 'dynasty'. We have thus at least three monographs on the Yādavas and the same number of works on the Candellas. For a very useful critique of dynastic reconstruction, through 'concatenation' of distinct segments of the same ruling lineage, see David P. Henige, 'Some Phantom Dynasties of Early and Medieval India: Epigraphic Evidence and the Abhorrence of a Vacuum', *Bulletin of the School of Oriental and African Studies*, 38.3 (1975).

[5] I have only to refer here to the statement made by Perry Anderson in the Foreword to his *Lineages of the Absolutist State* (Verso Edition, London, 1979, p. 11): 'Today, when "history from below" has become a watch-word in both Marxist and non-Marxist circles, and has produced major gains in our understanding of the past, it is nevertheless necessary to recall one of the basic axioms of historical materialism: that secular struggle between classes is ultimately resolved at the *political*—not at the economic or cultural level of society. In other words, it is the construction and destruction of State which seal the basic shifts in the relations of production . . . A "history from above" . . . is thus no less necessary than a "history from below".' Elsewhere (p. 404) he writes: ' . . . pre-capitalist modes of production cannot be defined *except* via their political, legal and ideological superstructures, since these are what determine the extra-economic coercion that specifies them'.

doms, the rapidity of the rise and fall of centres of power—are ultimately manifestations of the way in which the polity evolved in the period and hence is worthy, not so much of cataloguing, but of serious analysis. I make an additional point in justification of my plea for the study of political history by saying that an occasional comparison of notes with the historiography of medieval India would help, because medieval historians have continued to enrich our knowledge of political history and its study is essential for our understanding of that period.[6]

I

The relevant approaches to the study of the early medieval polity will be discussed later; I will begin with a brief reference to the basic opposition between the two broad strands of assumptions that bear upon a study of the Indian polity. In one assumption, polity in pre-modern India is variously characterized as 'traditional'[7] or 'Oriental Despotic';[8] in fact, it has been considered possible by different

[6] A few works which illustrate this interest in what may be called the post-J.N. Sarkar phase may be cited: Satish Chandra, *Parties and Politics at the Mughal Court, 1707–1740*, 3rd edition (Delhi, 1979); M. Athar Ali, *The Mughal Nobility Under Aurangzeb* (Asia Publishing House, 1968); Iqtidar Alam Khan, *The Political Biography of a Mughal Noble Munim Khan Khan-i-Khanan: 1497–1575* (Orient Longman, 1973); and J.F. Richards, *Mughal Administration in Golconda* (Clarendon Press, Oxford, 1975).

[7] 'Traditional polity' is implied in the statements and titles of writings on disparate periods of Indian history, in which a long-term perspective is absent and in most of which the accent is on Kingship and rituals associated with Kingship; see, for example, the following collections, Richard G. Fox, ed., *Realm and Region in Traditional India* (Delhi, 1977); R.J. Moore, ed., *Tradition and Politics in South Asia* (Delhi, 1979); J.F. Richards, ed., *Kingship and Authority in South Asia* (South-Asian Studies, University of Wisconsin, Madison Publication Series, Publication No. 3, 1978). S.N. Eisenstadt's typologies of 'centralized historical bureaucratic empires or States' in which he curiously clubs together Gupta, Maurya and the Mughal empires as 'several ancient Hindu States' also essentially correspond to the notion of 'traditional polity', *The Political System of Empires* (New York, 1969).

[8] That 'Oriental Despotism' characterizes changeless polity and society will be clear from the following statement of K.A. Wittfogel, '. . . varying forms of semi-complex hydraulic property and society prevailed in India almost from the dawn of written history to the 19th Century', *Oriental Despotism: A Comparative Study of Total Power*, 7th Printing (Yale University Press, 1970), p. 260. For the genesis of

individual authors—all apparently subscribing to the assumption of 'traditional polity'—to view political ideas and structures of disparate periods of Indian history in terms of a model of pre-State polity.[9] It would of course be too simplistic to lump a wide variety of writings on traditional pre-modern polity together because both in their empirical and theoretical contents such contributions vary substantially, but basically the broad assumption underlying most of them remains that traditional polity was essentially changeless: 'a continual kaleidoscopic reorientation of a given political and social content'.[10] Opposed

---

the concept of Oriental Despotism, its incorporation into Marx's notion of 'Asiatic mode' and its relevance in the Indian context, see Perry Anderson; Irfan Habib, 'An Examination of Wittfogel's Theory of Oriental Despotism', *Enquiry*, 6, pp. 53–73; 'Problems of Marxist Historical Analysis', in *Science and Human Progress*, Essays in honour of Prof. D.D. Kosambi (Bombay, 1974), pp. 34–47; Romila Thapar, *The Past and Prejudice* (Delhi, 1975); H.J.M. Claessen and P. Skalnik, 'The Early State: Theories and Hypotheses' in *The Early State*, pp. 7–8. Recently D. Lorenzen has argued ('Imperialism and Ancient Indian Historiography' in S.N. Mukherjee, ed., *India: History and Thought*, Essays in honour of A.L. Basham (Calcutta, 1982), pp. 84–102) that Oriental Despotism was a key concept in the pro-Imperialist interpretations of the ancient Indian polity and society and that the concept is present in the writings of nationalist historians in its inverted version.

9 I refer here to the model of the 'segmentary state', constructed by A. Southall on the basis of his study of a pre-state polity in East Africa, *Alur Society: A Study of Processes and Types of Domination* (Cambridge, 1953); for further discussion, Idem, 'A Critique of the Typology of States and Political Systems', in M. Banton, ed., *Political Systems and the Distribution of Power* (ASA Monographs 2, Tavistock Publications, 1968), pp. 113–40. The model is found applicable in the Indian context in relation to the *maṇḍala* theory by J.C. Heesterman, 'Power and Authority in Indian Tradition', in R.J. Moore, pp. 77–8; by Burton Stein in relation to south Indian polity from the Cola period onward: 'The Segmentary State in South Indian History', in R.G. Fox, ed., pp. 1–51 and *Peasant State and Society in Medieval South India* (Oxford University Press, 1980); and by R.G. Fox in the context of the organization of the Rajput clans in Uttar Pradesh in the late Mughal period (without, however, much reference to the Mughals), *Kin, Clan, Raja and Rule: State-Hinterland Relations in Pre-industrial India* (Berkeley, The University of California Press, 1971). For recent vindications of the model in the context of Africa and India in terms of its empirical validity, see A. Southall, 'The Segmentary State in Asia and Africa', *Comparative Studies in Society and History*, vol. 30 (1988), pp. 52–82; B. Stein, 'The Segmentary State: Interim Reflections', in J. Pouchepadass and H. Stern, eds, *From Kingship to State: The Political in the Anthropology and History of the Indian World* (Paris, 1991), pp. 217–37.

10 Fraṇk Perlin, 'The Pre-colonial Indian State in History and Epistemology: A

to this view of 'traditional' polity within which 'early medieval' is not clearly demarcated, is the other assumption which envisages possibilities of change and, curiously, it is within this purview that most empirical studies on early medieval India can be located. Here too views on change or on mechanisms of change are not identical; the majority of works on early medieval political history and institutions in fact contain generalizations which are mutually contradictory. The king in all the monarchical states is the source of absolute power and wields control through bureaucracy; there is thus nothing much to distinguish him from the 'absolute despot' despite his benevolent disposition; and yet, the malaise of polity is generated by feudal tendencies.[11] Change, expressed mostly in terms of dynastic shifts, becomes, in the early medieval context, a concern over the size of the emperor's territory; imperial rulers down to the time of Harṣa endeavoured to stem the tide of disintegration and fragmentation, which is seen as a disastrous change from the ideal imperial pattern and which is invariably assessed against the ultimate failure to retain what used to be called—and I fear many of our much used text books continue to call—the Hindu political order.[12] Concern with the failure of the early medieval political order—a concern not only noticeable in works

---

Reconstruction of Societal Formation in the Western Deccan from the Fifteenth to the Early Nineteenth Century', in H.J.M. Claessen and Peter Skalnik, eds, *The Study of the State*, p. 276.

[11] See, for example, A.S. Altekar, *State and Government in Ancient India*, reprint of 3rd edition (Delhi, 1972), chs 16–17. In the context of south India, while T.V. Mahalingam (*South Indian Polity*, University of Madras, 2nd edition, 1967, ch. 1, sec. 2) talks of checks on royal absolutism and the presence of *sāmantas* or *maṇḍaleśvaras*, K.A. Nilakanta Sastri (*The Colas*, reprint of 2nd edition, University of Madras, 1975, pp. 447–48) characterizes Cola polity as indicating change from 'somewhat tribal chieftaincy of the earlier time' to 'the almost Byzantine royalty of Rājarāja and his successors'. For a relevant discussion, see Lorenzen.

[12] R.C. Majumdar, for example, writes in his preface to *The Struggle for Empire* (vol. 5 of the History and Culture of the Indian people, Bombay, 1957, xliii): 'This volume deals with the transition period that marks the end of independent Hindu rule'. See also K.M. Panikkar's Foreword to Dasarath Sharma's *Early Cauhan Dynasties* (Delhi, 1959). R.C.P. Singh (*Kingship in Northern India, Cir. 600 AD–1200 AD*, Delhi, 1968, ch. 8) analyzes this failure in terms of the nature of Hindu kingship. Most works on the political history of the period dealing with changes in the loci of power are charged with communal overtones, completely ignoring the fact that such shifts were constantly taking place in Indian history.

on political history[13] but a starting point in serious monographs on social and economic history[14] as well—has logically led to value-judgements on the structure of polity; a single quote from a widely-read text book on polity, out of many such available, will serve to illustrate the sentiment common to most historians of early medieval India: '(the) ideal of federal-feudal empire, with full liberty to each constituent state to strive for the imperial status but without permission to forge a unitary empire after the conquest, thus produced a state of continuous instability in ancient India'.[15] I have chosen this quote to underline the kind of ambivalence which permeates the writings even of those who tend to think in terms of change: there is dichotomy between 'constituent state' and 'unitary empire', the dichotomy deriving in the present case from adherence to the model provided by ancient political thinkers; the dichotomy is not timeless because its emergence is located in the fourth century AD and yet it 'produced a state of continuous instability in ancient India', instability being change from the norm, i.e. the centralized, unitary state.

Irrespective of the merit of the terminologies used in these writings, historiographically the interesting correlation is between change in polity and feudalism. 'Feudalism' is thus not a new historiographical convention; its use, limited to the political plane, has been as a synonym for political fragmentation and the term has in fact been shuttled back and forth in Indian history to suit any period in which no 'unitary empire' could be located on the political horizon.[16]

We know that a major breakthrough in the application of this term to the Indian context came in the form of a new genre of empirical works from the fifties;[17] here for the first time 'feudal polity'

[13] D. Sharma, ch. 27.

[14] B.P. Mazumdar, *Socio-economic History of Northern India (1030–1194 AD)* (Calcutta, 1960), preface.

[15] Altekar, p. 388.

[16] H.C. Raychaudhuri (*Political History of Ancient India*, 6th edition, University of Calcutta, 1953, p. 208) speaks of *māṇḍalika-rājas* in the period of Bimbisāra as 'corresponding perhaps to the Earls and Counts of medieval European polity'. A.L. Basham speaks of quasi-feudal order in the pre-Mauryan age, and when 'that empire broke up . . . Mauryan bureaucracy gave way to quasi-feudalism once more', *Studies in Indian History and Culture* (Calcutta, 1964), p. 5.

[17] Serious analytical work of this genre starts with D.D. Kosambi, *An Introduction*

is not an entity-in-itself; through a reasoned argument—irrespective of whether we accept the argument or not—'feudal polity' is shown to be a stage which represents a structural change in the Indian social and economic order; it envisages the emergence of a hierarchical structure of society in place of the binarily opposed entities of the state and the peasantry, and it is basically this hierarchical structure with its different tiers of intermediaries which explains the mechanism of exploitation and coercion of the early medieval state. The distinctive contribution of the study of 'Indian feudalism', from the perspective of the problem I have in view, consists in the attempt to bridge the gap between polity and society.

In concluding this brief review of various strands of opinions on early Indian polity, which tend to be organized into two opposite sets, I feel that the opposition cannot be pushed to any extreme limits. If the feeling represents a curious contradiction, the contradiction is embedded in available historiography. For, even those who work within the framework of traditional polity do not all necessarily work with such ahistorical models as 'Oriental Despotism';[18] similarly, the

---

to the Study of Indian History (Bombay, 1956), and R.S. Sharma's *Indian Feudalism, C. 300–1200* (University of Calcutta, 1965), is the first thoroughly researched monograph on the subject. In terms of documentation another important work is by B.N.S. Yadava, *Society and Culture in Northern India in the Twelfth Century* (Allahabad, 1973). The literature on 'Indian feudalism' is of course growing and useful bibliographical references will be found in R.S. Sharma and D.N. Jha, 'The Economic History of India upto AD 1200: Trends and Prospects', *Journal of the Economic and Social History of the Orient*, 17.1, pp. 48–80; D.N. Jha, 'Early Indian Feudalism: A Historiographical Critique', Presidential Address, Indian History Congress, Ancient India Section, 40th session (Waltair, 1979); H. Mukhia, 'Was there Feudalism in Indian History?', Presidential Address, Medieval India Section, Indian History Congress, 40th session (Waltair, 1979); B.N.S. Yadava, 'The Problem of the Emergence of Feudal Relations in Early India', Presidential Address, Ancient India Section, 41st session (Bombay, 1980).

[18] Compare, for example, two articles by Nicholas B. Dirks written on two different periods of south Indian history: (i) 'Political Authority and Structural Change in Early South Indian History', *The Indian Economic and Social History Review*, 13.2 (1976), pp. 125–158; (ii) 'The Structure and Meaning of Political Relations in a South Indian Little Kingdom', *Contributions to Indian Sociology*, 13.2 (1979), pp. 169–206. B. Stein too (*Peasant State and Society . . .*) attempts to see change from the Cola to the Vijayanagar period. Their perception of change is, of course, not in terms of feudal polity.

current construct of 'feudal polity' carries over elements from past historiography, which in a way hinder the formulation of a long-term perspective of change. The opposition perhaps ultimately lies in the realm of ideologies and perspectives than in the realization of the necessity of study of change. We turn now to the specificity of the problem which this historiographical situation has created for a study of early medieval polity.

II

The structure of the construct of Indian feudalism, which is spoken of as a variant form, rests, so far as the study of polity is concerned, on two interrelated arguments. Since detailed studies of early medieval political formation within the framework of the feudalism hypothesis are still a desideratum,[19] they therefore need to be stated: (i) feudal polity emerged from the gradual breakdown of a centralized bureaucratic state system, empirically represented by the Mauryan state, the implication of the argument being that the emergence of diverse centres of power of the later periods would correspond to a process of displacement of bureaucratic units. Feudal polity, however, crystallized eight centuries after the disintegration of the Mauryan state, although elements of feudal polity—suggested by a two-tier or three-tier structure of the administrative system—are identified in the Kuṣāṇa polity of north India and the Sātavāhana polity of the Deccan;[20] (ii) the system of assignment of land, apparently absent in the Mauryan state because of the practice of remuneration in cash, became wide-

[19] Detailed documentation is found only in R.S. Sharma, *Indian Feudalism*, ch. 2, which analyzes 'feudal polity' in three kingdoms; B.P. Majumdar, chs 1–2, and B.N.S. Yadava, *Society and Culture*, chs 3–4; for a regional pattern, see D.D. Kosambi, 'Origins of Feudalism in Kashmir', *Journal of the Bombay Branch of the Royal Asiatic Society*, 1956–57, pp. 108–120 and Krishna Mohan, *Early Medieval History of Kashmir (with special reference to the Loharas, AD 1003–1171)* (Delhi, 1981), ch. 4. An earlier work, not usually cited but deserving attention for its wealth of material, is N.C. Bandyopadhyaya, *Development of Hindu Polity and Political Theories*, ed. N.N. Bhattacharyya (Delhi, 1980). For recent contributions to the study of the early medieval state, see Y. Subbarayalu, 'The Cola State', *Studies in History*, vol. 4, No. 2 (1982), pp. 265–306; R.N. Nandi, 'Feudalization of the State in Medieval South India', *Social Science Probings* (March, 1984), pp. 33–59.

[20] R.S. Sharma, *Aspects of Political Ideas and Institutions in Ancient India*, 2nd

spread and intermixed with the transfer of the rights of administration, corroding the authority of the state and leading to the 'parcellization' of its sovereignty.[21] It may be interesting to dilate on this characterization of the Mauryan state and its choice as a starting point for the study of feudal polity because at one level it carries over from past historiography the equation: feudal polity=political fragmentation =dismemberment of a centralized state; at another, it represents an unstated search for a proto-type of the state system of the Classical West, the breakdown of which provides a starting point for the study of western feudalism. However, for our purpose, the validity of the arguments stated above can be subjected to a single test: do they sufficiently explain the total political configuration of what is called the feudal formation? The explanation has to relate not to the structures of individual monarchies alone but also to the political geography of the subcontinent at any given point of time—a requirement suggested by frequent shifts in the centres of power and the ongoing process of the formation of new polities as a result of transition from pre-state to state societies. It is considerations such as these which have led to considerable rethinking regarding the Mauryan state itself,[22] which—the focal point in the concentration area of the earlier

---

edition (Delhi, 1968), ch. 15; Kosambi, *An Introduction*, ch. 9; B.N.S. Yadava, 'Some Aspects of the Changing Order in India During the Śaka-Kuṣāṇa Age', in G.R. Sharma, ed., *Kuṣāṇa Studies* (University of Allahabad, 1968), pp. 75–90.

[21] This supposition is based on two sets of evidence: (i) reference in the *Arthaśāstra* (5.3) to payment of state officials in coined money; and (ii) actual circulation of coined money in the Mauryan period. However, there seems to be a contradiction in the *Arthaśāstra* itself; cf. 5.3 with 2.1.7. Even 5.3, which deals with the payment of state officials, states: '. . . He should fix (wages for) the work of servants at one quarter of the revenue, or by payment to servants . . . ' (R.P. Kangle's translation, 2nd edition, Bombay, 1972, p. 302). More importantly, there is no necessary correlation between the circulation of coined money and payment in cash. This will hold true not only for the post-Mauryan period to the fifth century at least but for the medieval period as well, although in the medieval period the remuneration was computed in cash.

[22] Interestingly, Beni Prasad, as early as in 1928, held the 'unitary' character of the Mauryan State as suspect, *The State in Ancient India* (Allahabad, 1928), p. 192; Romila Thapar has considerably changed her views on the character of the Mauryan State: compare *Aśoka And the Decline of the Mauryas*, 2nd edition (Oxford University Press, 1973), ch. 4 with her 'The State as Empire' in H.J.M. Claessen and P. Skalnik, *The Study of the State*, pp. 409–26 and *From Lineage to State*, ch. 3. For other

mahājanapadas of the upper and middle Ganges basin—represents basically a relationship between the nucleus which is the metropolitan state and a range of differentiated polities. The disappearance of the metropolitan Mauryan state did not create a political or economic crisis either in areas where state polity had been in existence or in areas of pre-state polity incorporated within the Mauryan empire. In fact, Mauryan territorial expansion and similar expansions at later times seem to have created a fresh spurt in the emergence of local states in areas of pre-state polity—a phenomenon certainly not to be confused with the process of the decentralization of a centralized administration.[23]

Two further points regarding the current historiography on the genesis of feudal polity need to be made. First, not all criticisms levelled against the use of landgrant evidence for explaining the genesis of feudal polity can be brushed aside lightly. The fact remains that the major bulk of epigraphic evidence relates to *brahmadeyas* and *devadānas*, grants to brāhmaṇas and religious establishments, and the element of contract is largely absent in the system of early and early-medieval landgrants. The presence of a contractual element cannot be altogether denied;[24] it would also be difficult to disagree with the view

---

discussions, I.W. Mabbett, *Truth, Myth and Politics in Ancient India* (Delhi, 1972), chs 5–6; S.J. Tambiah, *World Conqueror and World Renouncer* (Cambridge University Press, 1976), pt. I, ch. 5; Heesterman, 'Power and Authority . . . ', p. 66.

[23] S. Seneviratne, 'Kalinga and Andhra: The Process of Secondary State Formation in Early India', in H.J.M. Claessen and P. Skalnik, eds, *The Study of the State*, pp. 317–37.

[24] See N.C. Bandyopadhyaya; see the important paper of B.N.S. Yadava, 'Secular Landgrants of the Post-Gupta Period and Some Aspects of the Growth of Feudal Complex in North India', in D.C. Sircar, ed., *Land System and Feudalism in Ancient India* (University of Calcutta, 1966), pp. 72–94. The general absence of a contractual element in the vast corpus of epigraphic material seems to be irrefutable; for contents of grants in general, cf. the writings of D.C. Sircar, *Indian Epigraphy* (Delhi, 1965), ch. 5; *Political and Administrative System of Ancient and Medieval India* (Delhi, 1973); *Landlordism and Tenancy in Ancient and Medieval India as Revealed by Epigraphical Records* (Lucknow, 1969) and *The Emperor and the Subordinate Rulers* (Santiniketan, 1982). Sircar's critique of 'feudal polity' is curious since he freely uses such terms as 'fiefs' and 'vassals' in the Indian context; see R.S. Sharma's criticism of Sircar's approach to the problem: 'Indian Feudalism Retouched', *The Indian Historical Review*, 1.2 (1974), pp. 320–30. For me, however, the 'contractual'

that the system of assignments brought in important changes in agrarian relations in areas where such assignments were made[25]—but how does it all help us to understand the genesis of feudal polity? Let me clarify. The *sāmanta*-feudatory system has been considered to be the hallmark of the structure of polity in early medieval India[26]—and there is no reason to dispute the empirical validity of this point—but it has not been seriously examined as to how even the system of secular or service assignments to officials led to the emergence of a *sāmanta*-feudatory network. It has been conceded that the general chronology of the epigraphic evidence for service-assignments postdates the genesis of feudal polity.[27] The conclusion which ought to follow from it is that service grants present a facet and not the precondition for the emergence of the overall pattern of political dominance. Secondly, irrespective of whether administrative measures can bring in changes in societal formations or not,[28] there is the larger question: what generates administrative measures? Land assignments as administrative measures are, we have seen, presented as deliberate acts which corrode the authority of the state; the state not only parts with its sources of revenue but also with its coercive and administrative prerogatives.

---

element remains important as otherwise the logic of service assignments does not appear intelligible. See also fn. 26.

[25] See fn. 17 for references. A restatement of this will be available in R.S. Sharma, 'How Feudal was Indian Feudalism?', *The Journal of Peasant Studies,* vol. 12, nos. 2–3, pp. 19–43.

[26] Yadava, *Society and Culture . . .*, ch. 3.

[27] R.S. Sharma, 'Landgrants to Vassals and Officials in Northern India *c.* AD 1000–1200', *Journal of the Economic and Social History of the Orient,* 4 (1961), pp. 70–71; Idem, 'Rajasasana: Meaning, Scope and Application', *Proceedings of the Indian History Congress,* 37 session (Calicut, 1976), pp. 76–87. For other details of such grants known variously as *prasāda-likhita, prasāda-pattalā, jīvita, rakta-koḍagi* and so on, see N.C. Bandyopadyaya; Yadava, 'Secular Landgrants . . .'; *Society and Culture . . .*, ch. 3; K.K. Gopal, 'Assignment to Officials and Royal Kinsmen in Early Medieval India (*c.* 700–1200 AD)', *University of Allahabad Studies* (Ancient History Section) (1963–64), pp. 75–103. Three points may, however, be noted: (i) the generally late chronology of such grants in some of which only the 'contract' element is explicitly stated; (ii) they are, including *grāsas* and *aṅgabhogas,* more an evidence of the sharing of lineage patrimonial holdings than of service grants; (iii) in terms of total area controlled by dominant sections in a polity such grants may be found to constitute a relatively insignificant proportion.

[28] This point has been raised by H. Mukhia.

Thus feudal polity arises because pre-feudal polity decides, to use an all-too-familiar expression, to preside over the liquidation of its own power. This is a curious position to take, which could be understandable only in terms of a crisis of structural significance in pre-feudal political and economic order. We have argued earlier that the breakdown of the Mauryan State does not appear to have generated such a crisis;[29] in fact, in a situation in which the state polity was expanding horizontally and the final annihilation of the *gaṇa-saṃgha* system of polity was taking place,[30] it would be a difficult exercise indeed to construct a reasoned theory of crisis in state power.

One must then look for an alternative explanation. In presenting the above critique of the historiography of the genesis of early medieval polity, the differential distribution of power represented by the *sāmanta*-feudatory structure is not disputed; what is questioned is the rather one-track argument, wholly centred around a particular value attached to the evidence of the landgrants, for the emergence of the structure in pre-Gupta and Gupta times. In fact, in no state system, however centralized, can there be a single focus or level of power, and the specificity of the differential distribution of power in early medieval polity may be an issue more complex than has hitherto been assumed. And perhaps a revaluation of the evidence of the majority of landgrants may be called for within this complexity.

III

At one level this complexity derives from the presence of trans-political ideology in all state systems, even though in the context of early

[29] Recent attempts to 'construct' a crisis lean heavily on the Brāhmaṇical perception of the evils of Kaliyuga and on the correlation of the evils with actual changes in terms of shifts in the positions of *varṇas* and producing classes, decline of urbanism, decentralization of polity and so on; see B.N.S. Yadava, 'The Accounts of the Kali Age and the Social Transition from Antiquity to the Middle Ages', *The Indian Historical Review*, 5, pp. 1–2 (1979), pp. 31–64; R.S. Sharma, 'The Kali Age: A Period of Social Crisis', in S.N. Mukherjee, ed., pp. 186–203. The 'crisis', of course, is chronologically located several centuries after the Maurya period, but in any case, the historical roots of the 'crisis' are not clear.

[30] See note 22; also the Allahabad Pillar Inscription of Samudragupta in D.C. Sircar, *Select Inscriptions Bearing on Indian History and Civilization*, vol. I, 2nd edition (Calcutta University, 1965), pp. 262–8.

medieval India one may not perceive such an ideology from the perspective of anthropologists or anthropology-oriented historians. One dimension of this was the need for constant validation of power not only in areas where a community was passing from the pre-state to the state-society stage but even in established state societies. The root of this need which, in the early medieval context, may be understood by broadly labelling it as the 'legitimation' process, lay in the separation between the temporal and the sacred domain.[31] The do-

[31] The literature on the 'legitimatization' process in early medieval India is growing; relevant discussions will be found in Romila Thapar, 'Social Mobility in Ancient India with Special Reference to Elite Groups' in her *Ancient Indian Social History: Some Interpretations* (Delhi, 1978); B.D. Chattopadhyaya, 'Origin of the Rajputs: Political, Economic and Social Processes in Early Medieval Rajasthan', *The Indian Historical Review*, 3.1 (1976), pp. 59–82; H. Kulke, 'Early State Formation and Royal Legitimation in Tribal Areas of Eastern India', *Studia Ethnologica Bernensia*, R. Moser & M.K. Gautam, eds, 1 (1978), pp. 29–37; Idem, 'Legitimation and Town Planning in the Feudatory States of Central Orissa', *Cities in South Asia: History, Society and Culture*, H. Kulke, *et al*, eds (Wiesbaden, 1982), pp. 17–36; 'Royal Temple Policy and the Structure of Medieval Hindu Kingdoms' in A. Eschmann, *et al*, eds, *The Cult of Jagannath and the Regional Tradition of Orissa* (Delhi, 1978), pp. 125–138; N. Dirks, 'Political Authority . . . '; G.W. Spencer, 'Religious Networks and Royal Influence in Eleventh Century South India', *Journal of the Economic and Social History of the Orient*, 12 (1969), pp. 32–56; S. Jaiswal, 'Caste in the Socio-Economic Framework of Early India', Presidential Address, Ancient India Section, Indian History Congress, 38 session (Bhuvaneswar, 1977), pp. 16ff; Idem, 'Studies in Early Indian Social History: Trends and Possibilities', *The Indian Historical Review*, 6.1–2 (1979–80), pp. 1–63; J.G. De Casparis, 'Inscriptions and South Asian Dynastic Tradition' in R.J. Moore, ed., pp. 103–27. The discussions show that 'legitimatization' could take various forms: performance of rituals, including sacrificial rituals, genealogical sanctity and the construction of temple networks. The relationship between temporal authority and the sacred domain of which the 'legitimatization' process is a manifestation is explored in A.K. Coomaraswamy, *Spiritual Authority and Temporal Power in the Indian Theory of Government* (American Oriental Society, 1942). For a recent exploration into this problem, see S. Bhattacharyya, 'Political Authority and Brāhmaṇa-Kṣatriya Relations in Early India—An Aspect of the Power-Elite Configuration', *The Indian Historical Review*, vol. 10, Nos. 1–2 (1983–1984), pp. 1–20; also, L. Dumont, 'The Conception of Kingship in Ancient India', *Religion, Politics and History in India* (Mouton Publishers, 1970), ch. 4. The following statement of Dumont is important: 'While spiritually, absolutely, the priest is superior, he is at the same time, from a temporal or material point of view, subject and dependent' (p. 65). J.F. Richards (*Kingship and Authority in South Asia*, Introduction) claims that a recent perspective ' . . . has revealed that too facile usage of only half recognized Western terms and concepts

mains, if one goes beyond theory and tries to grasp their relationship in concrete existential terms, must be seen as interdependent; if temporal power needed 'legitimatization' from 'spiritual' authority, so did the human agents of 'spiritual' authority require sustenance from temporal power. Viewed from this perspective, it should not be surprising that priestly validation of temporal power continued beyond the period of 'Hindu' dynasties; the brāhmaṇa, in a situation of reciprocal relationship, could continue to prepare the *praśastis* of the rule of a Sultan and Sanskritize his title to *Suratrāṇa*.[32] Emphasis on legitimation alone obfuscates crucial aspects of the exercise of force and of the secular compulsions of state power, but as a part of the overall political process it nevertheless offers us a convenient vantage point from which to view the ideological dimension of the state. Temporal power, in early as well as in later theoretical writings, was required to guarantee protection; it would be too narrow a view of 'protection' to take it simply to mean the physical protection of subjects. Protection related to the ideal social order as defined by the guardians of the sacred domain. *Daṇḍa* or force which may have had both secular and non-secular connotations was intended by the guardians of the sacred domain primarily not as a political expedient but for the preservation of the social order.[33] Curiously, the ideal social

---

such as legitimation, and the Church-State dichotomy have obscured the complexity and true significance of Kingship in India', and Heesterman in his contribution ('The Conundrum of King's Authority', ibid., pp. 1–27) initially agrees with this claim but finally concedes that the 'King and brahmin were definitely separated and made into two mutually exclusive categories. The greater the King's power, the more he needs the brahmin'. Cf. also C.R. Lingat, *The Classical Law of India* (Berkeley, University of California Press, 1973), p. 216.

[32] See the Cambay Stambhana Parsvanath temple inscription of 1308 AD referring to Alauddin as *suratrāṇa*, Appendix to *Epigraphia Indica*, 19–23, Nos. 664. An interesting record from Kotihar in Kashmir, dated 1369 AD, refers to Shihab-u-din as Shāhabhadana and traces his descent from the Pāṇḍava lineage, B.K. Kaul Deambi, *Corpus of Śāradā Inscriptions Of Kashmir* (Delhi, 1982), pp. 113–18; the Veraval record of 1263 from Junagadh equates the prophet with Viśvanātha—viśvarūpa—and begins with his *praśasti* and refers to the Hijri era as *Śrīviśvanātha-pratibaddha-nau-janānām-bodhaka-rasula-Muhammada saṃvat*, D.C. Sircar, *Select Inscriptions*, vol. 2 (Delhi, 1983), p. 303.

[33] See Beni Prasad, *Theory of Government in Ancient India*, 2nd edition (Allahabad, 1968), pp. 333–35; Mabbett, ch. 8.

order was defined, but *dharma*, nevertheless, was not uniform, and although the king was required to preserve social order, he was at the same time enjoined to allow the disparate *dharmas* of regions, guilds and associations and of social groups to continue.[34] If there is an anomaly here, the anomaly may help us to understand the massive support which the ruling elites extended to the representatives of the sacred domain in the early medieval period. The territorial spread of the state society required cutting through the tangle of disparate *dharmas* through the territorial spread of the brāhmaṇas and of institutions representing a uniform norm in some form or the other; they did not necessarily eliminate the disparate norms but they could provide a central focus to such disparate norms by their physical presence, their style of functioning and their control over what could be projected as the 'transcendental' norm.[35]

Another dimension of this central focus becomes noticeable with the crystallization of the Purāṇic order, implying the ascendancy of the Bhakti ideology. In sectarian terms, Bhakti could lead to the growth of conflicts in society,[36] but from the standpoint of the state, Bhakti could, perhaps much more effectively than *Dharmaśāstra*-oriented norms, be an instrument of integration.[37] If there was opposition between *Dharmaśāstra*-oriented norms and community norms, Bhakti, at least ideally, provided no incompatibility: local cults and sacred

[34] For details, see P.V. Kane, *History of Dharmaśāstra* (Ancient and Medieval Religious and Civil Law), vol. 3, 2nd edition (Poona, 1973), ch. 33; also Heesterman, 'The conundrum . . .'.

[35] Heesterman, 'Power and Authority . . .'.

[36] R.N. Nandi, 'Origin and Nature of Saivite Monasticism: The Case of Kālāmukhas' in R.S. Sharma and V. Jha, eds, *Indian Society: Historical Probings* (In memory of D.D. Kosambi) (Delhi, 1974), pp. 190–201; R. Champakalakshmi, 'Religious Conflict in the Tamil Country: A Re-appraisal of Epigraphic Evidence', *Journal of the Epigraphical Society of India*, 5 (1978).

[37] Bhakti could provide the allusion of equality among the lower orders which in reality remained a delusion even in the ritual area; R.N. Nandi convincingly points to the shift in the ideology of the Bhakti movement as also to the change brought about by its temple base and Sanskrit-educated priesthood, supported by members of ruling families, 'Some Social Aspects of the Nalayira Prabandham', *Proceedings of the Indian History Congress*, 37 session (Calicut, 1976), pp. 118–23; Kesavan Veluthat, 'The Temple Base of the Bhakti Movement in South India', ibid., 40 session (Waltair, 1979), pp. 185–94.

centres could be brought within the expansive Purāṇic fold through the process of identification. Though originating in an earlier period, the temple grew to be the major institutional locus of Bhakti in the early medieval period,[38] and for temporal power, the temple, as a symbol in material space of the sacred domain, could provide a direct link with that domain in two ways: (i) The king could seek to approximate the sacred domain through a process of identification with the divinity enshrined in the temple. The practice initiated by the Pallavas and augmented by the Colas, taken to be similar to the Devarāja cult of south-east Asia, is an example of such a process;[39] (ii) the second way was to surrender temporal power to the divinity, the cult of which was raised to the status of the central cult and to act as its agent. This process is illustrated by the stages through which the cult of Jagannātha emerged as the central cult in Orissa and the ritual surrender of temporal power to the divinity by King Anaṅgabhīma.[40] The centrality of the cult in relation to others in this process implied the centrality of its agents as well.[41] The Cola and Coḍagaṅga practices are perhaps facets of the same concern—to have direct links with the sacred domain.

The process of legitimatization thus cannot be viewed simply in terms of a newly emerged local polity seeking validation through linkage with a respectable Kṣatriya ancestry or by underlining its local roots; the constant validation of temporal authority really relates to the complex of ideological apparatus through which temporal power was reaching out to its temporal domain. '(If) the State (is) a special apparatus, exhibiting a peculiar material framework that cannot be reduced to the given relations of political domination',[42] then it be-

[38] Nandi; Idem, *Religious Institutions and Cults in the Deccan* (Delhi, 1973), pp. 10ff; Veluthat.

[39] K. Veluthat, 'Royalty and Divinity: Legitimisation of Monarchical Power in the South', *Proceedings of the Indian History Congress*, 39 session (Hyderabad, 1979), pp. 241–39; see also B. Stein, *Peasant State*, pp. 334ff.

[40] H. Kulke, 'Royal Temple Policy . . . '; Idem, 'King Anaṅgabhīma III, the Veritable Founder of the Gajapati Kingship and of the Jagannatha Trinity at Puri', *Journal of the Royal Asiatic Society of Great Britain and Ireland*, 1 (1981), pp. 26–39.

[41] For an interesting analysis of this process, H. Kulke, 'Legitimation and Town-planning in the Feudatory States of Central Orissa', in *Ritual Space in India: Studies in Architectural Anthropology*, Jan Pieper, ed., offprint, pp. 30–40.

[42] N. Poulantzas, *State, Power, Socialism* (London, 1980), p. 12.

comes imperative to study the pattern of use of the available ideological apparatus which constituted an integral part of the overall political order.[43] From the perspective of the interdependence between temporal power and sacred authority, it becomes understandable that assignments such as *brahmadeyas* and *devadānas* were not an administrative but a socio-religious necessity for the temporal power; the earthly agents of the sacred domain—and such agents were ultimately defined by the changing contexts of both the temporal and the sacred order—generated a pattern of dominance in their areas of preserve, but it would not be compatible with the argument presented here to generalize either that temporal power in early medieval India was a tool in the hands of the brāhmaṇas and the temple managers,[44] or that massive support to the representatives of the sacred domain meant parcellization of temporal power, an assumption which in any case will have to presuppose that temporal power emanated from a single source. It needs also to be underlined that the duality of the temporal and sacred domains does not necessarily imply that the relationships between the domains remained unchanged from the Vedic times to eternity.[45] From the standpoint of temporal power, Vedism, Purāṇism, Tantrism and other forms of heterodoxism could simultaneously acquire the connotation of the sacred domain.[46] What is required is to

[43] Poulantzas further explains (ibid., p. 37): ' . . . ideological power is never exhausted by the State and its ideological apparatuses. For just as they do not create the dominant ideology, they are not the only, or even primary factors in the reproductions of the relations of ideological domination/subordination. The ideological apparatuses simply elaborate and inculcate the dominant ideology'.

[44] This view seems to be projected by both K. Veluthat, 'Royalty and Divinity . . . ' and P.M. Rajan Gurukkal who considers the Kulaśekhara state of Kerala to be 'in a way the creation' of a dominant landed group among the brāhmaṇas, 'Medieval Landrights: Structure and Pattern of Distribution', ibid., pp. 279–84.

[45] See footnotes 31 and 90.

[46] This requires to be underlined in view of the changing patterns of patronage in different periods. For the early medieval period, the relative neglect of the implications of the deep penetration of Tantrism into religion and polity will bear out the point I am trying to make. Devangana Desai argues that the patronage of Tantrism is reflective of feudal degeneration, as it served the two dominant interests of the kings and feudal chiefs of early medieval India: War and Sex, 'Art under Feudalism in India', *The Indian Historical Review*, 1.1 (1974), p. 12; also Idem, *Erotic Sculpture of India* (Delhi, 1975). This seems to be too narrow a view to take of the profound impact of Tantrism in early medieval society. If Tantrism represented

analyze the regional and group perception of the sacred domain. This will help us understand the curious contradiction between general support and cases of persecution; the overwhelming domination of the brāhmaṇa groups and temples in south India juxtaposed with the incorporation of Jaina tenets in the religious policies of individual rulers of western India[47] or the appointment of a *devotpāṭananāyaka*, an official in charge of uprooting images of gods from temples and of confiscation of temple property, by an early medieval ruler of Kashmir.[48] Taking even the uncommon cases as aberrations would be to bypass the issue; the point is how in the early medieval context the relevance of the sacred domain was defined by temporal power.

Another aspect of the complexity we have talked about concerns the territorial limits of the temporal domain. Temporal domain was defined by the extent of royal power but Kingdom was not defined in concrete territorial terms; even the *janapada* or *rāṣṭra*, one of the constituent limbs of the state in the *Saptāṅga* formulation, was not 'internally coherent and closed towards the outside'.[49] The state was thus not a static unit but one that was naturally dynamic.[50] Even the territory of the Mauryas, which for the period of Aśoka alone can be clearly defined by the distribution of his edicts, was designated as *vijita* or *rājaviṣaya*[51]—an area over which the rule of the emperor extended.

---

esoteric knowledge, then the remark of F. Edgerton, made in relation to the Upaniṣads, seems relevant here: 'Knowledge, true esoteric knowledge, is the magic key to Omnipotence, absolute power. By it one becomes autonomous . . . ', 'Upanisads: What Do They Seek and Why', in D.P. Chattopadhyaya, ed., *Studies in the History of Indian Philosophy*, vol. I (Calcutta, 1978), p. 136. For Tantric impact on Purāṇic as well as heterodox religious orders and its close association with temporal power, R.N. Nandi, *Religious Institutions* . . . ', David N. Lorenzen, *The Kāpālikas and Kālāmukhas: Two Lost Saivite Sects* (New Delhi, 1972); R.B.P. Singh, *Jainism in Early Medieval Karnataka, (c. AD 500–1200)* (Delhi, 1975); B.D. Chattopadhyaya, 'Religion in a Royal Household: A Study of Some Aspects of the *Karpūramañjarī*', in this volume.

47 A.K. Majumdar, *Chaulukyas of Gujarat* (A survey of the history and culture of Gujarat from the middle of the tenth to the end of the thirteenth century) (Bombay, 1956), pp. 310, 315.

48 *Rājataraṅgiṇī*, vol. VII, pp. 1146–48.

49 Heesterman, 'Power and Authority . . .'.

50 De Casparis, 'Inscriptions and South Asian Dynastic Tradition'.

51 Major Rock Edicts, II, XIII; see D.C. Sircar, *Select Inscriptions*, 1, pp. 17, 35–6.

The territorial composition of the Mauryan empire in Aśoka's period can be characterized as a combination of several nodes such as Pāṭaliputra, Ujjayinī, Takṣaśilā, Tosali and Suvarṇagiri as well as areas of such peoples as Bhojas, Raṭhikas, Pulindas, Nābhakas and that of the *āṭavikas* or forest people.[52] Such fluid situations—for there is no guarantee that this territorial composition remained static throughout the Mauryan period—are schematized in the *maṇḍala* concept of the political theorists who locate the *vijigīṣu* at the core of the *maṇḍala*,[53] and the 'royal mystique',[54] represented by the *Cakravartin* model of kingship, is a logical follow-up of this formulation. It has been the bane of writings on the political history of early and early-medieval India to search for approximations of the *Cakravartī* among the kings of big-sized states;[55] the ideal is only a recognition of the existence of disparate polities and of military success as a precondition of the *Cakravartī* status which was superior to the status represented by the heads of other polities.

IV

Within the parameters of the interdependence of temporal and sacred domains, and more precisely the essentially dynamic contours of these domains, the political processes of early medieval India may be sought to be identified. I would venture to begin by suggesting that political processes may be seen in terms of parallels with contemporary economic, social and religious processes. The essence of the economic process lay in the horizontal spread of rural agrarian settlements, and

[52] Ibid.

[53] The concept is found in such texts as *Arthaśāstra*, 6.2; *Kāmandakīya Nītisāra*, 8.45 and so on. See Beni Prasad, *Theory of Government* . . . , pp. 143ff; Altekar, pp. 293ff; for recent comments, Heesterman, 'Power and Authority . . . ', pp. 77–8.

[54] T.R. Trautmann, 'Tradition of Statecraft in Ancient India', in R.J. Moore, ed., pp. 86–102. Trautmann defines 'royal mystique' as 'a network of interrelated symbols' its vehicles being 'works of art such as courtly epics, royal biographies and ornate ideologies found in inscriptions'; he takes Rājendra Cola's expedition to the north and north-east as an expression of this 'mystique'.

[55] Even R. Inden, who by no means suffers from the limitations of traditional political historiography, cannot seem to resist the search for a 'paramount king of all India', 'Hierarchies of Kings in Early Medieval India', *Contributions to Indian Sociology*, N.S. 15, 1–2 (1981), p. 99.

this remains true even for the early historical period, despite the accent on urban economy or money economy of the period.[56] The process of caste formation, the chief mechanism of which was the horizontal spread of the dominant ideology of social order based on the *varṇa*-division—despite, again, the ascendancy of heterodoxism in the early historical period[57]—remained the essence of the social process which drew widely dispersed and originally outlying groups into a structure which allowed them in a large measure to retain their original character except that this character was now defined with reference to the structure.[58] In the related religious process too the major trend was the integration of local cults, rituals and sacred centres into a pan-theistic supra-local structure; the mechanism of integration was by seeking affiliation with a deity or a sacred centre which had come to acquire supra-local significance.[59] Applied to the study of the political

[56] R.S. Sharma, *Perspectives in Social and Economic History of Early India* (Delhi, 1983), ch. 10.

[57] For example, despite the substantial support extended to the Buddhist sects by both the Sātavāhanas and the Western Kṣatrapas, the dominance of *Varṇa* ideology is evident in their records; cf. the expression *vinivatitacātuvaṇasaṃkarasa* applied to Gautamīputra Sātakarṇi in a *praśasti* written in his memory, and the expression *sarvva-varṇairabhigamya-rakṣaṇārthaṃ patitve vṛteṇa* applied to Śaka Rudradāman I in the Junagadh inscription of AD 150; Sircar, *Select Inscriptions*, 1, pp. 177–204.

[58] Despite their differences in many respects, N.K. Bose's model of 'tribal absorption' and M.N. Srinivas's model of 'Sanskritization' are being drawn upon to make this generalization. A useful review of the contributions of these two authors, with complete bibliographical references, will be found in S. Munshi, 'Tribal Absorption and Sanskritization in Hindu Society', *Contributions to Indian Sociology*, N.S., 13.2 (1979), pp. 293–317. It must be made clear that 'tribal absorption' is merely a broadly defined process and not the only process, and that the continuity of internal organization in a large measure does not imply status of equality within the social order; a misreading of the caste formation process would totally miss the hierarchical ordering in the caste structure down to the level of the untouchables. Secondly, the ethnic group as a whole, in view of the complex operation of the social mobility process, does not retain its pre-caste character; otherwise, we would not have had brāhmaṇas, Kṣatriyas, Śūdras and so on emerging from the same stock. For a useful discussion, see Jaiswal, 'Studies in Early Indian Social History . . . '.

[59] Synoptic studies on processes of cult formation in early medieval India are not known to me but the excellent study on the cult of Jagannātha may help illuminate the process, A. Eschmann *et al*, eds, *The Cult of Jagannath and the Regional Tradition of Orissa*, particularly, pt. 1, chs 3, 5; pt. 2, chs 13–14. In the case of Tamilnadu in the Cola period, note the remark of R. Champakalakshmi, 'The early Chola temples

process, these parallels would suggest consideration at three levels: the presence of established norms and nuclei of the state society, the horizontal spread of state society implying the transformation of pre-state polities into state polities, and the integration of local polities into structures that transcended the bounds of local polities. In other words, in trying to understand the political processes and structures in early medieval India it may be more profitable to start by juxtaposing the processes of the formation of local state polities and supra-local polities than by assessing the structures in terms of a perennial oscillation between forces of centralization and decentralization.

The parallelism drawn here is in a sense misleading since in polity, as in society or religion, no given structures could be immutable in view of the underlying dynamism I have already drawn attention to, but the point about the process essentially being a range of interactions still remains valid. The specific complexities of early medieval political formation have, therefore, to be stated in clear empirical terms. The first major point which may be put forward with regard to the post-Gupta polity is that the state society, represented by the emergence of ruling lineages, had covered all nuclear regions and had progressed well into peripheral areas by the end of the Gupta period. I assume details of political geography need not be cited to substantiate this generalization. And yet, it is significant that inscriptions from the seventh century alone, from different regions of India, begin to produce elaborate genealogies, either aligning the alleged local roots of ruling lineages with a mythical tradition or by tracing their descent from mythical heroic lineages.[60] The emergence of genealogy has been taken as a shift from 'yajña to vaṃśa',[61] indicating a change in the nature of kingship, but in the totality of its geographical distribution, the genealogical evidence has a more significant implication: the pro-

. . . systematically used the *liṅga* mainly due to its assimilative character as the only aniconic form which could incorporate in canonical temples, local and popular cult practices centring round the *Kangu* or pillar and tree, thus providing a constantly widening orbit for bringing in divergent socio-economic and ethnic groups into Saiva worship', 'Peasant State and Society in Medieval South India: A Review Article', *The Indian Economic and Social History Review*, 18, 3–4 (1982), p. 420.

60 De Casparis.

61 Dirks, 'Political Authority and Structural Change . . . '.

liferation of actual ruling lineages defining the domain of political power. The state society even in nuclear areas did not have a stable locus; the mobilization of military strength could not only displace a ruling lineage but could create a new locus and a new network of political relations. The shift from the Badami Cālukyas to the Rāṣṭrakūṭas and then again to the Cālukyas of Kalyāṇa, or from the Pallavas and the Pāṇḍyas to the Colas was not simply a change from one lineage to another; each change redefined the locus of the state in a geographical context which had nevertheless experienced a long and uninterrupted history of the state society. In such contexts, the use of the term 'state formation', primary, secondary or even tertiary, would be highly inappropriate and would obscure the distinction with areas which were indeed experiencing the passage from the pre-state to the state society on a significant scale. The distinction remains valid throughout Indian history due to the uneven pace of change, and transitions from the pre-state to the state society have been documented through medieval to modern times.[62]

I have been using expressions such as 'lineage domain'[63] and 'state society'[64] without a clear reference to the state in the early medieval

[62] A. Guha, 'Tribalism to Feudalism in Assam: 1600–1750', *The Indian Historical Review*, 1.1 (1974), pp. 65–76; Surajit Sinha, 'State Formation and Rajput Myth in Tribal Central India', *Man in India*, 42.1 (1962), pp. 35–80; K. Suresh Singh, 'A Study in State-formation among Tribal Communities', in R.S. Sharma and V. Jha, eds, *Indian Society: Historical Probings*, pp. 317–36; H.R. Sanyal, 'Malla-bhum', in Surajit Sinha, ed., *Tribal Politics and State Systems in Pre-Colonial Eastern and North-Eastern India* (Calcutta, 1987), pp. 73–142.

[63] 'Lineage' is simply used here to translate such terms as *kula*, *vaṃśa* or *anvaya* which were suffixed to the names of the ruling families. 'Lineage' in this sense does not denote a pre-state stage of polity as it may have done in the nascent stage of the emergence of the state in early India (Romila Thapar, *From Lineage . . .*).

[64] The range of definitions of the state is enormous, and to view the state as opposed to chiefdom in terms of the former's capacity to arrest fission in society and in terms of a 'centralized and hierarchically organized political system' (R. Cohen, 'State Origins: A Reappraisal' in *The Early State*, pp. 35–6) will not be compatible with long-term histories of state societies. Morton Fried's definition (*The Evolution of Political Society*, New York, 1967, p. 229) of the state 'as a complex of institutions by means of which the power of the society is organized on a basis superior to kinship' also does not seem sufficient. The real question is the context of power. Since the basis of the state lies in separation between producing and non-producing groups, there is no incompatibility between state society and the

context. This is because of some definitional problems which could be clearly stated by working out the geography of the loci of political power over a few centuries. I can however make a very brief reference to a selected span of time—the eleventh century—the two reasons for considering the span as significant being: (i) evidence for this period—particularly from south India—has recently resulted in the urge for a revaluation of commonly used concepts on the state; (ii) the eleventh century, in relation to the centuries preceding and following it, does not present any major fluctuations in the list and geography of the distribution of ruling lineages. At a rough estimate the number of ruling lineages of this century could be put around forty;[65] the number is reconstructed on the basis of specific references to lineage names and excludes cases where, despite the use of a regal title or a title approximating it, descent is not clearly indicated. In a sense the reconstruction of such numbers would be futile since I am not sure that I can convert these numbers into the number of states and say that forty states existed in India in the eleventh century. Terms such as the Cola State, Cālukya State or Pāla State in place of 'kingdoms' or 'empires' may not raise serious objections, but I am doubtful if I would be equally justified in going ahead with the use of this terminology in relation to, say, the Kadambas of Vanavāsī, Hangal and Goa;[66] the Cāhamānas of Śākambharī, Broach, Dholpur, Pratabgarh, Nadol and Ranthambhor;[67] the Paramāras of Malwa, Lāṭa, Candrāvatī, Arbuda and Suvarṇagiri;[68] and similarly, Noḷamba State, Bāṇa State

---

organization of political power along lineage ties or/and in other terms. State society, however, only points to the existence of this separation and does not suggest the historical specificity of the total complex of a State structure.

[65] This estimate is based on: H.C. Ray, *The Dynastic History of Northern India (Early Medieval Period)*, 2 vols., reprint (Delhi, 1973); F. Kielhorn, 'A List of Inscriptions of Northern India', Appendix to *Epigraphia Indica*, 5, 1–96; D.R. Bhandarkar, 'A List of the Inscriptions of Northern India in Brāhmī and its Derivative Scripts, from about 200 A.C.', Appendix to *Epigraphia Indica*, vols. 19–23; F. Kielhorn, 'Synchronistic Tables for Southern India, AD 400–1400', *Epigraphia Indica*, 8.

[66] G.M. Moraes, *The Kadamba-Kula. A History of Ancient and Medieval Karnataka* (Bombay, 1931).

[67] Dasarath Sharma; also 2nd edition (Delhi, 1975).

[68] P. Bhatia, *The Paramāras* (Delhi, 1968); also, H.V. Trivedi, *Inscriptions of the Paramāras* (*Corpus Inscriptionum Indicarum*, vol. 7.2) (New Delhi, n.d.).

or Raṭṭa State,[69] signifying the domains of these respective lineages, may be found to be equally inappropriate. The reason is not simply the status of a lineage; the point really is whether there is always a necessary correspondence between a lineage and a static territorial limit. Early medieval evidence suggests that this is not so. I have cited the cases of the Kadambas and the Cāhamānas; many more are readily available. The Kalacuris, an ancient lineage, are found in western Deccan in a comparatively early period but they established several nuclei of power, as in Tripurī and Ratanpur, in the upper Narmada basin in the early medieval period, whereas one of its segments ventured into such a remote area of northeastern India that it came to be designated as Sarayūpāra.[70] The movements of the Karṇāṭas outside Karnataka, although the particular lineages involved are not always specified, led to the establishment of new ruling families in Bengal and Bihar,[71] and possibly also to the formation of such Rajput clans as the Solankis and Rathods.[72] The ruling lineage in its entirety is the point of reference in the case of major lineages in many records, as suggested by expressions like *Pallavānām* or *Kadambānām*.[73] What I am, therefore, arguing is that since the changing distribution patterns of ruling lineages do not necessarily correspond to static territorial limits, an initial study of polity has to start with an analysis of the

[69] See M.S. Krishnamurthy, *Nolambas: A Political and Cultural Study* (Mysore, 1980); D. Desai, *The Mahāmaṇḍaleśvaras Under the Cālukyas of Kālyaṇī* (Bombay, 1951); M.S. Govindaswamy, *The Role of Feudatories in Pallava History* (Annamalai University, 1965); Idem, 'The Role of Feudatories in Cola History', Ph.D. thesis (Annamalai University, 1973); V. Balambal, *Feudatories of South India* (Allahabad, 1978).

[70] For the records of different Kalacuri lines, see V.V. Mirashi, *Inscriptions of the Kalachuri-Chedi Era* (*Corpus Inscriptionum Indicarum*, vol. 4, pp. 1–2) (Ootacamund, 1955).

[71] For a recent discussion, see D.C. Sircar, *Pāla-Sena Yuger Vaṃśānucarita* (in Bengali) (Calcutta, 1982).

[72] The common origin of the Cālukyas of Karnataka and the Caulukyas or Solankis of Gujarat has been doubted by many, including A.K. Majumdar, but Majumdar himself points to the existence of common traditions among them, 5; Rathod is derived from Rāṣṭrakūṭa, the name being in existence at Dhalop and Hathundi in Rajasthan in the early medieval period, D. Sharma, ed., *Rajasthan Through the Ages*, I (Bikaner, 1966), p. 287; also Chattopadhyaya, 'The Origin of the Rajputs . . . ' in this volume.

[73] De Casparis.

formation of lineages and of the pattern of the network they represent, both territorially and in inter-lineage combinations, at *different levels in the organization of political power.* Such an analysis may ultimately clarify relations in the structures of supra-local polities, which alone seem to be issues in historiographical debates on the polity of early medieval India. The focus then will have to shift from extremities like 'virtual absence of' or 'construction and collapse of' the administrative apparatus. In fact, as the empirical evidence from regions like Rajasthan suggests, the distribution of political authority could be organized by a network of lineages within the framework of the monarchical form of polity, retaining at the same time areas of bureaucratic functioning.[74] A remark, made with reference to medieval Deccan, seems pertinent here: 'The development of State bureaucracy and private lordly organization was neither mutually exclusive nor confined to two different stages of a process. In this agrarian society private and State interests developed simultaneously and in terms of one another'.[75]

The formation and mobilization of lineage power did not, of course, develop along a single channel; it could involve the colonization of areas of pre-state polity and change of the economic pattern of the region by expansive lineages;[76] in particular contexts, the emergence of ruling lineages would correspond to 'primary state formation' and the introduction of the monarchical ideology of rule; it could even be the simple replacement of one lineage by another. All these processes could and did operate simultaneously but—and this needs to be underlined if we are to take an all-India perspective—not in isolation from one another. Polities were interactive and interlocking—if nothing else, inventories of battles fought in the early medieval period would be a sure index of this—and this often resulted in the formation of new blocks and networks of power in which the original identity of a lineage was obliterated.[77]

[74] Chattopadhyaya, 'Origin of the Rajputs . . . '.

[75] Perlin, p. 279.

[76] Yadava, *Society and Culture*, p. 103, fn. 623; Chattopadhyaya, pp. 63–4; an example of this is provided by the Ajayagadh rock inscription in which Ānanda, the brother of Candella Trailokyavarman, is said to have reduced to submission the 'wild tribes of Bhillas, Śabaras and Pulindas', *Epigraphia Indica*, I, p. 337.

[77] Apart from the cases of the Solankis and the Rathods, those of the Coḍagaṅgas

Two further points about lineages as bases for the study of political power may be made. First, the Kalacuri or Cāhamāna evidence has shown that lineages could be amazingly expansive but there are other levels at which the relationships between lineages and territories can be examined. Pre-tenth century evidence from Tamilnadu has been cited to show that the nucleus of the power of a lineage could be an area comprised of two or three districts. The relationship between the lineage and its territory was expressed in the form of the name of the area in which the lineage was dominant; examples of this are common in the south and in the Deccan: Cola-nāḍu, Cera-nāḍu, Toṇḍai-nāḍu, Oyma-nāḍu, Iruṅgola-pāḍi, Gaṅga-pāḍi, Nuḷamba-pāḍi, to mention a few, bear out this relationship. The growth of a lineage into a supra-local or supra-regional power would result in the reorganization of the *nāḍus* or *pāḍis* into administrative units, as suggested by the emergence of the *vaḷa-naḍus* and *maṇḍalams* in the Cola State,[78] but, from our point of view, what is important is that such administrative units emerged by integrating pre-existing lineage areas. It must be conceded that the pattern available for the south and the Deccan cannot be applied to all regions; in Bengal, for example, such details of lineage geography are simply not available. Elsewhere, as in early medieval Rajasthan and Gujarat, the trend seems to have been towards the parcellization of the area variously called Gurjara-bhūmi, Gurjaratrā, Gurjara-dharitrī and Gurjaradharā—all obviously derived from the ethnic term Gurjara[79]—into strongholds of several lineages, only some of which traced their descent from the Gurjara stock.[80]

Secondly, the formation of ruling lineages can be seen also from the perspective of the social mobility process in early medieval India.

---

and Veṅgi Cālukyas may be cited to illustrate this process.

[78] Y. Subbarayalu, 'Mandalam as a Politico-Geographical Unit in South India', *Proceedings of the Indian History Congress*, 39 session (Hyderabad, 1978), pp. 84–6. For details of the political geography of the Cola country, see Idem, *Political Geography of the Chola Country* (Madras, 1973). Subbarayalu convincingly argues to show that *nāḍus* were basically agrarian regions and not 'artificial administrative divisions' (*Political Geography*, pp. 32–3), but from the point of view of polity the important point is the correlation in many cases between 'chieftaincies' and *nāḍus* and *pāḍis* (*Political Geography* . . . , ch. 7); see also Stein, *Peasant State* . . . , ch. 3.

[79] A.K. Majumdar, pp. 17–22.

[80] Chattopadhyaya.

In a situation of open-ended polity and of a congenial climate for 'Kṣatriyization',[81] any lineage or segment of a larger ethnic group, with a coherent organization of force, could successfully make a bid for political power and lay the foundation of a large state structure. The origin of the Hoysaḷa State, which lasted for about three centuries and a half, goes back to the *mālepas* or the hill chiefs of the Soseyūr forests and the hill forces that the chiefs could command at that stage.[82] Here too the pattern of the formation of a lineage and the level of power a lineage would reach would not be identical in all areas. Generally, the mobility upward was from a base which could be broadly characterized as agrarian, and political changes from the seventh century, again in western India, provide an idea of the sequences in the political mobility process. We have noted that Gurjaratrā or Gurjarabhūmi was the base from which several lineages tracing descent from the Gurjaras emerged; the separation of the ruling lineages from the common stock is suggested by the general name Gurjara-Pratihāra used by the lineages, and while the base of one such lineage in the Jodhpur area seems to have been established by displacing pre-existing groups, in the Alwar area in eastern Rajasthan there is clear indication of a sharp distinction which had developed between Gurjara cultivators and the Gurjara-Pratihāra ruling lineage.[83] It is on this base that the Gurjara-Pratihāra supra-regional power, which began with the expansion of one of the lineages and extended at one stage possibly as far east as Bengal, was built up. Elsewhere, for example, the presence of Vellāla generals and warrior elements and of feudatories in the Pallava and Cola polities in south India[84] or the formation of the Ḍāmaras into a major political group in the Lohara period (*c.* AD 1000–1170) in Kashmir[85] would

[81] See references in note 31.

[82] J.D.M. Derrett, *The Hoysaḷas* (A Medieval Indian Royal Family) (Oxford University Press, 1957), pp. 7–8; S. Settar, *Hoysaḷa Sculptures in the National Museum, Copenhagen* (Copenhagen, 1975), p. 16; also Idem, *The Hoysaḷa Temples*, vol. I (Dharwad-Bangalore, 1992), ch. I.

[83] Rajorgadh Inscription of Mathanadeva, *Epigraphia Indica*, vol. 3, pp. 263–7.

[84] Dirks, 'Political Authority and Structural Change . . . ', p. 130; Stein, *Peasant State* . . . , p. 188; for reference to Velirs of Kodumbalur as feudatories of the Pallavas, see Govindaswamy, *The Role of Feudatories in Pallava History*, pp. 70ff.

[85] Kosambi writes, 'The essential question is: Were the Dāmaras feudal lords? Did they hold land as feudal property? The answer is fairly clear, in the affirmative',

suggest a similar process of the emergence of potentially dominant elements from within local agrarian bases.

V

The structure of supra-local or supra-regional polities has then to become understandable in a large measure with reference to its substratum components, and it is in the characterization of this reference that the perspectives of historians substantially differ. Before the debate is taken up for review, the geographical loci of large polities need to be briefly touched upon. The large polities tended to emerge, throughout Indian history, in what geographers call 'nuclear' regions,[86] providing such polities with a resource base potentially much richer and easier to integrate administratively than relatively isolated pockets where 'state formation', a chronologically phased phenomenon, would reveal less integrative patterns of polity. The Ganges basin, Kaveri basin, Krishna-Godavari *doab* and Raichur *doab* are cited as examples of 'nuclear' regions, and indeed the large state structures of the early medieval period all thrived in these regions. Two qualifications are, however, necessary. First, a 'nuclear' region is finally a historical-chronological and not purely a geographical region; the nuclearity of

'Origins of Feudalism in Kashmir'; Yadava, 'Secular Landgrants . . . ', p. 90 too refers to a merchant called Jayyaka who amassed wealth and became a Ḍāmara chief. These assertions seem to result from a misreading of the *Rājataraṅgiṇī* evidence. The reference relating to Jayyaka (VII. 93–95) seems to show him to be from a peasant family, who traded in foodgrains with foreign countries and achieved the status of a Ḍāmara (see also IV. 347–48). The possible tribal background of the Ḍāmaras, their transformation into peasantry and emergence into a dominant section may have striking parallels with the Vellālas and other dominant peasant sections elsewhere; see the Appendix on Ḍāmaras in Krishna Mohan.

[86] The concept of 'nuclear' regions or even 'sub-nuclear' regions has been used by historians working on this period: Kulke, 'Royal Temple Policy . . . '; B. Stein, 'Integration of the Agrarian System in South India', in R.E. Frykenberg, ed., *Land Control and Social Structure in Indian History* (Madison, 1969), pp. 175–216. Theoretical discussions will be found in R.I. Crane, ed., *Regions and Regionalism in South Asian Studies* (Duke University, 1966); J.E. Schwartzberg, 'The Evolution of Regional Power Configurations in the Indian Subcontinent', in R.G. Fox, ed., pp. 197–233. I have, however, mainly followed the idea of the relative order of regions outlined in O.H.K. Spate and A.T.A. Learmonth, *India and Pakistan* (University Paperback, Delhi, 1972), chs 6, 13.

a region is related to the way historical factors converge on it and not merely to its resource potential. Warangal, away from the nuclear Krishna-Godavari *doab*, remained a base of the large structure of the Kākatīya State;[87] the Caulukya State of Gujarat, with its base at Aṇahilapāṭaka, emerged in a region which, from the point of view of its basic agrarian resource potential, was not sufficiently 'nuclear'.[88] Secondly, larger polities did not necessarily originate in nuclear areas; military mobilization could generate a movement towards nuclear areas and result in major transformations in polity. The movement of the Pratihāras from Rajasthan to Kanauj, of the Pālas from southeast Bengal to the middle and the lower Ganges basin,[89] the descent of the Hoysaḷas from the hilly region of the Soseyūr forests into the areas of south Karnataka held by the Gaṅgas for centuries, produced a steady growth of political structures of substantial dimensions in these regions.

I have already noted in the beginning that recognition of the dispersed foci of political power was present even in traditional historiography in the form of the formulation of 'feudal tendencies', although the formulation was applied generally to a pattern of polity which was considered not sufficiently large in terms of its approximation to an all-India empire and which could not, therefore, be considered centralized. Recent perspectives specifically related to only early medieval India have shifted from acceptance of 'centralization' and 'bureaucracy' as essential characteristics of a large state structure to detailed analyses of dispersed foci of power within such structures. This concern appears to be common both to those who characterize these structures in terms of 'feudal polity' and their critics to whom the 'feudal' model is either 'outworn' or is an exclusively European formation which hinders a proper understanding of the uniqueness of the Indian political system.[90] Where then does the difference lie?

[87] G. Yazdani, ed., *Early History of the Deccan* (Oxford University Press, 1960), vol. 2.

[88] However, for irrigation and development of the agrarian base of the Caulukyan state structure, see V.K. Jain, *Trade and Traders in Western India (AD 1000–1300)* (Delhi, 1990), ch. 2; for Rajasthan, B.D. Chattopadhyaya, 'Irrigation in Early Medieval Rajasthan' in this collection.

[89] D.C. Sircar, *Pāla-Sena Yuger* . . . .

[90] This particular brand of criticism in respect of Indian polity has emanated,

Reducing the discussion to the level of political relations alone, the fundamental difference seems to lie, as I understand it, between their respective notions of 'parcellized sovereignty' and 'shared sovereignty'. Opposition to the 'feudal' model[91] is best articulated in the model of the 'segmentary state' which is currently bandied about, at least in the circle of Western Indologists, as a major breakthrough in our understanding of the traditional Indian political system. The model which is directly lifted from the analysis of a pre-state polity in East Africa but, in the Indian context, is mixed up with concepts of kingship derived from literature, presents the following characteristics of the 'segmentary state': (i) limited territorial sovereignty which further weakens gradually as one moves from the core to the periphery, and often 'shades off into ritual hegemony'; (ii) the existence of a centralized core with quasi-autonomous foci of administration; (iii) the pyramidal repetition of the administrative structure and functions in the peripheral foci; (iv) the absence of absolute monopoly of legitimate force at the centre; and (v) shifting allegiances of the periphery of the

---

curiously, from American academic institutions, and in the context of early medieval polity been initiated by B. Stein, 'The State and Agrarian Order in Medieval South India: A Historiographical Critique', in B. Stein, ed., *Essays on South India* (Delhi, 1976), pp. 64–91. Stein proposed the alternative model of a 'segmentary state' ('The Segmentary State . . . ') which has proved a rallying point for South Asia experts from these institutions and even for initial detractors. For example, Dirks ('Political Authority and Structural Change', p. 126) in 1976 declared: 'The segmentary state model is neither well calibrated to index changes in political or social relations, nor is it culturally sensitive enough to identify the differences between East Africa and India, or *even more particularly between north and south India* (emphasis added; the implication perhaps is that the differences between north India and south India are greater than those between East Africa and India); by 1979 his criticism of the model had mellowed down considerably ('Structure and Meaning of Political Relations' . . .). R. Inden considers the model a 'real break with previous approaches', 'Ritual, Authority, and Cyclic Time in Hindu Kingship', in J.F. Richards, ed., pp. 28–73; see also B. Stein, 'All the Kings' Mana: Perspectives on Kingship in Medieval South India', ibid., pp. 115–67; Idem, 'Mahanavami: Medieval and Modern Kingly Ritual in South India', in B.L. Smith, ed., *Essays on Gupta Culture* (Delhi, 1983), pp. 67–92. The real point of convergence in these writings is that they view the Indian State system, whatever be the period, as a ritual system.

[91] The discussion here is restricted only to the construct of 'feudal polity' and to the particular brand of criticism it has recently been subjected to. It does not take into account the total range of the critique of the feudal formation.

system.[92] In the schema of the segmentary state, as it has been variously worked out in the Indian context, the major integrative factor is 'ritual sovereignty' rather than 'political sovereignty', and attempts at explications of the concept of 'ritual sovereignty' locate the king as the principal ritualist. The 'new modality of relations between the chiefs and the King', one writer argues in the context of the later phase of Pallava polity, (which) 'represents the expansion of a regional system into a trans-regional system' is nothing more than a shift from an earlier ritual system, and the different foci of power nothing more than ritual accessories.[93] It is the kingship which is 'incorporative' and, one may say by extending this logic, whatever be the territorial spread of the state, it is ritual space.

All this is a fine example of the study of the state *sans* politics.

[92] See note 9 for references to Southall's writings in which the 'segmentary state' model has been constructed. The applicability of the model has been debated in the volume edited by R.G. Fox; various points regarding the empirical validity of its application to the Cola State by Stein have been raised by R. Champakalakshmi, 'Peasant State and Society . . . ', and in greater detail by D.N. Jha, 'Relevance of Peasant State and Society to Pallava and Cola times', *The Indian Historical Review*, vol. 8, Nos. 1–2 (1981–82), pp. 74–94. I do not wish to re-examine the question of empirical validity here, but will briefly touch upon the internal consistency or the validity of the model itself. Southall constructs his model by drawing a distinction between the 'segmentary state' and the 'unitary state', which is, for a historian, as irrelevant as the dichotomy between the 'early state' and the 'industrial state'. If pre-state polity has a varied range (and according to Southall's own characterization, his East African Alur polity would approximate the 'chiefdom' category), so too has State polity, and to equate the State with a 'unitary state' is to totally ignore historical experience. Curiously, Southall's 'segmentary state' and 'unitary state' are not ultimately distinctly separate categories either; they are two extreme points in the same structure, which change positions, depending on the degree of centralization or decentralization in existence in the structure at any given point of time (p. 260). Secondly, Southall posits the 'segmentary state' as a counter-point to 'feudal polity' but ends up by suggesting its applicability to a series of historical political structures ranging from feudal France to 'traditional states of India, China and inner Asia' (pp. 252–4). There is no dearth of models one can draw upon (for example, the model of a 'galactic' state constructed by Tambiah on the basis of evidence from Thailand), and Stein is certainly not unaware of the curious position taken by Southall (Stein, 'Segmentary State . . . '), but the point remains that the model is projected as a key to our understanding of polity in 'traditional' India. Is it that it is being used to fill the vacuum created by the decline of 'Oriental Despotism' or of the venerated tradition of East-West dichotomy?

[93] Dirks, 'Political Authority and Structural Change . . . '.

While the analytic inseparability of 'State structure from State ritual'[94] is understandable, particularly in south India where material for the study of such a relationship is plentiful, the subordination of the political and economic dimensions of the state structure to its ritual dimension has led to the inevitable neglect of two imperatives under which a state is expected to operate: (i) stability in its power structure; (ii) resource mobilization[95] which, logically, cannot be separated from the process of the redistribution of resources to integrative elements within the state structure. To briefly illustrate the implications of these omissions, too narrow a definition of the 'core' of the Cola territory would leave unanswered why the Cola territorial reorganizations included apparently peripheral areas like Gaṅga-vāḍi and Nolamba-vāḍi[96] or why territorial conquests of strategic areas and areas of resource potential sought to eliminate existing powerholders and to convert them, in some cases at least, into extensions of patrimonial holdings.[97] The concept of a 'core' area as remaining permanently limited to the lineage area in the context of a supra-local polity is untenable; its definition too has to be seen more as functional than geographical.[98] The second omission has resulted in the postulate of

[94] Dirks, 'Structure and Meaning of Political Relations . . . '.

[95] See Eisentadt, xv–xvi, pp. 7–8.

[96] Subbarayalu, 'Mandalam as a Politico-Geographical Unit . . . '.

[97] The emergence of Cola power had its basis in the elimination of Muttaraiyar power in the Kaveri basin and then its penetration into *Toṇḍaimaṇḍalam.* Koṅgudeśa, Pāṇḍya country, Gaṅgavāḍi and Veṅgi, to mention only a few regions, lay inside the orbit of the Cola political interests, irrespective of the duration and fluctuations in actual control, whereas on the fringes of the Cola region proper local lineages could continue, although Subbarayalu thinks that the families of the 'Chiefs' were enlisted for the 'Chola army and administrative staff' (*Political Geography*, p. 80). For an attempt to determine the core of the Cola dominion through a study of the distribution pattern of Cola records, see G.W. Spencer and K.R. Hall, 'Toward an Analysis of Dynastic Hinterlands: The Imperial Cholas of 11th Century South India', *Asian Profile*, 2.1 (1974), pp. 51–62.

[98] I have already referred to the dispersed nodes of the Mauryan State (note 52); in the case of the Kuṣāṇas too Gandhāra in the north-west was a 'core' region and Mathura in the upper Ganga-Yamuna basin was another such region (B.D. Chattopadhyaya, 'Mathurā from Śuṅga to Kuṣāṇa Times: An Historical Outline', in Doris M. Srinivasan, ed., *Mathurā: The Cultural Heritage* (Delhi, 1989), pp. 19–30). 'Core', in the context of supra-local polities, has thus to acquire a flexible connotation.

the 'politics of plunder' as the major mechanism of resource acquisition and redistribution[99]—in fact, a mechanism which is essentially identical with the one present in the polity of the 'chiefdoms' of the Sangam age.[100] It is indeed curious that the postulate of the 'politics of plunder' has been put forward in relation to the Cola State in which a vast agrarian surplus sustained integrative elements in society and in which the state penetration into growing networks of trade and exchange could diversify and expand its resource bases enormously.[101]

The 'segmentary state' model or the concept of 'ritual sovereignty' cannot in fact resolve the problem of the political basis of integration since a rigid use of the 'segmentary state' concept relegates the different foci of power to the 'periphery' and does not really see them as components of the state structure. The phenomenon of different foci

[99] Stein, 'The State and Agrarian Order . . . '; the idea has been elaborated by G.W. Spencer, 'The Politics of Plunder: The Cholas in Eleventh Century Cylon', *Journal of Asian Studies*, 33.3 (1976), pp. 405–19. (Since I have not been able to consult Spencer's new publication, *Politics of Expansion: The Chola Conquest of Sri Lanka and Sri Vijaya* (Madras, 1983), I can only state his formulations in the article cited here). Spencer's own evidence contradicts his conclusion since it shows that Cola expansion was motivated more by strategic-commercial considerations, particularly considerations relating to the Pāṇḍya country, than by resource acquisition through raids. One may suggest that despite the revenue survey evidence of the time of the Colas and the actual occurrence of revenue terms (N. Karashima & B. Sitaraman, 'Revenue Terms in Chola Inscriptions', *Journal of Asian and African Studies*, 5 (1972), pp. 88—117; N. Karashima, 'Land Revenue Assessment in Cola Times as Seen in the Inscriptions of the Thanjavur and Gangaikondacolapuram Temples', cyclostyled copy) the revenue yield may have been limited, but the real issue is whether it was 'plunder' or agricultural surplus which sustained the ruling and non-ruling elites of society in eleventh century India. The answer is, of course, obvious, and studies on both the north and the south suggest that revenue demand in the early medieval period was on the increase.

[100] R.S. Kennedy, 'The King in Early South India, as Chieftain and Emperor', *The Indian Historical Review*, 3, 1 (1976), pp. 1–15.

[101] A recent detailed study on this is K.R. Hall, *Trade and Statecraft in the Age of the Colas* (Delhi, 1980); Idem, 'International Trade and Foreign Diplomacy in Early Medieval South India', *Journal of the Economic and Social History of the Orient*, 21 (1978), pp. 75–98. In fact, the phenomenon of the emergence of networks of exchange from the ninth–tenth centuries, which, in littoral regions, converged with those of international trade of that period was widespread; for Gujarat, see V.K. Jain; for local centres of exchange coinciding with centres of ruling lineages in various parts of India, see B.D. Chattopadhyaya, 'Urban Centres in Early Medieval India: An Overview' in this volume.

of power was not peculiarly south Indian but cut across all major political structures of the early medieval period, and there is thus a need for a common perspective, irrespective of the quality or the volume of material available from different regions. These diffused foci of 'quasi-autonomous' power are represented by what is broadly labelled as the *sāmanta* system which, although present in some form or the other in all major polities, has not been taken proper cognizance of by the protagonists of the 'segmentary state' model.[102] *Sāmanta* is of course a broad-spectrum category and encompasses a proliferating range of designations in use in the early medieval period. Not all the designations emerge simultaneously, but by the twelfth-thirteenth centuries such terms as *mahāsāmanta, sāmanta, mahāmaṇḍaleśvara, maṇḍaleśvara, rāṇaka, rāuta, ṭhakkura* and so on came to indicate a political order which was non-bureaucratic and in the context of which, in the overall structure of polity, the *rājapuruṣas* constituting the bureaucracy had only a limited part to play.[103] The order assumed the characteristics of a hierarchical formation, and this is clear not only in the binary hierarchy of *mahāsāmanta* and *sāmanta* or *mahāmaṇḍaleśvara* and *maṇḍaleśvara* but in the attempted schematization of the order in early medieval texts like the *Aparājitapṛcchā* as well.[104] The *sāmanta* in its trans-political connotation corresponded to the 'landed aristocracy' of the period; in addition, the spate of land assignments and other forms of prestation to various categories of donees, including those rendering military service to the state,[105] were

[102] Stein (*Peasant State* . . . , ch. 3) talks of local, autonomous chiefs in connection with the *nāḍu*, but his study of the Cola State has virtually no reference to the actual political linkage between them and the organization of Cola power. The report presented by N. Karashima and Y. Subbarayalu ('Statistical Study of Personal Names in Tamil Inscriptions: Interim Report II', *Computational Analysis of Asian and African Languages*, No. 3, 1976, pp. 9–20), on records from seven districts, lists more than 28 titles as 'feudatory', refers to their association with the administration and to distinctions between these titles; for details of different patterns of political and kin linkages, see Balambal; also Govindaswamy, 'The Role of Feudatories in Chola History'.

[103] For details for north India, see Yadava, *Society and Culture* . . . , ch. 3.

[104] Ibid.; also R.S. Sharma, *Social Changes in Early Medieval India (circa AD 500–1200)* (Delhi, 1969); a detailed study of the evidence has recently been made by R. Inden, 'Hierarchies of Kings . . . '.

[105] See note 24.

factors which, apart from the presence of the *sāmanta* landed aristocracy, weakened, it is believed, the hold of the state over both the polity and the revenue potential of its constituent territorial units.

The composition of the elites in any given state structure may have varied, but my argument requires that we begin with an explanation of the formation of a political structure rather than with a statement of its decentralized character. In other words, if the *sāmanta* system was, as has been suggested, the keynote of early medieval polity, then it needs to be recognized that from a pattern of relations characterized by *grahaṇa-mokṣa* (i.e. capture and release) in the early Gupta phase,[106] there was a shift towards a pattern in which the *sāmantas* were integrated into the structure of polity and in which the overlord-subordinate relation came to be dominant over other levels of relations in the structure. The political exigency of this integration from the Gupta period specially—and I posit *political* integration as a counterpoint to the decentralized polity of the feudal model—lay in the interrelatedness of polities caused by what I have called the horizontal spread of the state society and represented, geographically, by the lineages at their varied local bases. The exigency is expressed with some clarity in the following quote: 'The larger the unit the greater the King's power, and hence the greater his chances of being efficient within his geographical scope. Hence the constant urge to conquer . . . '.[107] The structure of polities was only partly based on the elimination of existing bases of power, by the expansion of the kin network of the lineage that emerged as dominant or by the organization of a bureaucracy that could connect different nodes in the structure, but the fact that political relations were regularly expressed as those between the overlord and his feudatories suggests that the dominant mode in the formation of the structure was by encapsulation of the existing bases of power, the spearhead in the structure being the overlord.

[106] Allahabad Pillar inscription of Samudragupta, Sircar, *Select Inscriptions*, I, p. 265. The expression means the same as *gṛhīta-pratimuktasya* which occurs in Kālidāsa's *Raghuvaṃśam*, IV. 33. And yet, it is from the fifth–sixth century that the term *sāmanta* comes to denote a subordinate position in relation to an overlord, L. Gopal, 'Samanta—its Varying Significance in Ancient India', *Journal of the Royal Asiatic Society of Great Britain and Ireland*, 1963, pp. 21–37.

[107] Derrett, p. 177.

The current state of research on the political history of the period makes it impossible to advance any generalization, from the vast corpus of early medieval material, regarding the composition of the feudatories, but two suggestions may be made: (i) since the emergence of the overlord himself had its basis mostly in local lineage power, the expansion of a lineage into a supra-local power was through pooling military resources and perhaps other forms of support of other lineages;[108] (ii) more importantly, pooling not only required a circulation or redistribution of resources[109] acquired in the process of expansion but required a system of ranking as well. These suggestions are in consonance with integrative polity and the transformation of the *sāmanta* into a vital component of the political structure is itself an evidence of ranking and in turn clarifies the political basis of integration. Ranking was associated with roles and services, and it may be postulated that a correlation was worked out between such roles as those of the *dūtaka*, *sāndhivigrahika*, *daṇḍanāyaka* and so on and ranking in the *sāmanta* hierarchy.[110] The gradual crystallization of

[108] A detailed examination of this will prove that the basic mechanism of the growth of the overlord–feudatory axis was not through the assignment of land and the transfer of state power. The Pratīhāras, for example, in the process of their emergence as a supra-regional power received support from the Cālukyas of Gujarat, Cāhamānas and other minor Pratihāra lineages; see *Epigraphia Indica*, 9, pp. 107–9; ibid., vol. 18, pp. 87–99; the reference to the *samastāṭavikasāmantacakra* in the *Rāmacarita* will also hardly fit the suggestion that the *sāmantas* were basically created, K.K. Gopal, 'The assembly of the sāmantas in early medieval India', *Journal of Indian History*, 42 (1964), pp. 231–50. For similar evidence regarding Pallava and Cola polities, see Dirks, 'Political Authority . . . '; Stein, 'All the King's Mana . . . '; Govindaswamy and Balambal (works cited above).

[109] Cf. references in the records of Rāṣṭrakūṭa Kṛṣṇa III to the distribution of conquered dominions among his subordinates, *Epigraphia Indica*, 4, p. 285; ibid., 5, p. 35; for reference to the award, in the Cola period, of chieftainship for the suppression of *raja-drohis*, *Annual Report on South Indian Epigraphy*, 1913, p. 40.

[110] Sharma (*Social Changes* . . .) too uses the term 'feudal ranks' but not in the sense of a system which emerges in the context of interdependent polities. Ranking is suggested by the pairing or other forms of combination of *sāmanta/mahāsāmanta* with designations which are basically administrative in connotation. For details, see Yadava, *Society and Culture* . . . , ch. 3, although Yadava does not view the evidence from the position that I would like to take; also L. Gopal; for the south, see Karashima and Subbarayalu 'Statistical Study . . . '; D. Desai, *Mahāmaṇḍaleśvaras* . . . ; Balambal; and Govindaswamy.

ranking permeated the early medieval society to such an extent that the status of members within individual ruling lineages came to be expressed in terms of ranks[111] and that ranks extended to even non-ruling groups and individuals.[112] And in terms of the social process, the transformation of political ranking could in the long run take the form of caste ranking.[113]

Rank as the basis of political organization implies differential access to the centre as also shifts within the system of ranking. The description in the *Aparājitapṛcchā*, although built up around an overlord of the ideal *cakravartī* model, nevertheless points to the relative positioning of different categories of ruling elites including *daṇḍanāyakas, maṇḍaleśas, māṇḍalikas, mahāsāmantas, sāmantas, laghusāmantas, caturaśikas, rājaputras* and so on. The system of ranking in relation to the overlord as offered in the text which was composed at the Caulukyan court in Gujarat may be reflective more of the text's perception of *Cakravartī* power than an actual order, but significantly, a correlation between territorial political hold and rank can be detected in its description.[114] Since the basis of territorial and political hold was not static, rank was not static either. In fact, even inadequate studies available so far would suggest that ranks held by individual families underwent changes,[115] that ranks varied from one generation to the next[116] and that aspirations for higher ranks were operative within

[111] Cf. the interesting case of the great queen Baṃmaladevī being addressed as *Mahāmaṇḍaleśvarī* in a record of 1179, *Epigraphia Carnatica*, 12, Tm. 35; for evidence from Rajasthan, see Chattopadhyaya, 'Origin of the Rajputs . . .'.

[112] Śūlapāṇi who was the head of the *Varendraka-śilpī-goṣṭhī* (guild of *sūtradharas* of north Bengal) is mentioned as a *rāṇaka* in the Deopara *praśasti* of the twelfth century, Sircar, *Select Inscriptions*, 2, p. 121; a record of 1263 from Jalor refers to the 'head worshipper' of a Mahāvīra temple as *Bhaṭṭāraka Rāvala*, Appendix to *Epigraphia Indica*, 19–23, No. 563.

[113] K.P. Ammakutty, 'Origin of the Samanta Caste in Kerala', *Proceedings of the Indian History Congress*, 41 session (Bombay, 1980), pp. 86–92. In Bengal and Orissa, *sāmanta, mahāpātra, paṭṭanāyaka* and so on are related to caste position.

[114] R. Inden, 'Hierarchies of Kings . . .'.

[115] For example, a record of 1151 from Tumkur district, *Epigraphia Carnatica*, 12, Tm. 9: the range is between *Pañcamahāśabda mahāsāmanta* and *nāyaka*.

[116] Cf. the article by D. Shukla, 'The Trend of Demotion of Feudal Families in the Early Medieval Indian Complex', *Proceedings of the Indian History Congress*, 41 session (Bombay, 1980), pp. 177–183.

individual political structures.[117] If the idea of ranking as the political basis of the organization of both local and supra-local structures be accepted, then it may be followed up for locating the potential sources of tension on the political plane: between the rank-holders as also between them and the overlord. Channels open for the diffusion of such tensions would not have been many; expansion of the kinship network, itself encompassed by the system of ranking, assignments in return for services as a means of displacing locally entrenched lineage power or diversification of the composition of ruling elites by drawing in non-ruling groups in the system of ranking[118] could only create new loci of power. Crisis was thus built into the process of the formation of the structures; a concrete statement of the crisis as it manifested itself in individual cases is a detail which has still to be satisfactorily worked out.

VI

Before concluding, I wish to reiterate what I said in the beginning: what has been presented is essentially a statement of my groping for a framework for the study of early medieval polity. I have said that the genesis of the specific features of early medieval polity cannot be satisfactorily comprehended either by isolating a single unit and analyzing the relationship of its segments in ritual terms or by the notion of decentralized polity in which bases of power are created from above through individual or institutional agents. If we take an all-India perspective, the shifting political geography of the lineages of the period seems, on the other hand, to suggest that the structure of early medieval polity was a logical development from the territorially limited state society of the early historical period to a gradual but far greater penetration of the state society into local agrarian and peripheral levels, generating continuous fissions at such levels. The feudatory and other intermediary strata in the early medieval structures of polity, in the absence of a definite correlation between service assignments and the

117 Derrett, p. 179.

118 For examples of big merchants and merchant families being elevated to the ranks of *daṇḍa-pati*, *daṇḍādhipati* and even *nṛpati* with appropriate insignias, see V.K. Jain, pp. 323ff.

formation of these strata, may thus be seen in terms of an 'integrative polity',[119] with potential sources of tension built into the structures. The early medieval phase of polity was perhaps in a way an intermediate phase—a prelude to the exercise of greater control by the medieval state through its nobility and its regulated system of service assignments, but then if the broad-spectrum *sāmanta* category was a dominant element in early medieval polity, so did the broad-spectrum category of 'zamindars' continue as an 'irritant' in the medieval state structure.[120]

All this, at the moment, is essentially a hypothesis, but I venture to place the hypothesis before you because of my conviction that historical studies progress through sharing, though not necessarily through consensus, and that History is not only a continuous dialogue between historians and their material from the past but is also an equally continuous dialogue between historians themselves.

[119] H. Kulke ('Fragmentation and Segmentation Versus Integration? Reflections on the Concepts of Indian Feudalism and the Segmentary State in Indian History', *Studies in History*, vol. 4, No. 2 (1982), pp. 236–7), also speaks of integration at the regional level but generally avoids discussing the political mechanism of integration.

[120] I. Habib, *The Agrarian System of Mughal India* (Asia Publishing House, 1963), ch. 5; Idem, 'The Peasant in Indian History', General President's Address, Indian History Congress, 43 session (Kurukshetra, 1982); S. Nurul Hasan, 'Zamindars Under the Mughals' in R.E. Frykenberg, ed., pp. 17–32; also A.R. Khan, *Chieftains in the Mughal Empire During the Reign of Akbar* (Simla, 1977), Introduction.

9

Religion in a Royal Household: A Study of Some Aspects of Rājaśekhara's Karpūramañjarī*

Rājaśekhara, who lived between the close of the ninth and the early part of the tenth century, was, in many ways, a man of the world and a man of worldly connections.[1] His ancestry is made to look impeccable in his own works: he was descended from *Yāyāvara-kula*, a lineage which is repeatedly eulogised in his works and with which were believed to have been connected such eminent litterateurs as Akāla-Jalada, Surānanda, Tarala and Kavirāja. In fact, it is quite possible that Akāla-Jalada was Rājaśekhara's grandfather and was a source of poetic inspiration to him. Two other connections must have substantially enriched his direct experience regarding contemporary elite society: (i) the association of his family with royalty; and (ii) his marriage. Rājaśekhara's father, Durduka, was a *mahāmantrī*, and his own connections with the Pratīhāra family, one of the most eminent royal families of the period, opened up for him the exclusive world of the courtly culture of early medieval India. He was a *Kavirāja* at the court of Mahendrapāla who regarded Rājaśekhara as his *guru*; he continued his association with the Pratīhāra court during the period of Mahīpāla but later shifted to Tripurī which was rising to

* Reprinted from P. Jash, ed., *Religion and Society in Ancient India* (Sudhakar Chattopadhyaya Commemoration Volume) (Calcutta, 1984).

[1] The biographical sketch of Rājaśekhara is prepared mainly on the basis of details available in the following works: S. Konow and C.R. Lanman, *Rājaśekhara's Karpūramañjarī*, second issue (Delhi, 1963), pp. 177–82; C.D. Dalal and R.A. Sastry, *Kāvyamīmāṃsā of Rājaśekhara*, 3rd edition (Baroda, 1934), Introduction, XII–XLV; Nagendranath Chakrabarti, *Rājaśekhara O Kāvyamīmāṃsā* (in Bengali) (Santiniketan, 1960), pp. 4–23; V.V. Mirashi, *Inscriptions of the Kalachuri-Chedi Era* (Corpus Inscriptionum Indicarum), vol. 4, pt. I (Ootacamund, 1955), pp. CLXXIV–CLXXVI; Manomohan Ghosh, *Rājaśekhara's Karpūramañjarī* (a Prakrit play), with translations, revised third edition (Calcutta, 1972), pp. 65–72.

prominence under the Kalacuris. His Kalacuri connection is curiously reflected in a verse in the Bilhari stone inscription of Yuvarāja II which puts forward the claim that the composition of the epigraph would evoke admiration from the great poet Rājaśekhara.[2] Rājaśekhara was married to Avantisundarī who is described as *Cāhüānakulamolimāliya* in the *Karpūramañjarī*;[3] the Cāhamāna clan was already on the way to becoming one of the major Rajput families in the early medieval period.[4]

Rājaśekhara was thus, by virtue of his descent and personal connections, eminently suited to assess the courtly culture of his period. In one respect, they must have given him an opportunity to grasp the essentials of the political and cultural situation on a pan-Indian scale. Even if we do not consider him as primarily a commentator of politics and culture of his time, his awareness of the key politico-cultural areas of his period comes out clearly in the repeated references he makes in his works to the contemporary *janapadas* and their linguistic, literary and other cultural traits. It was perhaps almost an obsession with him, so much so that a fellow litterateur, Kṣemendra, could not resist making a bawdy joke at Rājaśekhara's expense in his *Aucitya-vicāra-carcā*:

Kārṇāṭīdaśanāṃkita-sitamahārāṣṭrīkaṭākṣakṣataḥ
Prauḍhāndhrīstanapīḍita-praṇayinībhrubhaṅga-Vitrāsitaḥ
Lāṭībāhuviveṣṭitaśca-Malayastrītarjanī-tarjitaḥ
So'yam samprati Rājaśekhara-Vārāṇasīṃ bāñchati.[5]

[Our translation:

'Rājaśekhara, who has acquired marks (on his body by being bitten) with the teeth of the females of Karṇāṭa, who has been wounded by the sideways glances of the fair women of Mahārāṣṭra, who has been oppressed (being

[2] Mirashi, p. 207.

[3] *Karpūramañjarī*, I, II. In the preparation of this paper the text and translation of *Karpūramañjarī* as available in Konow and Lanman and in Manomohan Ghosh have been followed.

[4] See D. Sharma, *Early Chauhan Dynasties* (A study of Chauhan political history, Chauhan political institutions and life in the Chauhan dominions from *c.* 800 to 1316 AD) (Delhi, 1959), *passim*; also, B.D. Chattopadhyaya, 'Origin of the Rajputs: Political, Economic and Social Processes in Early Medieval Rajasthan' in this volume.

[5] Cited in N. Chakrabarti, p. 22.

pressed) by the breasts of the mature women of Andhra and threatened by the artfully twisted eyebrows of the beloved, who has been encircled by the arms of the females of Lāṭa, and who has received threats from the rebuking forefingers of the women of Malaya, now desires (refuge) in Vārāṇasī'.]

All this points to a rich possibility for the historian. As Rājaśekhara must have observed the royalty and the court culture from close quarters, it may be legitimately presumed that his works constitute valuable source material for the study of early medieval society. The point is, to what extent do his works actually reflect his awareness? This brief essay does not purport to answer this question fully; in it an attempt is made to explore a single work of Rājaśekhara, namely the *Karpūramañjarī*, and to analyse how trends in religion which are a vital part of the social orientation of this period are reflected in his work, at least at the level of the royalty. It is hoped that the sections that follow will provide the *raison d'être* of the selection of the text for such an analysis.

II

There are a few useful references in the *Karpūramañjarī* to the daily rites performed by the members of the royal household. At the end of Act I, the king retires to his evening worship (*saṃjhaṃ vandidum*).[6] In Act II, the application of sectarian marks (*ṭikkidā*) forms a part of the toiletry of the heroine, *Karpūramañjarī*.[7] These incidental notices however do not really relate structurally to the play, and in the case of *Karpūramañjarī* it is only an analysis of its central elements that may be expected to reveal the religious nuances embedded in it.

The cast of *Karpūramañjarī* is small and stereotyped, as is its plot. Almost throughout the play the king, who is on the way to becoming a *cakkavatti* (*cakravartī*) is in the company of his jester and their combined thoughts and efforts are directed to winning, for the king, the hand of *Karpūramañjarī*, the heroine. What makes the plot significant for our purpose is the character of Bhairavānanda who is at the centre of all that happens in the play, and even if all that happens

[6] Konow and Lanman, p. 242.
[7] *Karpūramañjarī*, II–12.

verges on the realm of the supernatural, it is the element of supernaturality which ultimately connects the play with the religious world of the early medieval period.

Bhairavānanda enters the play in Act I and gains easy access to the king and the queen as he is popularly reported to be an *atyadbhūtasiddhi*, i.e. 'one who has achieved miracles'.[8] His maiden speech is revealing in several ways and merits close study:

Manto ṇa tanto ṇa-a kiṃ-pi jāṇe
Jhāṃṇaṃ-ca ṇa Kiṃ-pi guruppasādā
Majjaṃ pivāmo mahilaṃ ramāmo
Mokkhaṃ-ca jāmo kulamaggalaggā.

[M. Ghosh's translation:

'I do not know any mantra or ritual, nor do I know any meditation. (But) by favour of my master I shall drink wine and have intercourse with the wife (lit. woman) and attain liberation attached to the Kaula way.'][9]

Bhairavānanda thus makes a frank confession of his ignorance of *mantra* and *tantra* but this negative side has a complementary positive aspect. Bhairavānanda is primarily interested in the pleasures of the flesh (*majja, māṃsa* and *mahilā*) but that they do not constitute purely secular pleasures is amply clear from what follows. The speech continues:

Raṇḍā Caṇḍā dikkhidā dhammadārā
Maṃjjaṃ māṃsaṃ piñjae khajjae-a
Bhikkhā bhojjaṃ Cammakhaṇḍam-ca sejjā
Kolo dhammo Kassa ṇo bhādi rammo.

[M. Ghosh's translation:

'A widow or a Caṇḍāla woman I may take as my legal wife. Wine may be drunk and meat may be eaten; begging may bring me food and a piece of hide may be my bed. To whom will the Kaula way not appear as lovely?'][10]

[8] Ibid., I, 21.

[9] M. Ghosh, pp. 91, 193. The translation offered by Ghosh requires some form of correction. For example, his translation, 'My Master' has to be understood in the sense of 'my guru' or 'preceptor', and 'wife' in the sense of 'female'.

[10] Ibid., I. 22; M. Ghosh, pp. 91, 193.

The text thus firmly establishes the *kaula-dharma* or *kaula* sectarian affiliation of Bhairavānanda. For comparison, a summary of *Kaula* practices in early medieval India may be cited: 'Kaulas believed in *trikamata* which consists in indulgence in drink and meat, and worship of Śiva in the company of a female partner sitting on the left during the rites. The *kaula* worshipper played the role of Śiva as united with Pārvatī and exhibited the *yoni-mudrā*.'[11] For the Kaula, Bhairavānanda, the path of salvation is not through trance, holy rites and the Vedas preached by Viṣṇu and Brahmā; his source of salvation is Umā's dear lover, through *suraakeli surārasehim*.[12]

The relevant passage runs as follows:

Muttiṃ bhaṇanti Haribamhamuhā-vi devā
Jhāṇeṇa Veapaḍhaṇeṇa Kadukkiāhiṃ
Ekkeṇa Kevalamumādaideṇa diṭṭho
Mokkho samaṃ suraakelisurārasehiṃ.

[M. Ghosh's translation:

'Even gods like Hari and Brahmā say that salvation comes from meditation, recitation of the Vedas and performing sacrifices. Only the dear consort of Umā (i.e. Śiva) sees salvation with love-sports and drinking of liquor.'][13]

Bhairavānanda's maiden speech thus appears to be of great significance in several ways. To the *Kaulācārī*, Śiva is not only the supreme god-head; to him the Purāṇic Trinity and orthopraxy of the form of reference to the Vedas as the fountainhead of religion is totally redundant. That it confirms the picture of the emergence of new sects and of growing sectarian separation in the early medieval period needs hardly to be stated. What is important is the context of the royal court in which the king and his brahmin *vidūṣaka* become subservient to the supernatural powers wielded by Bhairavānanda, for the supernatural power operates towards an end which is the ultimate objective of a king, namely the attainment of the status of a *cakravartī*. Unlike in Rājaśekhara's *Viddhaśālabhañjikā*, in the *Karpūramañjarī* this seems to happen without any military feat. Bhairavānanda produces Karpūra-

[11] Devangana Desai, *Erotic Sculpture of India* (New Delhi, 1975), p. 121.
[12] *Karpūramañjarī*, I–24.
[13] M. Ghosh, pp. 91, 193.

mañjarī, the heroine, at the court through his supernatural powers, and it is her marriage with the king, again accomplished through Bhairavānanda's intervention, that bestows upon the king the desired sovereign status.[14]

Perhaps Rājaśekhara was trying to offer an explanation, in line with what was considered plausible in the period, for a widespread contemporary phenomenon, namely the presence of Tāntric elements close to the royalty. Tāntrism permeated a wide range of sectarian practices from the Gupta period onward, and there is a curiously ambivalent attitude towards the practitioners of the Tāntric cults among the litterateurs. The attitude generally is one of disdain, but esoterism also commands fear and respect from a distance and this may explain why, despite the tone of disapprobation towards the Tāntric practitioners, there was no way of avoiding referring to them altogether. Devangana Desai has collected a few references where the Tāntrikas are spoken of disapprovingly.[15] For example, in the *Mālatī-Mādhava*, the Kāpālika Aghoraghaṇṭa and his female disciple, Kapālakuṇḍalā, are called *caṇḍālas.* And yet in the same play, Mādhava, the son of a minister who condemns the Kāpālikas, himself goes to the cremation ground for offering his own flesh. King Puṣpabhūti, Harṣa's forefather, is said to have visited a cremation ground with Bhairavācārya. Puṣpabhūti even offered to place himself, his harem, his court and his treasury at the ascetic's disposal. Kaulācārī Bhairavānanda, around whom Rājaśekhara weaves the *Karpūramañjarī* has thus a long ancestry and is not a creation of pure imagination.

III

Two other references in the *Karpūramañjarī*, to practices associated with the ladies of the royal seraglio, are worth analyzing. One is to the swing festival of Gaurī mentioned in Act II.[16] The swing festival has normally a Vaiṣṇavite association but the *Karpūramañjarī* certainly

[14] For the English translation of *Viddhaśālabhañjikā*, see *Journal of the American Oriental Society*, vol. 27, pp. 1–71.

[15] Devangana Desai, pp. 123–4.

[16] Konow and Lanman, p. 246.

points to the existence of its Śaivite counterpart. This phenomenon was perhaps early medieval in origin, although one cannot be too certain on this score.[17] In the *Karpūramañjarī* reference what is significant is not really the swing festival of Gaurī by itself but rather Bhairavānanda's association with it. On the fourth day of the festival the queen pays homage to the goddess by offering *Ketaka* flowers—an offering made possible by Bhairavānanda who makes the *Ketaka* blossom in *Caitra*[18] which, unlike the swing festival associated with Kṛṣṇa, is when the swing festival of Pārvatī takes place. It is believed that the swing festival in honour of Gaurī represents a *vrata*, spoken of as *Gaurīvrata* in other texts, which takes place on the third day of the bright half of *Caitra*.[19] This is not unlikely because the *Karpūramañjarī* contains another and more direct reference to a *vrata* called *Vaḍasāvittimahusava*.[20] *Vaḍasāvittimahusava* definitely corresponds to *Vaṭasāvitrīvrata* mentioned in a number of early medieval and medieval texts. It generally took place on the fourteenth day of the bright half of Jyeṣṭha and was performed by women whose husbands were living or even by sonless widows.[21] Kane has compiled some details of this *vrata* and it is necessary to examine these details in order to understand the significance of the *Karpūramañjarī* evidence. 'The procedure of the *vrata*, as set out in the *Vratārka* . . . and other later medieval works, is briefly as follows: The woman should make a *saṅkalpa* in the form: "I shall perform Sāvitrīvrata for securing long life and health to my husband and my sons and for securing freedom from widowhood in this and subsequent lives." She should then sprinkle water at the root of the *vaṭa* tree and surround it with cotton threads and should perform its worship with the *upacāras* and then offer worship to Sāvitrī (with image or mentally) . . . '[22]

Vaṭasāvitrīvrata is, as all other *vratas* are, clearly magical in import.

[17] Several references to the swing festival with Śaivite associations, compiled by B.P. Mazumdar, all occur in the context of the early medieval period, *Socio-Economic History of North India (1030–1194 AD)* (Calcutta, 1960), p. 277.

[18] *Karpūramañjarī*, II. 7.

[19] Konow and Lanman, p. 246, fn. 6; also B.P. Mazumdar, p. 280.

[20] *Karpūramañjarī*, IV. 10.

[21] P.V. Kane, *History of Dharmaśāstra*, vol. 5, pt. I, second edition (Poona, 1974), pp. 91–4.

[22] Ibid., p. 93.

However, in the *Karpūramañjarī*, *Vaḍasāvittimahusava* does not seem to be a mere domestic magical rite, and there are several elements which somewhat distinguish it from the corresponding *vrata* mentioned in the texts. Act IV of the play refers several times[23] to the installation of an image of Cāmuṇḍā, a Kaula-Kapalika deity per excellence,[24] in a sanctuary by Bhairavānanda. The sanctuary is constructed at the foot of a *vaṭa* tree. A close scrutiny of Act IV thus easily establishes the connection between the image of Cāmuṇḍā (a surrogate for Sāvitrī?) and the *vaṭa* in the context of the performance of the festival. Second, the king is invited by the queen to witness from the palace terrace certain spectacles in connection with the *vrata*, and what the king witnesses is a series of dances, performed only by women, which are distinctly connected with the *vrata* ritual. The description of the item may bring out further the affiliation of the ritual:

'Yet others, bearing in their hands offering of human flesh and terrible with their groans and shrieks and cries and wearing the masks of night-wondering ogresses, are enacting a cemetery-scene.'[25]

The *Vaḍasāvittimahusava* of *Karpūramañjarī* thus does not exactly correspond to the ideal type of the *vrata* which Kane has reconstructed. It has a different significance and fits in more closely with the ritual activities, throughout the play, of Bhairavānanda and with the incantation that he offers to Cāmuṇḍā: 'A dissolution of the universe is her pleasure-house; the blood of the demons is her fiery drought; victorious is Kālī as she quaffs it, in presence of Kāla, from a goblet made of the skull of Parameṣṭhin.'[26]

[23] *Karpūramañjarī*, IV. 19.
[24] Devangana Desai, p. 124. For a discussion of the reference in the *Mālatī-Mādhava* to the temple of Karāla-Cāmuṇḍā and her worshipper Aghoraghaṇṭa, see J.N. Banerjee, *Pauranic and Tantric Religion* (Calcutta University, 1966), p. 117.
[25] Konow and Lanman, p. 281.
[26] Ibid., p. 283.

IV

In the final section of this essay it is necessary to point out that through his use of various elements associated with the Kaula-Kāpālika rites in the *Karpūramañjarī* Rājaśekhara has not projected a situation which may be considered universal. Nevertheless, in several ways the play makes a significant contribution to our understanding of the early medieval religious world and of the contemporary attitude towards it. Rājaśekhara has brought—one cannot be entirely sure whether he has done so deliberately or not—two streams of magical rites to converge in the *Karpūramañjarī*. 'The magical aspect was basic to Tāntrism,'[27] and it was basic to *vrata* rites as well.[28] Perhaps through effecting a convergence of these two streams in the *Karpūramañjarī* Rājaśekhara was trying to posit a contrast between what may be broadly labelled as the Tāntric and the non-Tāntric world, although he is not seen to indulge in any direct value-judgement. It has already been remarked that in many ways the early medieval attitude towards the world of Tāntrism was ambivalent; this is understandable because of its wide prevalence as also the character of its clientele, apart from its sheer esoterism. Rājaśekhara does not, like Kṛṣṇa Miśra, the author of *Prabodhacandrodaya* and also a recipient of courtly favour from the contemporary Candellas, offer *Viṣṇubhakti* as the panacea for all Tāntric and heterodox evils;[29] as one sharing the same type of clientele he concludes *Karpūramañjarī* with a prayer in the form of a quotation from Bharata:

'May the forest-fire of Poverty, which day after day gleams far and wide,

[27] Devangana Desai, p. 145.

[28] Kane, p. 94, has disparaged the attempt of B.A. Gupte to find symbolism in the *vrata* ritual. According to Gupte, 'The Savitri vrata . . . is the annual celebration of Mother Earth's marriage with nature . . . reviving after the few showers of the monsoon', 'The Symbolism of Savitri-vrata', *The Indian Antiquary*, vol. 35 (1906), pp. 116–19. Gupte's specific interpretation may not be valid, but this does not invalidate the magical character of the *vrata* rites. See Abanindranath Tagore, *Banglar Vrata* (in Bengali), B.S. 1356, *passim.*

[29] See S.K. Nambiar, *Prabodhachandrodaya of Kṛṣṇa Miśra* (Delhi-Varanasi-Patna, 1971), ch. IV and *passim.* The *Prabodhachandrodaya* also contains valuable data relating to sectarian rivalry and the attitude of hostility towards Tāntric schools.

which brings to naught all the excellences of men of learning, be quenched by the rain of the side-long glances of fortune.'[30]

[30] Konow and Lanman, p. 288. For an understanding of the sentiment expressed in these lines, refer to the statement made by D.D. Kosambi in his analysis of Bhartṛhari, despite the obvious differences which may have existed between Bharata, Bhartṛhari and Rājaśekhara: 'He is unmistakably the Indian intellectual of his period, limited by caste and tradition in fields of activity and therefore limited in his real grip on life. The only alternatives open to any member of his class seem to have been the attainment of patronage at court, or retirement to the life of an almsman. The inner conflict, the contradiction latent in the very position of this class, could not have been made clearer than by the poet's verses'. D.D. Kosambi, 'The Quality of Renunciation in Bhartrihari's Poetry', in *Exasperating Essays* (Exercise in the Dialectical Method) (reprinted in Pune, 1986), pp. 72–93. The ambivalence of Rājaśekhara, present among his contemporaries as well with regard to the Kaula Kāpālika practices, represents perhaps more acutely an attitude of compromise characterizing patronage-seeking orthodox elements in society.

Bibliography

A. PRIMARY SOURCES

1. Texts (Indigenous and Non-Indigenous: In Original and in Translation)

A Record of the Buddhist Religion as practised in India and Malay Archipelago, translated by J. Takakusu (Oxford, 1896).

Arthaśāstra of Kauṭilya: translated by R.P. Kangle (University of Bombay, Bombay, 1972).

Karpūramañjarī: S. Konow and C.R. Lanman, *Rājaśekhara's Karpūramañjarī*, reprint (Delhi, 1963).

Manomohan Ghosh, *Rājaśekhara's Karpūramañjarī* (A Prakrit play), with translation, revised third edition (Calcutta, 1972).

Kāvyamīmāṃsā:

1. edited by G.S. Rai (Varanasi, 1964).
2. C.D. Dalal and R.A. Sastry, *Kāvyamīmāṃsā of Rājaśekhara*, third edition (Baroda, 1934).
3. Nagendranath Chakravarti, *Rājaśekhara O Kāvyamīmāṃsā* (in Bengali) (Santiniketan, 1960).

Manusmṛti:

The Laws of Manu, with the Bhāṣya of Medhātithi, 4 vols., translated by Ganganath Jha (Calcutta, 1922–27).

Meghadūtam: C.R. Devadhar, *Works of Kālidāsa* (edited with a critical introduction, translation and notes) vol. 2 (Poetry) (Delhi, 1984).

Prabodhacandrodaya: S.K. Nambiar, *Prabodhacandrodaya of Kṛṣṇa Miśra* (Delhi, 1971).

Rājataraṅgiṇī of Kalhaṇa:

M.A. Stein, *Kalhaṇa's Rājataraṅgiṇī: A Chronicle of the Kings of Kashmir*, vol. I, reprint (Delhi, 1961).

Rāmacaritam of Sandhyākaranandi: R.C. Majumdar, Radhagovinda Basak and Pandit Nanigopal Banerji, *The Rāmacaritam of Sandhyākaranandin* (Rajshahi, 1939).

Samarāïcca-Kahā:

H. Jacobi, *Samarāïcca-kahā, A Jaina Prākṛta work*, vol. I (Calcutta, 1926).

Samarāṅganasūtradhāra: edited by T. Ganapati Sastri and V.S. Agrawal (Baroda, 1966).

Si-Yu-Ki:

(1) *Si-Yu-Ki: Buddhist Records of the Western World*, translated by S. Beal, vol. I, reprint (Delhi, 1969).

(2) *On Yuan Chwang's Travels in India*, translated by T. Watters and edited by T.W. Rhys Davis and S.W. Bushell, reprint (Delhi, 1961).

Tabaqāt-i-Nāsirī: translated by H.G. Raverty, reprint (New Delhi, 1970).

The Periplus of the Erythraean Sea:

(1) translated and edited by W.H. Schoff, reprint (Delhi, 1974).

(2) translated and edited by G.W.B. Huntingford (London, 1980).

Vāstuśāstra: vol. I *(Hindu Science of Architecture)*, edited by D.N. Sukla (Chandigarh, n.d.).

2. *Archaeological Material*

Archaeological Survey of India, Annual Report: 1903–4, 1925–26.

Annual Report on the Working of the Rajputana Museum (Ajmer), from 1909–1936.

Archaeological Remains and Excavations at Bairat by D.R. Sahni (Department of Archaeology and Historical Research, Jaipur, n.d.).

Excavations at Ahar (Tamvavati) by H.D. Sankalia, S.B. Deo and Z.D. Ansari (Poona, 1969).

Excavations at Rairh during 1938–39 and 1939–40 by K.N. Puri (Department of Archaeology and Historical Research, Jaipur, n.d.).

Excavations at Tilaura-Kot and Explorations in the Nepalese-Tarai by Debala Mitra (The Department of Archaeology, Nepal, 1972).

Indian Archaeology—A Review (Archaeological Survey of India): 1956–57 to 1970–71.

Progress Report of the Archaeological Survey, Western Circle: 1905–6; 1907–8; 1908–9; 1909–10; 1910–11; 1911–12; 1914–15; 1916–17; 1920–21.

Rang-Mahal (The Swedish Archaeological Expedition to India) by Hanna Rydh (Lund-Bonn-Bombay, 1959).

The Archaeological Remains and Excavations at Nagari (Memoirs of the Archaeological Survey of India, No. 4) by D.R. Bhandarkar (Calcutta, 1920).

3. *Epigraphic and Numismatic Material*

A Collection of Prakrit and Sanskrit Inscriptions (Bhavanagar Archaeological Department, Bhavanagar, n.d.).

Annual Report of Indian Epigraphy. 1952–53, 1954–55, 1959–60, 1960–62, 1964–65.

Annual Report on South Indian Epigraphy. 1913.

Annual Report on the Working of the Rajputana Museum (Ajmer): 1909–1936.

Corpus of Śāradā Inscriptions of Kashmir by B.K. Kaul Deambi (Delhi, 1982).

Epigraphia Carnatica, vol. 12.

Epigraphia Indica, vols. 1–37 (Archaeological Survey of India, 1892 onward).

Epigraphic Discoveries in East Pakistan by D.C. Sircar (Calcutta, 1973).

Historical Inscriptions of Gujrat (in Gujrati), Sri Forbes Gujrati Sabha Series, No. 15, by G.V. Acharyya, part 2 (Bombay, 1935).

Inscriptions of the Kalachuri-Chedi Era (Corpus Inscriptionum Indicarum, vol. 4, 2 parts), edited by V.V. Mirashi (Ootacamund, 1955).

Inscriptions of the Paramāras, Chandellas, Kachchhapaghātas and two minor dynasties (Corpus Inscriptionum Indicarum, vol. 7, part 2), edited by H.V. Trivedi (Archaeological Survey of India, New Delhi, n.d.).

Jaina Inscriptions of Rajasthan by R.V. Somani (Jaipur, 1982).

Jaina Lekha Saṃgraha by P.C. Nahar, vol. I (Calcutta, 1918); vol. II (Calcutta, 1927).

Progress Report of the Archaeological Survey, Western Circle. 1905–6; 1907–8; 1908–9; 1909–10; 1910–11; 1911–12; 1914–15; 1916–17; 1920–21.

Roman Coins from Andhra Pradesh by P.L. Gupta (Andhra Pradesh Government Museum Series, No. 10, Hyderabad, 1965).

Select Inscriptions bearing on Indian History and Civilization, vol. 1, by D.C. Sircar, second edition (University of Calcutta, Calcutta, 1965).

Select Inscriptions bearing on Indian History and Civilization, vol. 2, by D.C. Sircar (Delhi, 1983).

B. LEXICONS

Deb, Raja Radhakanta, *Śabdakalpadruma,* part I (Calcutta, Saka 1808–1886; reprinted, Delhi, 1961).

Monier-Williams, M., *A Sanskrit-English Dictionary,* reprint (Oxford, 1964).

C. SECONDARY PUBLICATIONS

1. *Books and Dissertations*

Adams, R.M., *The Evolution of Urban Society (Early Mesopotamia and pre-Hispanic Mexico)* (Chicago, 1966).

Adhya, G.L., *Early Indian Economics (Studies in the Economic Life of Northern and Western India, C. 200 BC–300 AD)* (Bombay, 1966).

Altekar, A.S., *The Rāshṭrakūṭas and Their Times* (Poona, 1934).

—— *State and Government in Ancient India*, reprint of 3rd edition (Delhi, 1972).

Anderson, Perry, *Lineages of the Absolutist State* (Verso edition, London, 1974).

Appadorai, A., *Economic Conditions in Southern India (1000–1500 AD)*, 2 parts (University of Madras, Madras, 1936).

Aquique, Md., *Economic History of Mithila (C. 600 BC–1097 AD)* (New Delhi, 1974).

Asopa, J.N., *Origin of the Rajputs* (Delhi, 1976).

Bagai, Anjali, 'Merchandise and Mercantile Community in post-Gupta times in Northern India' (Ph.D dissertation, University of Delhi, 1985).

Balambal, V., *Feudatories of South India* (Allahabad, 1978).

Bandyopadhyaya, N.C., *Development of Hindu Polity and Political Theories*, edited by N.N. Bhattacharyya (New Delhi, 1980).

Banerjea, J.N., *Paurāṇic and Tāntrik Religion* (University of Calcutta, Calcutta, 1966).

Basham, A.L., *Studies in Indian History and Culture* (Calcutta, 1964).

Belshaw, Cyril, *Traditional Exchange and Modern Markets*, Indian reprint (Prentice Hall, New Delhi, 1969).

Bhatia, P., *The Paramāras* (Delhi, 1968).

Bhattacharyya, B., *Urban Development in India (Since Prehistoric Times)* (Delhi, 1979).

Bhattacharyya, P.K., *Historical Geography of Madhya Pradesh from Early Records* (Delhi-Varanasi-Patna, 1977).

Biardeau, Madeleine, *Hinduism: The Anthropology of a Civilization* (New Delhi, 1989).

Bose, M.K., *Late Classical India* (Calcutta, 1988).

Braudel, Fernand, *The Structure of Everyday Life* (London, 1981).

Chattopadhayaya, B.D., *Aspects of Rural Settlements and Rural Society in Early Medieval India* (Calcutta, 1990).

Chaudhary, A.K., *Early Medieval Village in North-eastern India (AD 600–1200)* (Calcutta, 1971).

Chicherov, A.I., *India: Economic Development in the 16th–18th Centuries* (Moscow, 1971).

Cipolla, Carlo, M. (ed.), *The Fontana Economic History of Europe*, vol. 1 (The Middle Ages), Collins/Fontana Books (London-Glasgow, 1973).

Claessen, H.J.M. and Skalnik, Peter (eds), *The Early State* (Mouton, The Hague, 1978).

—— (eds), *The Study of the State* (Mouton, The Hague, 1981).

Claessen, H.J.M. and P. Van de Velde (eds), *Early State Dynamics* (Leiden, 1987).

Coedes, G., *The Indianized States of Southeast Asia* (East-West Center Press, Hawaii, 1968).

Coomaraswamy, A.K., *Spiritual Authority and Temporal Power in the Indian Theory of Government*, reprinted (New Delhi, Munshiram Manoharlal, 1978; reprint of 1942 edition).

Crane, R.I. (ed.), *Regions and Regionalism in South Asian Studies: An Exploratory Study* (Durham, N.C.: Duke University Monograph Series, 1966).

Derrett, J.D.M., *The Hoysaḷas (A Medieval Indian Royal Family)* (Oxford University Press, 1957).

Desai, Devangana, *Erotic Sculpture of India* (New Delhi, 1975).

Desai, Dinkar, *The Mahāmaṇḍaleśvaras under the Chālukyas of Kalyāṇī* (Bombay, 1951).

Devakunjari, D., *Hampi* (Archaeological Survey of India, New Delhi, 1970).

Deyell, John S., *Living Without Silver: The Monetary History of Early Medieval North India* (Delhi, 1990).

Dikshit, G.S., *Local Selfgovernment in Medieval Karnataka* (Dharwar, 1964).

Dutt, B.B., *Townplanning in Ancient India* (Calcutta, 1925; reprinted, Delhi, 1977).

Eisenstadt, S.N., *The Political System of Empires* (New York, 1969).

Eschmann, A., Kulke, H. and Tripathi, G.C., *The Cult of Jagannath and the Regional Tradition of Orissa* (New Delhi, 1978).

Fox, Richard, G., *Kin, Clan, Raja and Rule: State-hinterland Relations in Pre-Industrial India* (The University of California Press, Berkeley, 1971).

—— (ed.), *Realm and Region in Traditional India* (Delhi, 1977).

Fried, Morton, *The Evolution of Political Society* (New York, 1967).

Ghosh, A., *The City in Early Historical India* (Simla, 1973).

Ghoshal, U.N., *Contributions to the History of the Hindu Revenue System*, second edition (Calcutta, 1972).

Goetz, Hermann, *The Art and Architecture of Bikaner State* (Oxford, 1960).

Gopal, L., *The Economic Life of Northern India (C. AD 700–1200)* (Delhi, 1965).

—— *Early Medieval Cointypes of Northern India* (Numismatic Notes and Monographs, No. 12) (Varanasi, 1966).

—— *Aspects of History of Agriculture in Ancient India* (Varanasi, 1980).

Govindaswamy, M.S., *The Role of Feudatories in Pallava History* (Annamalai University, Annamalai, 1965).

—— 'The Role of Feudatories in Chola History' (Ph.D dissertation, Annamalai University, Annamalai, 1973).

Gururajachar, S., *Some Aspects of Economic and Social Life in Karnataka (AD 1000–1300)* (Mysore, 1974).

Hall, K.R., *Trade and Statecraft in the Age of the Coḷas* (Delhi, 1980).

Handa, Devendra, *Osian: History, Archaeology, Art and Architecture* (Delhi, 1984).

Hardy, F., *Viraha-Bhakti: The Early History of Kṛṣṇa Devotion in South India* (Delhi, 1983).

Inden, Ronald, *Imagining India* (Oxford-Cambridge, Mass, 1990).

Jain, K.C., *Ancient Cities and Towns of Rajasthan (A Study of Culture and Civilization)* (Delhi-Varanasi-Patna, 1972).

Jain, V.K., *Trade and Traders in Western India (AD 1000–1300)* (New Delhi, 1990).

Jha, D.N., *Studies in Early Indian Economic History* (Delhi, 1980).

—— (ed.), *Feudal Social Formation in Early India* (Delhi, 1987).

Kakati, Banikanta, *The Mother Goddess Kāmakhyā* (or Studies in the Fusion of Aryan and Primitive Beliefs of Assam), Third impression (Gauhati, 1967).

Kane, P.V., *History of Dharmasastra (Ancient and Medieval Religious and Civil Law)*, vol. 3, second edition (Poona, 1973); vol. 5, part I (Poona, 1974).

Karashima, N., *South Indian History and Society: Studies from Inscriptions: AD 850–1800* (Delhi, 1984).

Kooij, K.R. Van, *Worship of the Goddess According to the Kālikā Purāṇa*, part I (A translation with an Introduction and notes on Chapters 54–69) (Leiden, 1972).

Kosambi, D.D., *An Introduction to the Study of Indian History* (Bombay, 1956).

Krishnamurthy, M.S., *Nolambas: A Political and Cultural Study* (Mysore, 1980).

Kuppuswamy, G.R., *Economic Conditions in Karnataka, AD 973–AD 1336* (Dharwar, 1975).

Lahiri, N., *Pre-Ahom Assam (Studies in the Inscriptions of Assam between the Fifth and the Thirteenth Centuries AD* (Delhi, 1991).

Lingat, C.R., *The Classical Law of India*, translated from the French with additions by J.D.M. Derrett (New Delhi, 1973).

Longhurst, A.H., *Hampi Ruins Described and Illustrated* (Madras, 1917).

Lorenzen, David, N., *The Kāpālikas and Kālāmukhas: Two Lost Śaivite Sects* (New Delhi, 1975).

Mabbett, I.W., *Truth, Myth and Politics in Ancient India* (Delhi, 1972).

Mahalingam, T.V., *South Indian Polity*, second edition (University of Madras, Madras, 1967).

Maity, S.K., *Economic Life of Northern India in the Gupta Period*, second edition (Delhi-Varanasi-Patna, 1970).

Majumdar, A.K., *Chaulukyas of Gujrat (A Survey of the History and Culture of Gujrat from the middle of the tenth to the end of the thirteenth century)* (Bombay, 1956).

Majumdar, R.C. (ed.), *The Age of Imperial Unity* (vol. 2 of *The History and Culture of the Indian People)*, Third impression (Bombay, 1960).

—— *The Struggle for Empire* (vol. 5 of *The History and Culture of the Indian People)* (Bombay, 1957).

—— *Corporate Life in Ancient India*, third edition (Calcutta, 1969).

Marx, Karl, *Capital*, vol. 3 (Foreign Languages Publishing House, Moscow, 1962)

—— *Grundrisse*, Penguin Edition (Harmondworth, 1973).

Mazumdar, B.P., *Socio-Economic History of Northern India (1030–1194 AD)* (Calcutta, 1960).

Mehta, R.N., *Medieval Archaeology* (Delhi, 1979).

Misra, S.C., 'An Inscriptional Approach to the Study of the *Arthaśāstra* of Kauṭilya', (Ph.D dissertation, University Delhi, 1984).

Misra, V.C., *Geography of Rajasthan* (New Delhi, 1967).

Misra, V.N., *Pre-and Protohistory of the Berach Basin, South Rajasthan* (Poona, 1967).

Mohan, Krishna, *Early Medieval History of Kashmir (with special reference to the Loharas, AD 1003–1171)* (Delhi, 1981).

Moore, R.J. (ed.), *Tradition and Politics in South Asia* (Delhi, 1979).

Moraes, G.M., *The Kadamba-Kula: A History of Ancient and Medieval Karnataka* (Bombay, 1931).

Morrison, B.M., *Political Centers and Cultural Regions in Early Bengal* (The University of Arizona Press, Tucson, 1970).

Mukherjee, B.N., *Post Gupta Coinages of Bengal* (Coin Study Circle, Calcutta, 1989).

Nandi, R.N., *Religious Institutions and Cults in the Deccan* (Delhi, 1973).

Nilakanta Sastri, K.A., *The Colas*, reprint of second edition (University of Madras, Madras, 1975).

—— (ed.), *A Comprehensive History of India*, vol. 2 (*The Mauryas and Satavahanas)* (Bombay, 1957).

Niyogi, P., *Contributions to the Economic History of Northern India (from the tenth to the twelfth century AD)* (Calcutta, 1962).

Obeyesekere, Gananath, *The Cult of Goddess Pattini*, First Indian Edition (Delhi, 1987).

O'Leary, Brendan, *The Asiatic Mode of Production: Oriental Despotism, Historical Materialism and Indian History* (Oxford-Cambridge, Mass, 1989).

Pathak, V.S., *Ancient Historians of India: A Study in Historical Biography* (Bombay, 1966).

Poulantzas, N., *State, Power and Socialism* (London, 1980).

Prasad, Beni, *The State in Ancient India* (Allahabad, 1928).

—— *Theory of Government in Ancient India*, second edition (Allahabad, 1964).

Prasad, O.P., *Decay and Revival of Urban Centres in Medieval South India (C. AD 600–1200)* (New Delhi, 1989).

Puri, B.N., *The History of the Gurjara-Pratihāras* (Bombay, 1957).

Rao, R. Narasimha, *Corporate Life in Medieval Andhradesa* (Secunderabad, 1967).

Rao, T. Venkateswara, 'Local Bodies in pre-Vijayanagara Andhra' (Ph.D dissertation, Karnataka University, Dharwad, 1975).

Ray, H.C., *The Dynastic History of Northern India (Early Medieval Period)*, 2 volumes, reprinted (New Delhi, 1973).

Ray, Niharranjan, *Bāṅgālīr Itihās* (Adi Parva), third revised edition in two parts (Calcutta, 1980).

Raychaudhuri, H.C., *Political History of Ancient India*, sixth edition (University of Calcutta, Calcutta, 1953).

Sarkar, H. and Misra, B.N., *Nagarjunakonda* (Archaeological Survey of India, New Delhi, 1980).

Settar, S., *Hoysaḷa Sculptures in the National Museum, Copenhagen* (Copenhagen, 1975).

—— *Hampi* (Bangalore, 1990).

—— *The Hoysaḷa Temples*, parts I and II (Dharwad-Bangalore, 1992).

Sharma, D., *Early Chauhan Dynasties (A Study of Chauhan Political History, Chauhan Political Institutions and Life in the Chauhan Dominions from C. 800 to 1316 AD)* (Delhi, 1959).

—— (general ed.), *Rajasthan Through the Ages*, vol. I (Rajasthan State Archives, Bikaner, 1966).

Sharma, R.C., *Settlement Geography of the Indian Desert* (New Delhi, 1972).

Sharma, R.S., *Indian Feudalism, C. 300–1200* (University of Calcutta, Calcutta, 1965).

—— *Social Changes in Early Medieval India (circa AD 500–1200)* (The first Devraj Chanana Memorial Lecture, Delhi, 1969).

—— *Aspects of Political Ideas and Institutions in Ancient India*, second revised and enlarged edition (Delhi, 1968); third revised edition (Delhi, 1991).

—— *Śūdras in Ancient India*, second revised and enlarged edition (Delhi, 1980).

—— *Material Culture and Social Formations in Ancient India* (Delhi, 1983).

—— *Perspectives in Social and Economic History of Early India* (Delhi, 1983).

—— *Urban Decay in India, C. AD 300–C. 1000* (Delhi, 1987).

Shrimali, K.M., *Agrarian Structure in Central India and the Northern Deccan (A Study in Vākāṭaka Inscriptions)* (Delhi, 1987).

Singer, C., *et al* (eds), *A History of Technology*, vol. 2 (Oxford, 1957).

Singh, R.B.P., *Jainism in Early Medieval Karnataka (C. AD 500–1200)* (Delhi, 1975).

Singh, R.C.P., *Kingship in Northern India C. 600 AD–1200 AD* (Delhi, 1968).

Singh, Upinder, 'Kings, Brāhmaṇas and Temples in Orissa: An Epigraphic Study (300–1147 CE.)' (Doctorate Dissertation, McGill University, Montreal, 1990).

Sinha, Nandini, 'The Guhila Lineages and the Emergence of State in Early Medieval Mewar', M. Phil dissertation, Centre for Historical Studies, Jawaharlal Nehru University (New Delhi, 1988).

Sircar, D.C., *Indian Epigraphy* (Delhi, 1965).

—— (ed.), *Landsystem and Feudalism in Ancient India* (University of Calcutta, 1966).

—— *Landlordism and Tenancy in Ancient and Medieval India as Revealed by Epigraphical Records* (Lucknow, 1969).

—— *The Guhilas of Kiṣkindhā* (Calcutta, 1965).

—— *Some Problems of Kuṣāṇa and Rajput History* (University of Calcutta, Calcutta, 1969).

—— *Political and Administrative Systems of Ancient and Medieval India* (Delhi, 1973).

—— *The Emperor and the Subordinate Rulers* (Vishva Bharati University, Santiniketan, 1982).

—— *Pāla-Sena Yuger Vaṃśānucarita* (in Bengali) (Calcutta, 1982).

Sontheimer, G.D., *The Joint Hindu Family (Its Evolution as a Legal Institution)* (New Delhi, 1977).

Southall, A., *Alur Society: A Study in Processes and Types of Domination* (Cambridge, 1953).

Spate, O.H.K. and Learmonth, A.T.A., *India and Pakistan: A General and Regional Geography*, third edition (London, 1967).

Srivastava, B., *Trade and Commerce in Ancient India (from the earliest times to C. AD 300)* (Varanasi, 1968).

Stein, Burton, *Peasant State and Society in Medieval South India* (Oxford University Press, Delhi, 1980).

Subbarao, B., *The Personality of India*, second edition (Baroda, 1958).

Subbarayalu, Y., *Political Geography of the Chola Country* (Madras, 1973).

Suryavamsi, B., *The Ābhīras: Their History and Culture* (Baroda, 1962).

Tambiah, S.J., *World Conqueror and World Renouncer* (Cambridge University Press, 1976).

Thakur, Abanindranath, *Bānglār Vrata* (in Bengali) (Santiniketan, B.S., 1356).

Thakur, V.K., *Urbanization in Ancient India* (New Delhi, 1981).

—— *Historiography of Indian Feudalism* (Patna, 1989).

Thapar, Romila, *The Past and Prejudice* (National Book Trust, New Delhi, 1975).

—— *Exile and the Kingdom: Some Thoughts on the Rāmāyaṇa* (The Mythic Society, Bangalore, 1978).

—— *Ancient Indian Social History: Some Interpretations* (Delhi, 1978).

—— *From Lineage to State (Social Formations in the Mid-First Millennium BC in the Ganga Valley)* (Bombay, 1984).

—— *The Mauryas Revisited* (S.G. Deuskar Lectures on Indian History, 1984) (Centre for Studies in Social Sciences, Calcutta, 1987).

Tod, James, *Annals and Antiquities of Rajasthan*, edited by William Crooke, reprint, vol. I (Delhi, 1971).

Usher, A.P., *A History of Mechanical Inventions* (Boston, 1959).

Vaidya, C.V., *History of Medieval Hindu India*, vol. 2 *(Early History of Rajputs: 750 to 1000 AD)* (Poona, 1924).

Wagle, Narendra, *Society at the time of the Buddha* (Bombay, 1966).

Warmington, E.H., *The Commerce between the Roman Empire and India* (Cambridge, 1928).

Wheeler, R.E.M., *Rome Beyond the Imperial Frontiers* (London, 1954).

Wittfogel, K.A., *Oriental Despotism: A Comparative Study of Total Power*, seventh printing (Yale University Press, 1970).

Yadava, B.N.S., *Society and Culture in Northern India in the Twelfth Century* (Allahabad, 1973).

Yazdani, G. (ed.), *Early History of the Deccan*, 2 volumes (Oxford University Press, 1960).

2. Articles, Addresses and Chapters in Edited Volumes

Agrawala, R.C., 'Dramma in Ancient Indian Epigraphs and Literature', *The Journal of the Numismatic Society of India*, vol. 17, No. 2 (1955), pp. 64–82.

—— 'Paśchimī Rājasthan ke kuchh prārambhik smritistambha', *Varadā* (in Hindi) (April, 1963).

—— 'Persian wheel in Rajasthani sculpture', *Man in India*, vol. 46 (1966), pp. 87–8.

Agrawala, V.S., 'A cultural note on the *Kuvalayamālā*', in A.N. Upadhye (ed.), *Kuvalayamālā*, pt. 2 (Bombay, 1970).

Ammakutty, K.P., 'Origin of the Samanta Caste in Kerala', *Proceedings of the Indian History Congress*, 41 session (Bombay, 1980), pp. 86–92.

Avasthy, R.S. and Ghosh, A., 'References to Muhammadans in Sanskrit Inscriptions in Northern India—AD 730 to 1320', *Journal of Indian History*, vol. 15 (1936), pp. 161–84.

Aymard, Maurice, 'Money and Peasant Economy', *Studies in History*, vol. 2, No. 2 (1980), pp. 11–20.

Bernard, J., 'Trade and Finance in the Middle Ages: 900–1500', in C.M. Cipolla (ed.), *The Fontana Economic History of Europe: The Middle Ages*, vol. I (London-Glasgow, 1973), pp. 274–338.

Bhandarkar, D.R., 'Foreign Elements in the Hindu Population', *The Indian Antiquary*, vol. 40 (1911), pp. 7–37.

Bhattacharyya, S., 'Political Authority and Brāhmaṇa-Kṣatriya Relations in Early India—An Aspect of the Power-Elite Configuration', *The Indian Historical Review*, vol. 10, Nos. 1–2 (1983–84), pp. 1–20.

Chakrabarti, Dilip, K., 'Concept of Urban Revolution and the Indian Context', *Puratattva* (Bulletin of the Indian Archaeological Society), No. 6 (1972–73), pp. 27–32.

—— 'Beginning of Iron and Social Change in India', *Indian Studies: Past and Present*, vol. 14, No. 4 (1972–73), pp. 329–38.

Champakalakshmi, R., 'Religious Conflict in the Tamil Country: A Re-appraisal of Epigraphic Evidence', *Journal of the Epigraphical Society of India*, vol. 5 (1978).

—— 'Peasant State and Society in Medieval South India: A Review Article', *The Indian Economic and Social History Review*, vol. 18, pts. 3–4 (1981), pp. 411–26.

—— 'Growth of Urban Centres in South India: Kuḍamūkku-Paḻaiyāṟai, the Twin-city of the Colas', *Studies in History*, vol. I, pt. I (1979), pp. 1–29.

—— 'Urban Process in Early Medieval Tamilnadu', Occasional Papers Series, No. 3 (Urban History Association of India).

—— 'Urbanization in South India: The Role of Ideology and Polity', Presidential Address, Ancient India Section, Indian History Congress, 47th session (Srinagar, 1986).

—— 'Religion and Social Change in Tamilnadu (C. AD 600–1300)', in N.N. Bhattacharyya (ed.), *Medieval Bhakti Movements in India* (Sri Caitanya Quin-centenary Commemoration volume) (New Delhi, 1989), pp. 162–73.

—— 'The Study of the Settlement Patterns in the Coḷa Period: Some Perspectives', *Man and Environment*, vol. 14, No. I (1989), pp. 91–101.

Chattopadhyaya, B.D., 'Currency in Early Bengal', *Journal of Indian History*, vol. 55, pt. 3 (1977), pp. 41–60.

—— 'Mathurā From the Śuṅga to the Kuṣāṇa Times: An Historical Outline', in Doris M. Srinivasan (ed.), *Mathura: The Cultural Heritage* (Delhi, 1989), pp. 19–30.

—— 'Transition to the Early Historical Phase in the Deccan: A Note', in B.M. Pande and B.D. Chattopadhyaya (eds), *Archaeology and History* (Essays in Memory of Sri A. Ghosh) (Delhi, 1987), pp. 727–32.

—— 'State and Economy in North India: 4th Century to 12th Century' (forthcoming).

Cohen, R., 'State Origins: A Re-appraisal', in H.J.M. Claessen and Peter Skalnik (eds), *The Early State* (Mouton, The Hague, 1978), pp. 31–75.

De Casparis, J.G., 'Inscriptions and South Asian Dynastic Tradition', in R.J. Moore (ed.), *Tradition and Politics in South Asia* (Delhi, 1979), pp. 103–27.

Desai, Devangana, 'Art under Feudalism in India', *The Indian Historical Review*, vol. I, pt. I (1974), pp. 10–17.

—— 'Social Dimensions of Art in Early India', Presidential Address, Section

I, Ancient India, Indian History Congress, 50th session (Gorakhpur, 1989).

Digby, Simon, 'Economic Conditions before 1200' in Tapan Raychaudhuri and Irfan Habib (eds), *The Cambridge Economic History of India*, vol. I (*c.* 1200–*c.* 1750) (Cambridge University Press, Cambridge, 1982), pp. 45–7.

Dirks, Nicholas, B., 'Political Authority and Structural Change in Early South Indian History', *The Indian Economic and Social History Review*, vol. 13, pt. 2 (1976), pp. 125–58.

—— 'The Structure and Meaning of Political Relations in a South Indian Little Kingdom', *Contributions to Indian Sociology*, vol. 13, pt. 2 (1979), pp. 169–206.

Dumont, Louis, 'The Conception of Kingship in Ancient India', in *Religion, Politics and History in India* (Mouton, Paris-The Hague, 1970), pp. 63–88.

Edgerton, F., 'Upanishads: What Do They Seek and Why', in D.P. Chattopadhyaya (ed.), *Studies in the History of Indian Philosophy*, vol. I (Calcutta, 1978), pp. 110–40.

Erdosy, G., 'Early Historic Cities of Northern India', *South Asian Studies*, vol. 3 (1987), pp. 1–23.

Ghosh, A. and Panigrahi, K.C., 'The Pottery of Ahichchhatra, District Bareilly, U.P', *Ancient India*, No. I (1946), pp. 37–59.

Gopal, K.K., 'Assignments to Officials and Royal Kinsmen in Early Medieval India (*c.* AD 700–1200)', *University of Allahabad Studies* (Ancient Indian Section, 1963–64), pp. 75–103.

Gopal, L., 'Sāmanta—its Varying Significance in Ancient India', *Journal of the Royal Asiatic Society of Great Britain and Ireland*, parts I and II (April 1963), pp. 21–37.

—— 'The Textile Industry in Early Medieval India', *Journal of the Asiatic Society of Bombay*, vols. 39/40 (1964–65), pp. 95–103.

—— 'Coins in the Epigraphic and Literary Records of Northern India in the Early Medieval Period', *Journal of the Numismatic Society of India*, vol. 25 (1963), pp. 1–16.

Guha, A., 'Tribalism to Feudalism in Assam: 1600–1750', *The Indian Historical Review*, vol. I, No. I (1974), pp. 65–76.

Gupta, Chitrarekha, 'The Writers' Class of Ancient India—A Case Study in Social Mobility', *The Indian Economic and Social History Review*, vol. 20, No. 2 (1983), pp. 191–204.

—— 'Horse Trade in North India: Some Reflections on Socio-economic

Life', *Journal of Ancient Indian History*, vol. 14, pts. 1–2 (1983–84), pp. 186–206.

Gupte, B.A., 'The Symbolism of Savitri-vrata', *The Indian Antiquary*, vol. 35 (1906), pp. 116–19.

Gurukkal, Rajan, 'Medieval Landrights: Structure and Pattern of Distribution', *Proceedings of the Indian History Congress*, 39th session (Hyderabad, 1978), pp. 279–84.

—— 'Aspects of the Reservoir System of Irrigation in the Early Pāṇḍya State', *Studies in History*, N.S. vol. 2, No. 2 (1986), pp. 155–64.

Habib, Irfan, 'An Examination of Wittfogel's Theory of Oriental Despotism', *Enquiry*, No. 6 (1961), pp. 54–73.

—— 'Problems of Marxist Historical Analysis', *Science and Human Progress* (Essays in Honour of Late Professor D.D. Kosambi) (Bombay, 1974), pp. 34–47.

—— 'Technological Changes and Society: 13th and 14th Centuries', Presidential Address, Medieval Indian Section, Indian History Congress, 31 session (Varanasi, 1969), pp. 139–61.

—— 'Usury in Medieval India', *Comparative Studies in Society and History*, vol. 6, No. 4 (1964), pp. 393–419.

—— 'The Social Distribution of Landed Property in Pre-British India (A Historical Survey)', in R.S. Sharma and V. Jha (eds), *Indian Society: Historical Probings* (In Memory of D.D. Kosambi) (Delhi, 1974), pp. 264–316.

—— 'Classifying Pre-colonial India', in T.J. Byres and Harbans Mukhia (eds), *Feudalism and Non-European Societies* (Special issue of *The Journal of Peasant Studies*, vol. 12, Nos. 2–3) (London, 1985), pp. 44–53.

—— 'Pursuing the History of Indian Technology: Pre-modern Modes of Transmission of Power' (The Rajiv Bambawale Memorial Lecture, Indian Institute of Technology, New Delhi, 1990), manuscript.

Hall, K.R., 'Towards an Analysis of Dynastic Hinterlands: The Imperial Cholas of 11th Century South India', *Asian profile*, vol. 2, No. I (1974).

—— 'International Trade and Foreign Diplomacy in Early Medieval South India', *Journal of the Economic and Social History of the Orient*, vol. 21 (1978), pp. 75–98.

Handa, Devendra, 'Coins of Somalladevi', *Numismatic Digest*, vol. 2, pt. 2 (1978), pp. 42–57.

Heesterman, J.C., 'Power and Authority in Indian Tradition', in R.J. Moore (ed.), *Tradition and Politics in South Asia* (Delhi, 1979), pp. 60–85.

Henige, David, P., 'Some Phantom Dynasties of Early and Medieval India:

Epigraphic Evidence and the Abhorrence of a Vacuum', *Bulletin of the School of Oriental and African Studies*, vol. 38, pt. 3 (1975), pp. 525–49.

Inden, Ronald, 'Hierarchies of Kings in Early Medieval India', *Contributions to Indian Sociology*, New Series, vol. 15, pts. 1–2 (1981), pp. 99–125.

Irwin, John, 'Asokan Pillars: A Reassessment of the Evidence', *The Burlington Magazine* (1973), pp. 706–20.

Jaiswal, Suvira, 'Caste in the Socio-economic Framework of Early India', Presidential Address, Ancient India Section, Indian History Congress, 38 session (Bhuvaneswar, 1977), pp. 23–48.

—— 'Studies in Early Indian Social History: Trends and Possibilities', *The Indian Historical Review*, vol. 6, pts. 1–2 (1979–80), pp. 1–63.

—— 'Varṇa Ideology and Social Change', *Social Scientist*, vol. 19, Nos. 3–4 (1991), pp. 41–8.

Jha, D.N., 'Early Indian Feudalism: A Historiographical Critique', Presidential Address, Ancient India Section, Indian History Congress, 40 session (Waltair, 1979).

—— 'Relevance of Peasant State and Society to Pallava and Cola Times', *The Indian Historical Review*, vol. 8, Nos. 1–2 (1981–82), pp. 74–94.

Joshi, M.C., 'An Early Inscriptional Reference to Persian Wheel', in *Professor K.A. Nilakanta Sastri Felicitation Volume*, edited by S. Ganesan, S. Rajam, N.S. Ramaswami and M.D. Sampath (Madras, 1971), pp. 214–217.

Karashima, N., 'Revenue Terms in Chola Inscriptions', *Journal of Asian and African Studies* (Tokyo), vol. 5 (1972), pp. 87–117.

—— 'Land Revenue Assessment in Coḷa Times as Seen in the Inscriptions of the Thanjavur and Gangaikondacolapuram Temples', in *Studies in Socio-cultural Change in Rural Villages in Tiruchirapalli District, Tamilnadu, India*, No. 1, N . Karashima, Y. Subbarayalu and P. Shanmugam (eds) (Tokyo, 1980), pp. 33–50.

Karashima, N. and Subbarayalu, Y., 'Statistical Study of Personal Names in Tamil Inscriptions: Interim Report II (March 1976)', *Computational Analysis of Asian and African Languages*, No. 3, pp. 9–21.

Kennedy, R.S., 'The King in Early South India as Chieftain and Emperor', *The Indian Historical Review*, vol. 3, No. I (1976), pp. 1–15.

Kosambi, D.D., 'The Quality of Renunciation in Bhartrihari's Poetry', in *Exasperating Essays* (Exercise in Dialectical Method), reprinted (Pune, 1986), pp. 72–93.

—— 'Origins of Feudalism in Kashmir', *Journal of the Bombay Branch of the Royal Asiatic Society* (1956–57), pp. 108–20.

Kulke, Hermann, 'Kṣatriyaization and Social Change: A Study in Orissa Setting', in S.D. Pillai (ed.), *Aspects of Changing India: Studies in Honour of Professor G.S. Ghurye* (Bombay, 1976), pp. 398–409.

—— 'Royal Temple Policy and the Structure of Medieval Hindu Kingdoms', in A. Eschmann, H. Kulke and G.C. Tripathi (eds), *The Cult of Jagannath and the Regional Tradition of Orissa* (New Delhi, 1978), pp. 125–38.

—— 'Early State Formation and Royal Legitimation in Tribal Areas of Eastern India', in R. Moser and M.K. Gautam (eds), *Aspects of Tribal Life in South Asia I: Strategy and Survival* (Berne, 1978), pp. 29–38.

—— 'Legitimation and Town-planning in the Feudatory States of Central Orissa', in J. Peiper (ed.), *Ritual Space in India: Studies in Architectural Anthropology* (London, 1980).

—— 'Fragmentation and Segmentation versus Integration? Reflections on the Concept of Indian Feudalism and the Segmentary State in Indian History', *Studies in History*, vol. 4, No. 2 (1982), pp. 237–63.

—— 'The Early and the Imperial Kingdom in Early Medieval India' (forthcoming).

Lahiri, N., 'Landholding and Peasantry in the Brahmaputra Valley, C. 5th–13th Centuries AD', *Journal of the Economic and Social History of the Orient*, vol. 33 (1990), pp. 157–68.

Lal, B.B., 'Perhaps the Earliest Ploughed Field So Far Excavated Anywhere in the World', *Puratattva* (Bulletin of the Indian Archaeological Society), No. 4 (1970–71).

Lorenzen, David, 'Imperialism and Ancient Indian Historiography', in S.N. Mukherjee (ed.), *India: History and Thought* (Essays in Honour of A.L. Basham) (Calcutta, 1982), pp. 84–102.

Medvedev, E.M., 'The Towns of Northern India During the 6th–7th Centuries (according to Hiuen Tsang)' in *India-Land and People*, Book 3 (vol. 14 of Countries and Peoples of the East), compiled and edited by I.V. Sakharov (Moscow, 1972), pp. 168–83.

Mukhia, H., 'Was there Feudalism in Indian History?', *The Journal of Peasant Studies*, vol. 8, No. 3 (1981), pp. 273–310.

—— 'Peasant Production and Medieval Indian Society', T.J. Byres and Harbans Mukhia (eds), *Feudalism and Non-European Societies* (Special issue of *The Journal of Peasant Studies*, vol. 12, Nos. 2–3) (London, 1985), pp. 228–50.

Munshi, S., 'Tribal Absorption and Sanskritization in Hindu Society', *Contributions to Indian Sociology*, New Series, vol. 13, pt. 2 (1979), pp. 293–317.

Nandi, R.N., 'Origin and Nature of Śaivite Monasticism: The Case of Kālāmukhas', in R.S. Sharma and V. Jha (eds), *Indian Society: Historical Probings* (in memory of D.D. Kosambi) (Delhi, 1974), pp. 190–201.

—— 'Origin of the Vīraśaiva Movement', *The Indian Historical Review*, vol. 2, No. 1 (1975), pp. 32–46.

—— 'Some Social Aspects of the Nalayira Prabandham', *Proceedings of the Indian History Congress*, 37 session (Calicut, 1976), pp. 118–23.

—— 'Gotra and Social Mobility in the Deccan', *Proceedings of the Indian History Congress*, 32nd session (Jabalpur, 1970), pp. 118–24.

—— 'Growth of Rural Economy in Early Feudal India', Presidential Address, Ancient India Section, Indian History Congress, 45th session (Annamalai, 1984).

—— 'Feudalization of the State in Medieval South India', *Social Science Probings* (March, 1985), pp. 33–59.

Narayanan, M.G.S. and Kesavan Veluthat, 'Bhakti Movement in South India', in D.N. Jha (ed.), *Feudal Social Formation in Early India*, pp. 348–75.

Nath, R., 'Rehant versus the Persian Wheel', *Journal of the Asiatic Society, Bengal*, New Series, vol. 12, Nos. 1–4 (1970), pp. 81–4.

Perlin, Frank, 'The Pre-colonial Indian State in History and Epistemology: A Reconstruction of Societal Formation in the Western Deccan from the Fifteenth to the Early Nineteenth Century', in H.J.M. Claessen and Peter Skalnik (eds), *The Study of the State* (The Hague, 1981), pp. 275–302.

Proceedings of the Symposium on the Rajputana Desert (Bulletin of the National Institute of Sciences in India), No. 1 (New Delhi, 1952).

Raheja, R.C., 'Influence of Climatic Changes on the Vegetation of the Arid Zone in India', *Annals of Arid Zone* (Arid Zone Research Association of India), vol. 4, No. 1 (1965), pp. 64–8.

Rao, T. Venketeswara, 'Numerical Figures Affixed to the Names of Territorial Divisions in Medieval Andhra', *Itihās* (Journal of the Andhra Pradesh Archives), vol. 2, No. 1 (1974).

Ray, Niharranjan, 'The Medieval Factor in Indian History', General President's Address, Indian History Congress, 29th session (Patiala, 1967), pp. 1–29.

Sanyal, Hiteshranjan, 'Mallabhum', in Surjit Sinha (ed.), *Tribal Politics and State Systems in Pre-colonial Eastern and North Eastern India* (Calcutta, 1987), pp. 73–142.

Sarkar, H., 'Chhayastambhas from Nagarjunakonda', in R. Nagaswamy (ed.), *Seminar on Herostones* (Madras, 1974).

Seneviratne, S., 'Kalinga and Andhra: The Process of Secondary State Formation in Early India', in H.J.M. Claessen and Peter Skalnik (eds), *The Study of the State* (The Hague, 1981), pp. 317–38.

Sharma, R.S., 'Origins of Feudalism in India (C. AD 400–650)', *Journal of the Economic and Social History of the Orient*, vol. 1, No. 3 (1958), pp. 297–328.

—— 'Landgrants to Vassals and Officials in Northern India, C. AD 1000–1200', *Journal of the Economic and Social History of the Orient*, vol. 4 (1961), pp. 70–105.

—— 'Rajasasana: Meaning, Scope and Application', *Proceedings of the Indian History Congress*, 37 session (Calicut, 1976), pp. 76–86.

—— 'Problem of Transition from Ancient to Medieval in Indian History', *The Indian Historical Review*, vol. I, No. I (1974), pp. 1–9.

—— 'Indian Feudalism Re-touched', *The Indian Historical Review*, vol. I, No. 2 (1974), pp. 320–30.

Sharma, R.S. (and D.N. Jha), 'The Economic History of India up to AD 1200: Trends and Prospects', *Journal of the Economic and Social History of the Orient*, vol. 17 (1974), pp. 48–80.

—— 'Decay of Gangetic Towns in Gupta and post-Gupta Times', *Proceedings of the Indian History Congress*, 33 session (Muzaffarpur, 1972), pp. 94–104.

—— 'Taxation and State Formation in Northern India in Pre-Mauryan Times (C. 600–300 BC)', included in R.S. Sharma, *Aspects of Political Ideas and Institutions in Ancient India*, third revised edition (Delhi, 1991), pp. 197–232.

—— 'Problems of Peasant Protest in Early Medieval India', *Social Scientist*, vol. 16, No. 9 (1988), pp. 3–16.

—— 'From Gopati to Bhūpati (A review of the changing position of the king)', *Studies in History*, vol. 2, No. 2 (1980), pp. 1–10.

—— 'The Kali Age: A Period of Social Crisis', in S.N. Mukherjee (ed.), *India: History and Thought* (Essays in honour of A.L. Basham) (Calcutta, 1982), pp. 186–203.

—— 'How Feudal was Indian Feudalism?' in T.J. Byres and Harbans Mukhia (eds), *Feudalism and Non-European Societies* (Special issue of *The Journal of Peasant Studies*, vol. 12, Nos. 2–3) (London, 1985), pp. 19–43.

Singh, K. Suresh, 'A Study in State-formation Among Tribal Communities', in R.S. Sharma and V. Jha (eds), *Indian Society: Historical Probings* (In memory of D.D. Kosambi) (Delhi, 1974), pp. 317–36.

Sinha, Surajit, 'State Formation and Rajput Myth in Tribal Central India', *Man in India*, vol. 42, No. I (1962), pp. 35–80.

Southall, A., 'A Critique of the Typology of States and Political Systems', in M. Banton (ed.), *Political Systems and the Distribution of Power* (ASA Monographs, No. 2, Tavistock Publications, London, 1969), pp. 113–40.

—— 'The Segmentary State in Africa and Asia', *Comparative Studies in Society and History*, vol. 30 (1988), pp. 52–82.

Spencer, G.W., 'Religious Networks and Royal Influence in the Eleventh Century South India', *Journal of the Economic and Social History of the Orient*, vol. 12, pt. I (1969), pp. 42–57.

—— 'The Politics of Plunder: The Cholas in Eleventh Century Ceylon', *Journal of Asian Studies*, vol. 35, No. 3 (1976), pp. 405–19.

Stein, Burton, 'Integration of the Agrarian System of South India', in R. Frykenberg (ed.), *Land Control and Social Structure in Indian History* (Madison, 1969), pp. 175–216.

—— 'The State and the Agrarian Order in Medieval South India: A Historiographical Critique', in Burton Stein (ed.), *Essays on South India* (New Delhi, 1976), pp. 64–92.

—— 'The Segmentary State in South Indian History', in R.G. Fox (ed.), *Realm and Region in Traditional India* (New Delhi, 1977), pp. 3–51.

—— 'All the King's Mana: Perspectives on Kingship in Medieval South India', in J.F. Richards (ed.), *Kingship and Authority in South Asia* (Madison, 1981).

—— 'Mahanavami: Medieval and Modern Kingly Ritual in South India', in B.L. Smith (ed.), *Essays on Gupta Culture* (Delhi, 1983), pp. 67–90.

—— 'The Segmentary State: Interim Reflections', in J. Pouchepadass and H. Stern (eds), *From Kingship to State: The Political in the Anthropology and History of the Indian World, Puruṣārtha*, 13 (1991), pp. 217–37.

Subbarayalu, Y., 'Mandalam as Politico-Geographical Unit in South India', *Proceedings of the Indian History Congress*, 39 session (Hyderabad, 1978), pp. 84–6.

—— 'The Coḷa State', *Studies in History*, vol. 4, No. 2 (1982), pp. 265–306.

Takahashi, H.K., 'A Contribution to the Discussion', in *The Transition from Feudalism to Capitalism* (A Symposium by Paul M. Sweezy *et al*) (London, 1954), pp. 30–5.

Thakur, V.K., 'Towns in Early Medieval India', in K.V. Raman *et al*, *Srinidhiḥ (Perspectives in Indian Archaeology, Art and Culture: K.R. Srinivasan Festschrift)* (Madras, 1983), pp. 389–97.

Thapar, Romila, 'The Image of the Barbarian in Early India', *Comparative*

Studies in Society and History, vol. 13, No. 4 (1971), pp. 408–36; reprinted in Romila Thapar, *Ancient Indian Social History* (New Delhi, 1978), pp. 152–92.

—— 'State Formation in Early India', *International Social Science Journal*, vol. 32, pt. 4 (1980), pp. 655–9.

—— 'The State as Empire' in H. Claessen and P. Skalnik (eds), *The Study of the State* (The Hague, 1981), pp. 409–26.

Veluthat, Kesavan, 'Royalty and Divinity: Legitimisation of Monarchical Power in the South', *Proceedings of the Indian History Congress*, 39 session (Hyderabad, 1978), pp. 241–49.

—— 'The Temple Base of the Bhakti Movement in South India', *Proceedings of the Indian History Congress*, 40 session (Waltair, 1979), pp. 185–94.

Venkayya, V., 'Irrigation in Southern India in Pallava Times', *Archaeological Survey of India: Annual Report, 1903–04*, pp. 202–11.

Vishnu-Mittre, 'Remains of Rice and Millet', Appendix II in H.D. Sankalia, *et al*, *Excavations at Ahar (Tamvavati)* (Poona, 1969).

Wills, C.U., 'The Territorial System of Rajput Kingdoms of Medieval Chattisgarh', *Journal and Proceedings of the Asiatic Society of Bengal*, New Series, vol. 15 (1919), pp. 197–262.

Yadava, B.N.S., 'Secular Landgrants of the Post-Gupta Period and Some Aspects of the Growth of Feudal Complex in North India', in D.C. Sircar (ed.), *Land System and Feudalism in Ancient India* (University of Calcutta, Calcutta, 1966).

—— 'Some Aspects of the Changing Order in India During the Śaka-Kuṣāṇa Age', in G.R. Sharma (ed.), *Kuṣāṇa Studies* (University of Allahabad, Allahabad, 1964).

—— 'Immobility and Subjection of Indian Peasantry in Early Medieval Complex', *The Indian Historical Review*, vol. 1, No. 1 (1974), pp. 18–27.

—— 'The Accounts of the Kali Age and the Social Transition from Antiquity to the Middle Ages', *The Indian Historical Review*, vol. 5, Nos. 1–2 (1979), pp. 31–63.

—— 'The Problem of the Emergence of Feudal Relations in Early India', Presidential Address, Ancient India Section, Indian History Congress, 41 session (Bombay, 1980), pp. 19–78.

Yamazaki, T., 'Some Aspects of Land-sale Inscriptions in Fifth and Sixth Century Bengal', *Acta Asiatica* (Bulletin of the Institute of Eastern Culture), No. 43 (Tokyo, 1982), pp. 17–36.

Ziegler, N.P., 'Marvari Historical Chronicles: Sources for the Social and Cultural History of Rajasthan', *The Indian Economic and Social History Review*, vol. 13, No. 2 (1976), pp. 219–50.

Index